T0298968

This book focusses on the relationship between the process of commodity production and the process of social reproduction of labour. It seeks to restore that relationship to the central place it had in the classical surplus approach, where profit was defined primarily in terms of the difference between production and the costs of social reproduction of labour.

The argument is directly opposed to that of the wages fund theorists, who rejected the Ricardian view that wages were exogenously determined by material, historical and institutional factors. By substituting a strict supply-and-demand mechanism, they and their modern followers actually removed the whole question of the exogeneity of the process of social reproduction from the analysis of the labour market. This rendered marginal and analytically invisible certain fundamental aspects of the economic system – in particular, the function of the state and that of women's work, in the process of social reproduction. Examination of the 1909 Poor Law Report and of the women's labour market shows that what disappeared from theory remained crucial for economic policy.

The production–reproduction perspective, on which this book is based, makes it possible to recover some essential aspects of the social reproduction of labour and its fundamental role in the structure of the waged labour market, opening new directions for economic analysis.

Social reproduction: the political
economy of the labour market

Social reproduction: the political economy of the labour market

ANTONELLA PICCHIO

CAMBRIDGE
UNIVERSITY PRESS

CAMBRIDGE UNIVERSITY PRESS
Cambridge, New York, Melbourne, Madrid, Cape Town, Singapore,
São Paulo, Delhi, Dubai, Tokyo

Cambridge University Press
The Edinburgh Building, Cambridge CB2 8RU, UK

Published in the United States of America by Cambridge University Press, New York

www.cambridge.org
Information on this title: www.cambridge.org/9780521418720

First published 1992
Reprinted 1994

A catalogue record for this publication is available from the British Library

Library of Congress Cataloguing in Publication data
Picchio, Antonella.
Social reproduction: the political economy of the labour market /
Antonella Picchio.
p.   cm.
Includes bibliographical references.
ISBN 0 521 41872 0
1. Labor economics.   2. Labor market.   3. Labor supply.   4. Labor
policy.   5. Working class.   6. Social classes.   I. Title.
HD4901.P515   1992
331.12 – dc20   92–3371   CIP

ISBN 978-0-521-41872-0 Hardback

Transferred to digital printing 2010

To my sisters: Joan, Laura, Pina

For cognition is neither passive contemplation nor acquisition of the only possible insight into something given. It is an active, live interrelationship, a reshaping and being reshaped, in short, an act of creation.

Ludwik Fleck
'On the Crisis of Reality'

Contents

Contents

Acknowledgements

The research work for this book was done at the University of Cambridge When I began the project I was a visiting scholar at the Faculty of Economics and Politics; then I continued it as a Ph.D. thesis. The luxury of studying in a satisfying way, free from the tensions of daily academic work in Italy, has been financed over several years by the Consiglio Nazionale delle Ricerche, the Ministero della Pubblica Istruzione, and the Ente per gli Studi Monetari, Bancari e Finanziari L. Einaudi (Rome).

The Faculty of Economics of the University of Modena has allowed me, within the constraints of my teaching responsibilities, periods of leave enabling me to carry out my research.

Many people have helped me in the course of this work. John Eatwell supervised my research with great commitment and generosity, and his encouragement has been of decisive importance to me. While he was on leave I had the good fortune to be guided by Phyllis Deane, who continued to offer me friendly support. Pierangelo Garegnani supervised my work while I was in Italy. I am indebted for valuable comments on various parts of this work to Francesca Bettio, Sergio Bruno, Bastiano Brusco, Anna Carabelli, Marco Dardi, Nicolò De Vecchi, Andrea Ginzburg, Cristina Marcuzzo, Fernando Vianello, Paola Villa and Frank Wilkinson. Neil De Marchi read the last draft of chapters 1 to 4 and gave me encouragement in the final, most difficult phase. Pier Luigi Porta read the first chapter and sympathetically disagreed. The Introduction was read, edited and pruned by Michele Salvati, Joan Hall and Ted Hall.

Clare Hall College has offered me hospitality of a warmth and kindness very rare in any institution. To be one of its members is a great honour and a great pleasure.

My work has been discussed in several seminars in Cambridge and elsewhere, at the Conference of the American Economic Associations in Atlanta, at the European University of Florence, and at various meetings of the International Working Party on Labour Market Segmentation (Berlin, Aix-en-Provence, Cambridge, Trento).

A preliminary version of the first chapter was published in *Ricerche Economiche* (1981a), and some results of my research were published in Wilkinson (1981) and in *The New Palgrave Dictionary* (1986a).

The main influence on my perspective has come from my political activity in the feminist movement. This is a collective contribution, which I acknowledge with gratitude and pride.

Acknowledgements

Last but not least, Joan Hall has translated some parts of the book from Italian, edited my English, and often helped to clarify my ideas. For her generosity and affection I include her among my sisters, to whom I dedicate this book. Her husband Ted Hall adopted me as part of the family, providing excellent music and support.

Bobbie Coe, who word-processed the whole book, took me to the end of my task with incredible patience and kindness when I most needed both. Computers have in no way spoiled her warm personality.

I have no wife to thank for endurance. I have two children, Andrea and Barbara Del Mercato, whom I love and respect deeply.

Cambridge   December 1990

Introduction

Capitalism, like every other social system, imposes a specific relationship between the process of production of goods and services and the process of social reproduction of the population. The capitalist system is defined by the use of waged labour to produce commodities. In this system access to the means of subsistence is mediated by wages for the vast majority of the population. This mediation, a consequence of the private ownership of the means of production, determines the specifically capitalist relation between the process of production and the process of social reproduction.[1]

Polanyi (1944, 1977) points out that when the problem of social reproduction was excluded from direct and general analysis, the scope of scientific significance was diminished; but he did not fully acknowledge the deep divergence on this question between classical political economy and neoclassical economics. If the capitalist labour market is defined merely in terms of allocation (relative scarcity and fluidity), as in neoclassical economics, the analysis of the social process of reproduction is bound to be treated as a mere appendage to economic analysis.

The critique of the neoclassical theory of distribution undertaken by Sraffa (1960) provided a firm logical ground for rejection of an allocative determination of prices. It also offers a sound basis for recovering the classical view of wages as institutionally determined, focussing on the inverse relationship between wages and profit and, more precisely, between profit and costs of reproduction of labour. My approach, starting from this critique, permits the inclusion of the process of social reproduction in the general analytical framework of political economy: reproduction, in all its aspects, is the touchstone for my criticism of the narrowness of modern economics and my assessment of the specific, historically determined, capitalist relationship between production of commodities and social reproduction of the labouring population.

As seen by classical economists, some of the most important features of the capitalist economic system can be summarized as follows: a general possibility of producing wealth; the purpose of the productive process as the creation of exchange values; the existence of a surplus of production over the necessary costs of production (essentially the subsistence of the labourers); the profit form of part of that surplus; the use of the surplus for the progressive broadening of productive capacity; and, last but not least, the institution of a waged labour market which guarantees social control over labour through the general dependence on wages for subsistence.

1

Social reproduction of labour

In the first chapter I argue that classical political economy – in its definition of the natural price of labour, in its definition of profit as part of the surplus and in its assumption of a non-clearing labour market – directly reflects some of the complexities inherent in waged labour. I give particular attention to the natural price of labour because in the history of economic thought this concept has been used with different meanings, and some fundamental confusions have resulted. It began as a concept of socially determined cost of social reproduction of the labouring population but was later transformed into the idea of a supply-and-demand equilibrium price of labour (in the limited sense of work done at the work place).

In the classical surplus approach the relationship between concepts and reality was immediately evident: wages were prices because labour was considered a commodity; they were separately determined because the process of reproduction of labour was separate from the production of other commodities; they were costs of production because labour was considered producible; and they were inversely related to profit because the distribution of the product between classes was determined within the institutional context of private ownership of the means of production. Thus the analytical concepts fully reflect the main characteristics of the capitalist labour market, and take into account some of the historical characteristics of labour as a commodity.

This is not the case in the neoclassical analytical framework. There the specificity of labour is generally not acknowledged, as Solow recognizes:

one important tradition within economics, perhaps the dominant tradition right now, especially in macroeconomics, holds that in nearly all respects the labor market is just like other markets . . . Common sense, on the other hand, seems to take it for granted that there is something special about labor as a commodity and therefore about the labour market too . . .

I want to make the case that the labour market really is different. In particular, I claim that it cannot be understood without taking account of the fact that participants, on both sides, have well developed notions of what is fair and what is not. (Solow, 1990, p. 3)

What makes labour a different commodity is in fact its process of reproduction, which is necessarily material and social and follows historically established social norms. What Solow does not acknowledge is that the failure to recognize the peculiarity of the labour market is not due to naivety – or excessive sophistication – on the part of economists, but to the methodological foundations of neoclassical economics which assumes systematic relationships between prices and quantities, purged of all social and institutional processes. In the case of labour this method is fatal.

Introduction

The specific experience of the process of reproduction of labour is common to all. But to comprehend the reality of the capitalist system common sense alone is not enough: we also need an analytical framework that can organize that experience into a meaningful structure. Our task is not simply to name the problems and tack them on to existing schemes, in the hope of restoring some of the complexities formerly omitted from the analysis. We have to see if the analytical framework can handle these complexities within its general theory – not as details but as substantive questions, not as exceptions but as norms. While the specific reality of the process of reproduction of waged labour need not be described in detail with all the minutiae of daily domestic life, it cannot be ignored or left outside the analytical framework used for dealing with the economic system. If the analytical scheme cannot accommodate that reality, efforts to add it by treating families as firms (Becker, 1965, 1981, 1986) cannot provide adequate tools for understanding.

The present climate is one of widespread uneasiness about the capacity of economic science to provide adequate tools for comprehending reality. Some prominent representatives of the profession express dissatisfaction with the way formalism in recent years has been pursued as an end in itself (Parker, 1986). Others openly criticize the scientific methodology used (Mirowsky, 1984, 1989). Certain developing schools of thought show a renewed interest in the role of historical and institutional factors (Hodgson, 1988; Samuels, 1988). The technical rationality of choices is being moderated by a more empirical rationality (Simon, 1983). The 'social engineering' concepts of welfare formulated by Utilitarians are being questioned (Sen and Williams, 1982). The proponents of games theory are prepared to include the idea of conflict, though they think they can resolve it with rules of technical rationality rather than through the sedimentation in time of moral norms legitimated by social consensus (Ullmann-Margalit, 1977). The evolutionists are looking for models of dynamic systems that can take account of endogenous qualitative modifications, though they are forced to recognize that it is difficult to make them include people's expectations and habits (Allen, 1988, p. 116).[2]

Working on this terrain, which is unstable but no longer constricted by arrogance, I maintain that the analytical concept of wages as a cost of social reproduction, a cost which is determined exogenously with respect to the prices of other commodities, can be extremely valuable for the analysis of the labour market. My alignment with the tradition of the theories of surplus is not motivated by a search for new orthodoxies. The aim is to preserve analytical tools which in my view are better adapted – though not yet satisfactory – for dealing with the problems I consider important.

3

I believe that the need to maintain the distinction between the natural price and the market price of labour, constantly emphasized by Ricardo and then by Marx, is central for understanding certain fundamental aspects of the system. When that distinction is lost, the economic analysis loses the capacity it had in Smith, Ricardo and Marx for illuminating the nature of the labour market. The introduction of a theory of wages as the allocation of scarcities, rather than as the reflection of the historical process of reproduction, led to an analytical shift. In the second chapter this is discussed in connection with the theory of the wages fund, hence unencumbered by later complications related to the neoclassical theory of distribution.

The concept of the natural price of labour as an exogenous cost of reproduction is the line of demarcation between Ricardo's economic theory and theories based on the idea that wages are determined by supply and demand, so that prices and quantities are systematically linked in a context of scarcity (Garegnani, 1983, 1984, 1987). These theories are not necessarily neoclassical (Bharadwaj, 1978a, 1989); that is to say, they are not all tied to a particular theory of distribution in which profit is determined by the productivity of capital and wages by the productivity of labour. It is important to note, however, that all these theories presuppose that the size and living standards of the population are disciplined by the market, understood exclusively as a process of allocation of relative scarcities. The determination of wages in a theory of exogenous distribution, historically given by social norms and institutions and by material processes, is thus completely different from the systematic, more or less mechanical, determination of wages within a process of allocation of given factors of production.

Neoclassical theory includes a particular notion of labour supply as a systematic price–quantity relation. This relation is part of an analytical scheme which generally expresses relations between quantities, without reference to historical or – still less – political processes. This is done not simply for the sake of abstraction, but to purge the theory of any complications arising from the labour market. It is no accident, then, that institutions and material processes of reproduction find no place in the general scheme of neoclassical economics. In going back to the classical approach in which the natural price of labour is a norm that is not systematically dependent on relations of exchange of scarce quantities, but given by the historical process of social reproduction, I aim to place institutions and historical living standards at the very centre of the analytical scheme. What is involved, therefore, is not only a difference in concepts, but a radical difference in method. But my aim is not to provide a theory or a history of the social reproduction of labour; it is to return the question of the capitalist relationship between production and reproduction in its former position at the core of the analytical framework of political economy. In order to do this my first task is to recover an essential tool – the classical idea of the natural price of labour (chapters 1 and 2).

Having reestablished an analytical perspective based on 'subsistence', in chapters 3, 4 and 5 I present some historical cases that bring out the persistence and the importance of the problems inherent in the capitalist relation between production and reproduction: one such example is the Poor Laws, another is women's labour in reproduction. Lastly, on the basis of these cases and using the analytical tools recovered from the history of economic analysis, in chapter 6 I propose my approach to the labour supply, based not on a systematic relation between price and quantity of labour but on its social process of reproduction. In the neoclassical perspective population size and standards of living depend on the quantity of capital – i.e. the aggregate demand for labour; in the Ricardian tradition wages are determined by the historical process of reproduction.

The difference between the two theories of wages is crucial for social policy. A natural or 'objective' limit on the resources available for the working population – impersonally determined by the quantity of capital – necessarily implies that problems of adaptation between accumulation and the process of social reproduction must be solved (or at any rate absorbed) within the process of reproduction of the population, without impinging significantly on the formation and accumulation of profit. According to theories of this type, the state should be called upon only in exceptional, limited and temporary cases, although in reality it is forced to take measures to ensure that the adaptation is accomplished. An application of such a theory, based on scarcity of resources and on the principle that resources for workers' subsistence are more scarce than others, appears in the Poor Law Report of 1834; but equally crude versions of the same scheme appear in the formulation of economic policies today. Thus the underlying analytical malpractice should be identified. Moreover, as we see in the third chapter, the failure of the 1834 policies – unanimously recognized by the 1905–9 Royal Committee on the Poor Laws – brings out the gravity of the problems affecting the capitalist labour market. Though these problems were excluded from the general analysis, they remained central and persistent at the level of economic reality.

An important aspect of the analytical scheme proposed here is the view of the capitalist system which emerges from it. Ricardian economics is based on a view that is undoubtedly partial both in its range and in its class outlook, but it is certainly more useful than neoclassical economics for understanding the inner workings of the labour market. First of all, Ricardo's concept of surplus helps to bring out the historical subordination of social reproduction to the requirements of profit accumulation. Thus it facilitates criticism not only of neoclassical economics but also of classical political economy itself, in terms of the complexities and tensions inherent in the capitalist relation between the processes of production and social reproduction.

These tensions impinge very directly and specifically on women, as I will try to show in chapters 4 and 5. The difficulty of women's reproductive work lies not so much in physical exertion or long hours, but in the struggle to give priority to the needs of people within the constraints of profit. Women find themselves more and more isolated in this increasingly stressful effort to change the balance of social imperatives, because the market and other institutions respond mainly to the requirements of capitalist accumulation, with all the limitations imposed by those requirements.

The difficult position of women in the process of social reproduction cannot be hidden, and in any case women are no longer inclined to hide it. The insecurity which appears to be an individual problem is in reality a systemic one, profoundly rooted in a general indifference towards the living conditions of the population. It stems not only from the material conditions of life, which may be adequate or even opulent for some sections of the labouring population, but from social and psychological conditions linked with people's deep needs for security, growth and autonomy.

The labour market, the fundamental institution of the capitalist system, has perhaps come out best among the historically existing systems for commanding labour and distributing the means of subsistence. But because it is necessarily based on collective insecurity and on subordination of the process of social reproduction to the process of accumulation, it is far from being the best of all possible worlds. The separation between the processes of production and reproduction hides the ways in which the proportion between the value of production and costs of reproduction has historically been held within limits compatible with capitalist accumulation. But what is compatible is actually dictated by the rate of profit – by definition historical – and not by natural scarcities or technological dynamics. To expose the feigned 'objectivity' of profit and 'endogeneity' of wages is one of the aims of this book.

Two fundamental questions emerge from the foregoing discussion, one theoretical and the other political. The theoretical question is whether the balance between production and reproduction is determined by natural or technical laws, or by historically evolving norms and institutions. From the latter position, on which my argument is clearly based, arises the political question: how to reverse the priorities in favour of reproduction.

Women can contribute to both questions by presenting the bill for the enormous amount of work they do in reproducing the population. To accomplish this they need allies, including men dissatisfied with their own gender-based solution to the contradictions inherent in the capitalist relationship between accumulation and reproduction. Other potential allies are all persons aware of the world-wide risks which an exclusively profit-oriented system of production has by now created because of its perverse relationship between the production of commodities and the reproduction of individuals, the human race and the planet. But all the alliances must be based on the recognition of the specificity of women's exploitation in the process of social reproduction of the population. Potential allies, therefore, must go beyond the false gender neutrality of exploitation of waged labour if they are Marxists; and, if they are ecologists, they must go beyond the romantic exaltation of the family (Illich, 1981, 1982).

1

Wages as exogenous costs of social reproduction

1.1 The historical context

By classical political economy I mean here the analytical structure in which the nascent capitalist economic system was analysed, especially by British economists, at the end of the eighteenth century and in the first decades of the nineteenth century. The analytical framework I refer to as 'classical' is basically limited to that of Ricardo's surplus approach, although Smith and Malthus are also used for their rich information and analytical considerations on the labour market.

Marx is not included here because his analysis of the labour market, as the locus of an unequal exchange – freed from the Malthusian demographic adjustments – and as the core of the dynamic process of capitalist accumulation, is a powerful critique of classical analysis. The concept of the natural price of labour, however, can be used as an introduction to Marx's analysis of wages. The analysis of the modes of subsistence is one of the roots of the Marxist materialist tradition (Meek, 1967a), but it goes far beyond that tradition. Marx's emphasis is more on the process of production and accumulation of profit than on the process of social reproduction; this leads to some deficiencies in his analysis of the family and the state as agents in the labour market. Moreover, the political implications of a social–reproduction perspective – involving, as a political subject, the whole labouring population and not merely waged workers – must be taken explicitly into consideration. Finally, while in the production process individuals can be aggregated on the basis of their common productive characteristics, in the process of social reproduction they retain specific identities which cannot be totally subsumed within social groups.[1]

To understand the basic features of a new system which was still in the process of formation, many disciplines were called into service. Social theorists used history, philosophy, political thought, moral philosophy, aesthetics, demography and natural history to explain a social system which was traditional in that it was based on private property, but which broke with tradition in its general use of waged labour.[2] Within the traditional subordination of labour to property, profound changes were occurring in the structure of classes. Thus the legitimization of a viable implicit social contract was as important as analytical consistency.

Smith was able to accomplish a shift of scientific perspective precisely because he merged jurisprudence, ethics, rhetoric, political thought and history in his powerful grasp of the new economic structure.[3] What he grasped in fact was not the industrial revolution, which was not yet established (Kindleberger, 1976), but the division of labour and the new social relations between labourers and employers, and between the labouring population and its means of subsistence.

The accumulation of capital introduced a separation between the processes of production and the processes of social reproduction of the labouring population. This separation occurred merely at the level of organization, as these processes were interconnected, and both were necessary for the reproduction of the system as a whole: commodities could not be produced without labour, and the labouring population could not survive without wages. The separation was not spontaneous and it was not accomplished by impersonal market forces: laws, orders, courts, evictions and workhouses forced the changes into social practice. Such measures were no longer used to enforce a brutal personal command over labour, but to induce, often brutally, a dependence of the labouring population on the waged labour market. Dependence was often forced not because production of subsistence goods in household agriculture was inadequate, but precisely because it was adequate. If households were independent of the labour market, the labouring population – once it produced what it needed for consumption or for exchange in order to pay rent – would choose leisure instead of more production.[4]

In a capitalist system the labouring population no longer reproduces itself with self-produced goods or with market goods acquired by direct exchange of its own products; its reproduction depends on the sale of its labour. In this respect, the capitalist system introduced a change in the meaning and objectives of the social system: the independent household produced for the reproduction of its members, the capitalist economy uses the reproduction of the labouring population for the accumulation of capital.[5] Hence capital must be understood not only physically, as tools or goods, but as a specific historical relationship between the labouring population and its means of reproduction. Since the surplus is the difference between production and costs of production – basically costs of reproduction of the labouring population – the relationship is a conflictual one.

The establishment of the capitalist labour market as a viable social institution was partly favoured by its implied democratic challenge against forms of command over labour by direct control over persons, whether brutal or paternalistic.[6] The direct sale of labour gained social acceptance because it led to higher standards of living, at least in some sections of the labouring population; but it concealed a loss of autonomy and an increased insecurity over the means of reproduction.[7]

The waged labour market required control over labour and its reproduction, and this was gained through two different and interrelated historical processes. One of these, the expropriation of the means of subsistence which forced the independent household into the labour market, has been well studied in the history of enclosures and primitive accumulation. The other is the attempt, mainly on the part of the state, to increase control over the process of reproduction of the labouring population. This is usually overlooked in the study of the origins of capitalism.

From the sixteenth century on, continuous attention was given by the state to the question of population, the human body, sexuality, infancy, marriage and the family. The search for 'laws' and regularities governing population and human bodies was itself part of a complex network of power forces, as Foucault points out:

As for population controls, one notes the emergence of demography, the evaluation of the relationship between resources and inhabitants, the constructing of tables analyzing wealth and its circulation . . .
This bio-power was without question an indispensable element in the development of capitalism; the latter would not have been possible without the controlled insertion of bodies into the machinery of production and the adjustment of the phenomena of population to economic processes. But this was not all it required; it also needed the growth of both these factors, their reinforcement as well as their availability and docility; . . . If the development of the great instruments of the state, as *institutions* of power, ensured the maintenance of production relations, the rudiments of anatomy and bio-politics, created in the eighteenth century as *techniques* of power, present at every level of the social body and utilized by very diverse institutions (the family and the army, schools and the police, individual medicine and the administration of collective bodies), operated in the sphere of economic processes, their development, and the forces working to sustain them . . . The adjustment of the accumulation of men to that of capital, the joining of the growth of human groups to the expansion of productive forces and the differential allocation of profit, were made possible in part by the exercise of bio-power in its many forms and modes of application. (Foucault, 1979, pp. 140–1)

Women play a key role in the process of reproduction and as such were a main target for control. A terrific amount of violence was used against them all over Europe when thousands of 'witches' were tortured and burnt in towns and villages by state officials after religious trials. Witches were in fact persecuted for their knowledge of gynaecology (childbirth, abortion, contraceptives), for rebellion against husbands (poisoning was a widespread practice), for social unrest (in a moment of increasing insecurity over the means of subsistence), for refusing marriage, for sexual intercourse outside marriage, etc. Fear and misogyny, as well as their own interest in controlling women's reproductive work, deterred men from intervening in women's support.[8]

When labour became waged labour, the work of reproduction became unwaged housework. The biological aspects of human reproduction were used to hide the historical and social aspects of gender division of labour. As time went by the separation involved different places, timings, power relationships, and, most of all, social values. The separation between the process of production and that of social reproduction of labour implied that the division of labour between men and women took new forms and shaped new power relationships within the traditional context of women's subordination.[9]

An exploitative division of labour and oppressive power relationships between genders were usually taken as natural by classical economists. This is explicable in terms of the cultural and civil context of their works. These were based on the assumption of increasing freedom for 'individuals' (which meant males) and limited freedom for women, whose economic, political and juridical dependence on the head of the family was taken for granted by the power structure as well as by the great majority of its radical opponents (Gobetti, 1983). The issue here, however, is not what political economists had to say about the role of women, but what they said about the capitalist relationship between accumulation of capital and reproduction of the labouring population.

1.2 The analytical context

The acceptance of the new institutional system of the waged labour market was the basis for the classical political economists' uncritical view of profit. Although they were uncritical, however, they were quite lucid in their acknowledgement of some of the system's basic characteristics. They had to be so in order to grasp its functioning and formulate abstract schemes to facilitate understanding of the real processes of production and distribution of wealth. They showed this lucidity – and their anxieties – in various ways: Smith referred explicitly to class conflicts, and Ricardo used Smith's analysis of the economic system as a basis for a theory of value which assumed an inverse relationship between profit and wages.

In the classical framework the wealth of the nation is seen as producible, and labour is the basic commodity capable of producing a surplus which allows for a continuous process of accumulation. In this context of producible commodities, prices are mainly determined by costs of production. In the same way, the price of labour is determined by the cost of its reproduction. The analogy is possible only if labour can be considered producible and not persistently and generally scarce.

The classical analytical framework directly reflects some historical facts: the fact that labour has itself become a commodity makes continuous accumulation possible; the fact that labour is a very peculiar commodity, whose production is not directly organized by capitalists, leads to the determination of wages separately from other prices; and, finally, the fact that labour is producible leads to the notion of wages as costs of social reproduction.

In a market economy prices play two roles: they have to cover the costs of production, and they are the impersonal mechanism for distribution of income among classes and within classes. The problem of the classical theory of value is precisely to explain how this happens and to reveal the functioning of the economic system behind the visible phenomena of market prices. The distribution between wages and profit makes the problem of values and relative prices more difficult than the one outlined in the Physiocratic surplus approach, where the distribution of surplus between independent labourers and landowners was visualized as an explicit institutional transfer of surplus in the form of rent. When labour is acknowledged as a commodity, relative prices must reflect first of all the relationship between profits and wages. The relevant aspects of the new distribution of surplus are more hidden but no less institutional.

Both Smith and Ricardo made judgements on the persistent or accidental nature of problems. The difference between the natural and the market price of labour implies different levels of analysis.[10] The social cost of reproduction of the labouring population reflects a basic problem inherent in the social system, arising from the role of private property as a filter mediating access to the means of subsistence. Political economy locates old questions in a new perspective: the debate on corn prices takes the form of a debate on natural wages; social justice is said to be guaranteed by the functioning of the labour market (Hont and Ignatieff, 1983)[11]; and the right to subsistence gives place to a debate on the right to work.

In order to reach a deeper understanding of the concept of the natural price of labour it is important to study its roots, which are based on the modes of subsistence. The forms of access to subsistence play a major part in the study of human societies. To grasp them one must take account of the productive processes and the social norms regulating the distribution of resources, as social stratifications imply different degrees of access to the means of subsistence. In Greece, for instance, working for the necessities of life was seen as the distinguishing feature of slaves (Arendt,

12

1958, p. 61).

Classical political economists took into account new solutions to the problems of subsistence but did not attempt to remove those problems from the analytical framework. The modes of subsistence were the crucial dynamic key in the four-stage theory of growth endorsed by Smith in the *Lectures on Jurisprudence* and a crucial issue in the *Wealth of Nations* as the moral basis of the social system, as Hont and Ignatieff point out in the following passage:[12]

If, as Smith too argued in the 'invisible hand' passage of the 'Theory of Moral Sentiments', the moral legitimacy in distribution in commercial society lay in the fact that those who were left out in the partition of property, i.e. the wage earning poor, received adequate subsistence, it remained for him to explain in the 'Wealth of Nations' exactly how this was achieved. In a commercial society wage labourers were 'independent': that is they did not depend upon their masters to provide them with subsistence, and their rate of remuneration was determined by supply and demand for labour and by the customs of their trade and only ultimately by what was necessary for their bare subsistence. (Hont and Ignatieff, 1983, p. 13)

As a matter of fact Hont and Ignatieff miss the difference between natural and market wages. This is unfortunate because the difference in nature and relative importance between wages as the costs of social reproduction and wages as prices set by supply and demand is essential for the classical analytical framework. What Ricardo and Smith attempted to do, at the level of the natural price of labour, was to evaluate some of the persistent forces which acted on wages: historical modes of production of wage goods, class power relationships, habits and tastes.

As we shall see, the analytical solutions proposed by classical economists could not cope with the complexities of all these factors. The distinctive feature of the classical system, however, is that some essential elements of the labour market were placed within the normal and general analytical framework as basic aspects of the economic system as a whole. These included not only wages and employment, but also living standards, social norms, class conflicts, social segmentation, demographic movements, the state and the family. They were seen as related to the problems inherent in the definition of labour as a commodity, and its peculiar process of production: other commodities do not subsist, they exist; they do not die, they are either consumed or destroyed; they are not born but they are produced. Last but not least, they do not acquire habits and tastes and are not politically active.

Some mercantilist institutions regulating the exchange of labour had to be removed (for example, direct control over wages and labour mobility).

However, the labour market necessarily maintained its political and institutional texture, which was the essence of the analytical notion of the natural (normal) price of labour. To disregard this complexity means to cut one of the deep roots essential for the understanding of the economic system and to remove the modes of subsistence from their central role in the structuring of the social system.

The significance of social reproduction as a foundation block of the classical analytical framework is almost completely lost today even in the modern reappraisal of the surplus approach. In this respect my work goes along different lines from the many speculations on the determinate character of the natural price of labour.[13] My aim, in fact, is to recover the complexity of the capitalist relationship between the process of accumulation of capital and the process of social reproduction of the labouring population. The way in which this relationship is analysed has important implications not only for the question of the determinacy of wages but also for the methodology of economic analysis.

1.3 Smith, Ricardo and Malthus on wages

A greater understanding of the essence of their theory of wages can be gained by rereading Smith, Ricardo and Malthus with particular attention to the notion of labour as a commodity, wages and the costs of social reproduction of the labouring population, and the role of the state and the family in the labour market.

In Smith there is already a full awareness that waged labour constitutes the general case of the labour–subsistence exchange:

It seldom happens that the person who tills the ground has wherewithal to maintain himself till he reaps the harvest. His maintenance is generally advanced to him from the stock of a master, the farmer who employs him, and who would have no interest to employ him, unless he was to share in the produce of his labour, or unless his stock was to be replaced to him with a profit.

This profit makes a second deduction from the produce of the labour which is employed upon land . . .

It sometimes happens, indeed, that a single independent workman has stock sufficient both to purchase the materials of his work, and to maintain himself till it be completed . . . Such cases, however, are not very frequent, and in every part of Europe, twenty workmen serve under a master for one that is independent; and the wages of labour are everywhere understood to be, what they usually are, when the labourer is one person, and the owner of the stock which employs him another. (A. Smith, 1976 (1776), p. 83)

Labour was considered not only as a commodity, but also as a producible commmodity. Smith expresses it like this: 'the demand for men, like that for any other commodity, necessarily regulates the production of men, quickens it when it goes on too slowly and stops it when it advances too fast' (p. 98). Ricardo, on the other hand, says: 'Labour, like all the other things which are purchased and sold, and which can be increased or diminished in quantity, has its natural and its market price' (Ricardo, 1951a (1817), p. 91). For Ricardo too, labour is a commodity – more precisely, a thing (for Smith it was men) – whose quantity is not fixed like that of land, and can in some way be adapted to the requirements of production. Men are now called 'labour', and they are considered, in the analysis and in the real system, as a specific section of the population, so specific that Ricardo and Smith call it a 'race'. Malthus insists on the definition of labour as a commodity, which assumes a more abstract connotation: 'The wages of labour are the remuneration of the labourer for his personal exertions. They may be divided like the prices of commodities, into real and nominal' (Malthus, 1820, p. 240).

Some analytical insights in the *Wealth of Nations* are particularly important with regard to the problems of the labour market. First of all, Smith opens chapter 8, 'Of the Wages of Labour', by introducing the capitalist separation between production and distribution, i.e. between the produce and the recompense of labour.[14] This reflects a separation between production of commodities and reproduction of the labouring population and corresponds to the historical process of expropriation of the means of subsistence from the labouring population. It also reflects the class structure of society which leads to the distribution of the product between wages, profits and rent and to a separate organization of production and reproduction with new forms of division of labour.

Smith noticed a fundamental effect of the separation between production and reproduction, i.e. the reduction of costs of reproduction inherent in the new social framework. In fact, the separation introduces a radical change into the organization of the process of reproduction of labour. He compares the waged labour market with the case of slavery, which involves a different form of social reproduction:

The wear and tear of a slave, it has been said, is at the expense of his master; but that of a free servant is at his own expense. The wear and tear of the latter, however, is, in reality, as much at the expense of his master as that of the former . . . But though the wear and tear of a free servant be equally at the expense of his master, it generally costs him much less than that of a slave. The fund destined for replacing or repairing, if I may say so, the wear and tear of the slave, is commonly managed by a negligent master or careless overseer. That destined for performing the same office with regard to the free man, is managed by the free man himself. The disorders which generally prevail in the economy of the rich, naturally introduce themselves into the management of the former: the strict frugality and the parsimonious attention of the poor naturally establish themselves in that of the latter. Under such different management, the same purpose must require very different degrees of expense to execute it . . . I believe that the work done by freemen comes cheaper in the end than that performed by slaves. It is found to do so even at Boston, New York, and Philadelphia, where the wages of common labour are so very high. (A. Smith, 1976 (1776), pp. 183–4)

In this very revealing and usually overlooked passage, Smith acknowledges that free (dependent) labour implies a separation between the organization of production and that of reproduction, and notes that this separation leads to a reduction in the costs of reproduction. The reduction of costs is here not attributed to an absolute impoverishment in standards of living, nor to an increase in the productivity of labour in the production of wage goods – which Smith discusses elsewhere – but it is clearly explained in terms of savings in the organization of the process of reproduction. This is one of the main threads of my argument.

On the basis of distribution, Smith develops the idea of an inherent class conflict in the social system, and this, as he clearly points out, is potentially so radical as to involve the very foundations of the state:

Avarice and ambition in the rich, in the poor the hatred of labour and the love of the present ease and enjoyment, are the passions much more steady in their operations . . . The affluence of the rich excites the indignation of the poor, who are often both driven by want, and prompted by envy, to invade his possession . . . The acquisition of valuable and expensive property therefore, necessarily requires the establishment of civil government. (pp. 709–10)

The main features of Smith's vision of the capitalist labour market can be schematically summarized as follows: (a) a full establishment of the exchange of labour for wages; (b) a separation between the organization of production and that of reproduction; (c) insecurity as the basis of command over work; (d) economic growth owing to the increase of productivity made possible by the division of labour; (e) a general increase of standards of living for all, in spite of widespread social inequality.

Ricardo explicitly stresses his dependence on Smith's analysis of the labour market. Although the problems related to the specificity of labour with regard to the process of social reproduction are given less descriptive attention, he is more stringent and consistent in dealing with distribution and relative prices, as he is pessimistic about long-term perspectives for capitalist growth.

Exogeneity of wages

The data on which Ricardo based his analysis of value and distribution can be summed up as: real wages, output, techniques (hence employment), and the conditions of social reproduction of the labouring population. From these data, which result from different historical processes, the surplus is determined as the difference between production and reproduction. Once the surplus is determined, the unknown elements of the system are the rate of profit and the system of relative prices (Sraffa, 1960; Eatwell, 1977; Garegnani, 1984).

In Smith and Ricardo the distribution of the social product to the various classes is explained by means of different analytical concepts. Wages, like all commodity prices, are first of all a cost of production; as necessary consumption they do not, by definition, figure in the net product. Profit, on the other hand, represents the net product that belongs to the owners of the means of production by virtue of their power relationship with the producers (the workers). Neither profit nor wages are explained on the basis of a specific contribution to production. Profit derives from the ownership of the means of production, and ownership is not a productive factor but a particular institutional relationship. The wages that go to the workers are based not on their productive capacity but on the cost of reproducing them as workers, and of reproducing the labouring population dependent on their wages.

In their definition of wages Smith and Ricardo follow the indications already given by Petty and Turgot of a subsistence wage seen as the necessary cost for the reproduction of the labouring population. According to Smith:

A man must always live by his work, and his wages must at least be sufficient to maintain him. They must even upon most occasions be somewhat more; otherwise it would be impossible for him to bring up a family, and the race of such workmen could not last beyond the first generation. (A. Smith, 1976 (1776), p. 85)

While Ricardo says:

The power of the labourer to support himself, and the family which may be necessary to keep up the number of labourers, does not depend on the quantity of money which he may receive for wages, but on the quantity of food, necessaries and conveniences become essential to him from habit, which that money will purchase. (Ricardo, 1951a (1817), p. 93)

The share of output distributed to the labouring population as a whole cannot exceed the limits consistent with capitalist accumulation. The lower limit of that share is defined by the need to reproduce the labouring population, and the upper limit is defined by the needs of accumulation. In

17

this double constraint lies the problem of the classical political economists and their view of the functioning of the labour market. The relationship is made more complicated by the fact that the natural drive towards a continuous refinement in standards of living is considered a dynamic element of economic growth. Historical standards of living of the labouring population are thus an exogenous dynamic force which has to be contained within the dynamics of the accumulation of capital.[15]

In the *Lectures on Jurisprudence* Smith – in a context of natural history[16] – refers to 'delicacy of mind' as one of the basic forces leading to the social division of labour:

As the delicacy of a man's body requires much greater provision than that of any other animal, the same or rather much greater delicacy of his mind requires a still greater provision, to which all the different arts (are) subservient.

Man is the only animal who is possessed of such a nicety that the very colour of an object hurts him. Among different objects a different division of arrangement of them pleases. The taste of beauty . . . is the cause of all this nicety. (A. Smith, 1978a (1767), p. 488)[17]

Ricardo uses the argument of insatiable needs to maintain that the economic system does not face problems of insufficiency of effective demand:

I consider the wants and tastes of mankind unlimited. We all wish to add to our enjoyments or to our power. Consumption adds to our enjoyments, accumulation to our power, and they equally promote demand. (Ricardo, 1952 (1816–18), vol. VII, p. 135)

Malthus includes luxuries in his definition of real wages: 'The real wages of labour consist of their value, estimated in the necessaries, conveniences, and luxuries of life' (Malthus, 1820, p. 240). Note that in a Ricardian context, if 'luxuries' become part of the necessary cost of guaranteeing the supply of labour, they must be considered 'necessary consumption' for the productive system: if bread is consumed by non-productive classes, that bread is not to be regarded necessary consumption, whereas flowers, if they become part of the general habits of the labouring population, should be considered as productive consumption.

The analytical concept of the natural price of labour, taken as the normal historical cost of social reproduction, serves to locate directly in the economic analysis some of the problems inherent in the peculiarity of the social and historical processes that structure the labour market. This concept is often confined to the limited meaning of a subsistence theory of wages, and is often confused with a downward rigidity of otherwise flexible wages. As such, it is considered applicable only to the specific case of low-waged sections of the population (S. Hollander, 1979, 1984) or to poor countries (Lewis, 1954).[18] Thus, the subsistence theory of wages is treated not as a general theory of the determination of wages – as exogenous historical costs of social reproduction of labour – but only as a theory of low wages. This is why Ricardo's theory of wages as costs of reproduction was confused with the 'iron law of wages', i.e. with a theory of constant minimum wages. This confusion between exogenous and constant was partly justified by Ricardo's endorsement of a specific theory of reproduction, that of Malthus, and by the assumption of the scarcity of land as systematically affecting the cost of production of wage goods. The idea of subsistence as mere rigidity conflicts with the notion of wages as costs of social reproduction, as we shall see in the next chapter.

Smith and Ricardo considered it methodologically essential to distinguish between systematic and accidental events. In natural prices, as opposed to market prices, they regarded the consideration of systematic and persistent social behaviour as the only valid analytical basis for defining the state of the system:

In making labour the foundation of the value of commodities, and the comparative quantity of labour which is necessary to their production, the rule which determines the respective quantities of goods which shall be given in exchange for each other, we must not be supposed to deny the accidental and temporary deviations of the actual or market price of commodities from this, their primary and natural price . . .
In speaking then of the exchangeable value of commodities, or the power of purchasing possessed by any one commodity, I mean always the power which it would possess, if not disturbed by any temporal or accidental cause, and which is its natural price. (Ricardo, 1951a (1817), pp. 88, 97)

The system of natural prices reflects the influence of the dominant and persistent forces acting on production, reproduction and distribution. Market prices, defined by their deviation from natural prices, reflect the flexibility of the economic system when it is affected by accidental and temporary scarcities superimposed on the system's structure of producible commodities, labour included. The course of market prices cannot be understood without first isolating the persistent centres of gravitation defined by the natural prices which reflect the basic productive forces of the system. Thus, for Ricardo, the natural price constitutes a fundamental point of reference for defining the state of the system in terms of its dominant characteristics, as revealed when the allocation of capital guarantees a uniform rate of profit. The difference is not one of time; it is rather in the quality of the forces acting behind natural prices and behind market prices (Garegnani, 1976; Eatwell, 1977).[19]

Schumpeter acknowledges Ricardo's distinction between market price and natural price, although he dismisses it as 'superficial and equivocal' and in any case a theoretical relic of the past.

> Cantillon paid much attention to the problem of market price as distinguished from normal price – exactly as did A. Smith later on. One feature of his treatment is worth noting because it persisted practically to J. S. Mill. Like all 'classics' of the nineteenth century, Ricardo especially, Cantillon never asked the question how market price is related to normal price and precisely how the latter emerges – if indeed it does emerge – from the supply-and-demand mechanism that produces the former. Taking this relation for granted, he was led to treat market price as a separate phenomenon and to restrict the supply-and-demand explanation to it.
>
> Thus emerged the superficial and, as the later development of the theory of value was to show, misleading formula – normal price is determined by cost, market price is determined by supply and demand. (Schumpeter, 1954, p. 220)

In the case of labour, the distinction between natural and market price plays a key role because labour is a basic commodity (i.e. necessary input for all other commodities), because the forces acting in the process of reproduction of the labouring population profoundly affect the social system, and because the labouring population is an active political subject. If the notion of natural price is applied to the commodity labour, the natural price of labour must mean the price towards which wages tend through the action of persistent and systematic forces in the labour market. The natural price is not constant, but changes from time to time and from place to place, thereby causing a shift in the centre towards which market wages gravitate.

The fact that natural prices, including wages, are not determined by the interplay of supply and demand as systematic price–quantity relationships does not mean that the production of commodities and labour can be separated from the functioning of the market. Nor is there a separation between non-market and market operations. The process of reproduction of the economic system has to be seen as a whole, and the existence of the labour market, as the general form of the labour–subsistence exchange, determines the essential character of the whole process of social reproduction.

The problem, in fact, is not to separate the process of production from that of exchange but to see how physical and social processes of production and reproduction systematically structure the relationships of exchange. The market is in fact an institution, or rather a complex of institutions, which enables agents to receive signals regarding the exchange and circulation of commodities at various levels. The phenomena signalled are diverse and so are the institutional behaviours that respond to the signals. A confusion about the analytical categories of prices reflects a deeply confused view of the functioning of the market. Instead of being seen within a multidimensional social structure based on processes and institutions, the latter is reduced to an allocative mechanism whereby quantities and prices respond systematically to each other. This levels and obscures the crucial problems of the economic system. In the case of the labour market this disregard of important social realities has a particularly mystifying effect, because it conceals the way exchange actually functions in a capitalist system where labour is a fundamental commodity.

The cost of social reproduction of labour, while highly important from the analytical point of view, is difficult to define and to measure precisely. But the problem, at least here, is not so much to define a specific wage bundle to be used as the physical index of that cost, as to analyse some of the basic forces which determine its level and composition, and to see how those forces are reflected in the analytical framework. The material standards of living expressed in the natural price of labour, at a given time, are determined by the consolidated habits and tastes of the labouring population. In this sense, the natural wage can be understood as the wage level which is conventionally accepted in the labour market as the basis for bargaining. Ricardo takes this wage bundle as constant for a given period of production, but in the course of time it can change in level and composition.

The cost of social reproduction can be specified as minimum, average, or otherwise. The definition of wages as costs of social reproduction does not imply any tendency of the natural price of labour towards either biological subsistence, a minimum wage or increasing standards of living. Lack of precision in defining the historical trends of the costs of reproduction, or different views as to their dynamics, do not in themselves indicate confusion in the use of the natural and the market price of labour. The lack of insight into the process of social reproduction of labour does not in itself preclude clarity about the role of the process of social reproduction of labour – and of its inherent conflicts – in the determination of wages and of relative prices. The issue under consideration here is not the classical (or any other) theory of reproduction, but the role of the historical process of reproduction in the classical analysis of the labour market and of the social system.[20]

The problem of indicating (at least in analytical terms) a given wage bundle reflected in the natural price of labour is greatly complicated by the fact that in classical political economy that wage bundle depends – in different ways – on power relationships between opposed political subjects. Smith, for instance, says:

21

Social reproduction of labour

What are the common wages of labour depends everywhere upon the contract usually made between those two parties, whose interests are by no means the same. The workmen desire to get as much, the masters to give as little as possible. The former are disposed to combine in order to raise, the latter in order to lower the wages of labour. (A. Smith, 1976 (1776), p. 83)

Ricardo expresses this potential conflict in terms which are sociologically less rich but analytically more cogent. Malthus in a certain sense assumes that the market can resolve the conflict, or at least regulate it through automatic mechanisms of exchange, reducing it to the play of supply and demand. This is perhaps why he feels free to introduce a definition of the supply of labour, which is given in terms of consent:

And if the resources of the country were to remain fixed, the comforts of the lower classes of society would depend upon their habits, or on the amount of those necessaries and conveniences without which they would not consent to keep up their numbers. (Malthus, 1820, p. 243)

So the natural wage reflects not only factors such as persistent habits of the labouring population and their material standards of living, but also the 'normal' historical and institutional forms of conflict between classes. Each period is characterized not only by a level of output and wages, but also by a complex set of social norms and 'rules of the game' in the class conflict. These are inherited from past organizational levels, and they form the basis of new modes of conflictual behaviour. The natural price is influenced both by the wage bundle considered 'normal' and by the organizations and political means through which that bundle has been obtained. In the analysis of the classical economists this aspect emerges, for example, in references to laws against workers' combinations, which belong to a particular epoch and cannot be considered permanent.

The inclusion of power relationships in the determination of wages and prices makes it impossible to see the economic system as a natural organism, or as a machine which incorporates enough automatic mechanisms to guarantee its continuous reproduction and growth (Meek, 1977). The power relationship between workers and capitalists turns precisely on the material standards of living of the labouring population. In the conflict with their employers, the workers' objective is not a mere trial of relative strength, but the maintenance and improvement of the standards of living that represent the 'passions and the interests' of the labouring population. This vital aspect of bargaining, closely linked with the material process of reproduction of labour, appears in the classical economists' definition of real wages as the real command of the workers over a specific wage bundle composed of 'the quantity of food, necessaries and conveniences become essential to him from habit' (Ricardo, 1951a (1817), p. 93).

Ricardo and Malthus differ considerably over the influence of demand on prices. For Ricardo natural prices are determined by the conditions of production of commodities, and this holds for labour too.

The natural price of labour is that price which is necessary to enable the labourers, one with another, to subsist and to perpetuate their race, without either increase or diminution . . .

The market price for labour is the price, which is really paid for it, from the natural operation of the proportion of supply to the demand; labour is dear when it is scarce, and cheap when it is plentiful. However much the market price of labour may deviate from its natural price, it has, like commodities, a tendency to conform to it. (Ricardo, 1951a (1817), pp. 93, 99)

As already noted, for Ricardo the variation in the relationship between supply and demand is caused by accidental and unsystematic events. The market price of labour is superimposed on the natural price of labour as an index of scarcity, without, however, changing the basic structure of the analytical system. Ricardo does not assume, even over time, a direct systematic relationship between the natural price of labour and the demand for labour:

Thus, then, with every improvement of society, with every increase in its capital, the market wages of labour will rise; but the permanence of their rise will depend on the question, whether the natural price of labour has also risen; and this again will depend on the rise in the natural price of those necessaries on which the wages of labour are expended.

It is not to be understood that the natural price of labour, even estimated in food and necessaries, is absolutely fixed and constant. It varies at different times in the same country, and very materially differs in different countries.

It essentially depends on the habits and customs of the people. (Ricardo, 1951a (1817), pp. 96–7)

For Ricardo, the difference between natural and market prices is precisely in the forces that lie behind them: in the first case the forces of production, in the second temporary or partial perturbations of the market caused by imbalances between the quantity supplied and the quantity demanded.[21] Still, to sustain the concept of the wage as the natural price of labour a mechanism is required through which the quantity of labour, as Smith said, can be 'quickened when it goes too slowly and stopped when it advances too fast' (A. Smith, 1976 (1776), p. 98).[22]

1.4 The supply of labour

Until the first half of the eighteenth century, social theorists for the most part considered the increase of population not only as a symptom but also as a cause of the increase of wealth; some of them considered the population itself as an asset.[23] In the second part of the eighteenth century this attitude was progressively modified; Godwin was to remain the last paladin of populationist optimism. In his isolation he made an easy target for Malthus, whose task it was to bury the expectations of well-being and increasing wealth for all which were widespread throughout Europe in the last decades of the eighteenth century (Meek, 1953, pp. 11–12; Himmelfarb, 1984, pp. 100–32).

In his work, *An Essay on the Principle of Population*, Malthus attempted to formulate a universal law demonstrating the powerlessness of any action on the part of the working classes, or reformist governments, to put an end to poverty. According to his theory, population tends to increase at a faster rate than productive resources. The effects of any demographic behaviour which might conflict with the requirements of accumulation must inevitably fall back on the workers in terms of poverty. This will be either 'voluntary' because it is due to foolishness, or 'ineluctable' because it can be attributed to nature.[24]

Ricardo adopts Malthus's theory of population, which assumes a natural mechanism to control the quantity and the living standards of the labouring population. A precise analytical problem drove him to accept Malthus's law. In Ricardo's scheme, where profit is defined as a residuum, the potential conflict between wages and profit is explicit. Thus the dynamics of wages must be circumscribed – at least at the analytical level – to avoid the hypothetical possibility that workers' consumption might absorb the whole product of labour and leave no margin for the reproduction of the capitalist system. Malthus's demographic mechanism allowed Ricardo to assume a non-explosive market price for labour, which oscillates around the natural price. Wages are prevented from dropping to levels too low for the reproduction of labour, or from reaching and maintaining levels too high for the system's needs for capital accumulation. The adjustments work at the level of market prices, being activated by relative changes in supply and demand.

In the Ricardian context a change in the quantity of the population could affect the natural price of labour via the basic forces working behind the whole process of social reproduction – for instance, a change in the market price of labour might eventually affect the general standards of living, health, and sexual behaviour of the labouring population. But the way in which accidents and temporary or partial movements of market prices produce persistent and general effects must be traced historically. It must include the complex network of reactions in the whole system of reproduction. This is why Smith mentions peculiar adjustment mechanisms which involve starvation, begging, criminal offences, etc. (A. Smith, 1976 (1776), pp. 90–1).

The issues involved in the distinction between natural and market prices on the basis of scarcity are troublesome because of the fact that the scarcity of fertile land is a persistent element of Ricardo's framework, and its effects are generalized because of the increasing costs of production of wage goods. But here too it is not the supply and demand for labour that affect the natural price of labour, but the conditions of its reproduction via the cost of production of wage goods.

In reality the direct correspondence between wages and population size, which is necessary to the Malthusian demographic mechanism, becomes highly disputable when the habits and tastes of the labouring population affect not simply their physical state but their readiness to accept the conditions of waged labour. The struggle for reproduction when standards of living are very low appears largely as a struggle against nature, on which the hardest attacks are blamed. Illnesses, climate, shortages and fertility seem to be exclusively natural factors, and so the weakness of the labouring population also appears to be natural. But when the standards of living of the population rise, the social aspects linked to the system of production become more evident and can be more easily confronted through the labourers' political organization.[25]

In Ricardo's analysis the labour supply is defined as an aggregate supply, determined by collective forms of behaviour which are strongly interdependent. The aggregation is based on the behaviour of the whole labouring population; it has a precise material basis in the normal wage bundle, and a strong social texture in conventional habits and tastes. Working hours and levels of job satisfact,ion are, in fact socially determined. The aggregate behaviour which defines the supply is a class behaviour, in the sense that it varies according to the role labourers play in production, in the conflict between the workers and the owners of the means of production, and in distribution. It is also a gender behaviour as it reflects the historical sexual division of labour. Thus in classical political economy there is no labour-supply function expressing a continuous relationship between wages and the quantity of labour supplied.[26]

In given circumstances the normal supply is defined by a single quantity which is determined by the material and political forces acting in the social reproduction of labour, including normal standards of living, hours, inclination to work, family structures and power relationships. Each state of the system is defined by a natural price of labour associated with a given supply.[27]

1.5 The family and the state

The social forces operating in the process of social reproduction affect not only wages, but also other sources of subsistence which are granted to the labouring population in addition to or instead of wages. Within the Ricardian context, profit is the residual of all the forms of consumption of the labouring classes, but whereas wages are transformed into capital, i.e. used in the production process to obtain a surplus, other forms of subsistence may be simply transfers of net product.

The classical economists paid particular attention to one of the institutional aspects which characterized the British labour market. This was the Poor Law, on the basis of which a minimum level of subsistence could be granted to the residents of the parish. The direct effects of this institution on the functioning of the labour market could not be ignored (Coats, 1972; Himmelfarb, 1984; Picchio, 1986a).

The polemics of classical economists against the Poor Law had a precise objective: to remove wages and working conditions from the direct influence of the state, which at the time was represented mainly by magistrates who had the power to fix minimum wages, to determine the financing and the functioning of workhouses, and to regulate the mobility of labour. The full development of capitalism required the free exchange of labour on the market, which meant first of all the removal of all institutional restraints from labour and its mobility. As Ricardo puts it, 'Like all other contracts, wages should be left to the fair and free competition of the market, and should never be controlled by the interference of the legislative' (Ricardo, 1951a (1817), p. 15).

But while on the one hand the classical economists upheld the liberalization of the exchange of labour, on the other they were not at all hostile to state intervention in the sectors of education and health. They recognized the regulation of the family, the government of urban settlements, and the control of criminality and deviation, as the primary task of the state.[28] Smith makes explicit reference to state intervention in labour disputes, and he was also explicit in recognizing where the state stood: in support of the employers (A. Smith, 1976 (1776), pp. 83–5). But the classical economists did not confuse legislation with social norms.

In the Ricardian system of natural prices, as already noted, both wages and employment are taken as given, and there is no assumption of structural full employment. In Ricardo's analytical framework the problem of coping with unemployment does not have a general solution at the level of the adjustment of prices and quantities. In his discussion of machinery, in the third edition of the *Principles*, Ricardo recognized the fact that an increase of capital does not automatically lead to an increase in the demand for labour. But this did not make him change his view of the economic system, which already assumed a non-clearing labour market. His basic distinction between the natural and the market price of labour, necessary for his theory of distribution, was in fact not affected by an historical displacement of labour by fixed capital – a process that can occur in various ways which have to be traced historically.[29] In the Ricardian context the problem is not to justify the possibility of unemployment due to a replacement of labour by machines, but rather to include specific cases of technological substitution in a general framework which generally does not assume full employment. Unemployment has to be traced mainly in the historical relationship between the process of accumulation of capital and the process of social reproduction – processes that involve different objectives and forces, and are managed separately.

Ricardo did express some concern about the effectiveness of the mechanism of population adjustment, and he made explicit if feeble references to some supportive institutional mechanisms, to be introduced when the labour market did not serve satisfactorily to adjust population size and quality to the needs of accumulation. The problem was to free the exchange of labour and at the same time to guarantee its social reproduction in the right quantitative and qualitative terms. The problem had no automatic or general solution.[30] In this context Ricardo refers explicitly to the state:

It is a truth which admits not a doubt, that the comforts and well-being of the poor cannot be permanently secured without some regard on their part, or some effort on the part of the legislature, to regulate the increase of their numbers, and to render less frequent among them early and improvident marriages. (Ricardo, 1951a (1817), pp. 106–7)

Malthus, too, refers to legislation as one of the state's tools for controlling the size of the population:

Even the practical legislators who encouraged marriage seemed to think that the supplies of children might sometimes follow too rapidly for the means of supporting them; and it appears to have been with a view to provide against this difficulty . . . that they frequently sanctioned the inhuman practice of infanticide. (Malthus, 1820, p. 254)

Equally notable are some of Ricardo's comments on the role of the international labour market in regulating the size of the labour force:

In new settlements . . . it is probable that capital has a tendency to increase faster than mankind; and if a deficiency of labour were not supplied by more populous countries, this tendency would very much raise the price of labour. (Ricardo,

27

1951a (1817), p. 97)

An international labour market also means different standards of living:

An English labourer would consider his wages under their natural rate, and too scanty to support a family, if they enable him to purchase no other food than potatoes, and to live in no better habitation than a mud cabin; yet these moderate demands of nature are often deemed sufficient where 'man's life is cheap' and his wants easily satisfied. (p. 98)

If the reproduction of labour is taken as part of the economic system, then the analysis must include the state as active participant in the labour market at the level of the basic structure of the social system (Picchio Del Mercato, 1981b). Even the classical political economists had to recognize it, although in their anti-mercantilist mood they were not too keen on state intervention. Political economists were not naive in dealing with the state – they were only trying, in different ways, to distinguish the different levels of its action.[31]

The family is the other basic institution to which classical political economists refer in connection with wages. Wages are understood as family wages (i.e. adequate to reproduce a family of normal size and standards of living), and also as capital. As we have seen, capital is in fact defined as 'food, clothing, tools, raw materials, machinery' (Ricardo, 1951a (1817), p. 95). Hence Ricardo clearly acknowledges the fact that the reproduction of the family is part of the reproduction of capital, although he takes into consideration only the production of commodities necessary for the family wage and dismisses the housework necessary to transform them.

Malthus offers interesting examples of the role of the family as an institutional source of flexibility for the labour market:

When the population of a country increases faster than usual, the labouring classes must have the command of a greater quantity of food than they had before possessed, or at least applied to the maintenance of their families. This may be obtained in various ways – by higher real wages, by saving in conveniences, by adopting a cheaper kind of food, by more task-work and the more general employment of the women and children, or by parish allowances. (Malthus, 1820, pp. 59–60)

If the price of labour is analysed according to the classical method, using the analysis followed for other commodities and in the meanwhile acknowledging the specificity of its reproduction, the picture of the economic system is broadened and deepened. This enables it to encompass even those phenomena, linked with the reproduction of labour, which are often relegated to a vague accessory, natural or precapitalist sphere outside the process of capitalist production, or to the level of cultural, psychological and institutional rigidities of the market.

Ricardo used the Malthusian law as the basic adjustment mechanism for the labour market, though he already showed some doubts about its functioning. While this mechanism is no longer acceptable because of its simplistic naturalism and deterministic economicism, the classical approach retains its potential usefulness as a starting point from which to construct an overall picture of the structure of the labour market with its intrinsic institutional characteristics.

The problem of classical political economy – and of the capitalist system – is the fact that the labouring population, despite the weakness inherent in its dependence for subsistence on waged work, manages to maintain, through resistance and attack, a certain control over the modes of its reproduction. This is why waged labourers are different from slaves. The fact that workers were in part able to negotiate the terms of exchange of labour for wages was fully recognized by Smith and Ricardo, as we have seen in the preceding sections. It has also been shown that the problem in defining the wage bundle is not only to formulate an accurate list of wage goods; it is also the political problem of determining the expectations and the relative strength of the labouring population, on which the definition of normal or 'natural' price is really based.[32]

Hence the natural price of labour is the conventional and historical value of labour, expressed in physical terms; as such, it is taken as given for the period under observation. Thus it produces a static image of a process of social reproduction characterized by a continuous conflict on the basis of which, as Smith says, 'the workers desire to get as much, the master to give as little as possible' (A. Smith, 1976 (1776), p. 83). The natural price of labour is, therefore, the outcome of a complex series of social and political forces, embodied in a variety of institutions and expressed through a variety of social norms. The interactions of institutions, in particular, constitute the adjustment mechanism necessary to maintain wages within the bounds necessary for a viable relationship between social reproduction and accumulation. The problems of defining the 'natural price' are hence both analytical and political. Political and institutional aspects need not be added to economic theory because they are already part of its core.

2
The displacement effect
of the wages fund theory

2.1 Introduction

In this chapter I shall try to follow the various ways in which some Ricardians managed to formulate a radically different theory of wages – a theory based on supply and demand, and thus inconsistent with the Ricardian assumption of an exogenous wage. The authors to be considered are James Mill, Robert Torrens and J. R. McCulloch. An attempt will be made to trace the various modifications introduced by each of them at different stages with regard to definitions, adjustment mechanisms, methods and policy perspectives. The end result of their efforts was the establishment of the wages fund theory, which constituted a step towards a radical change in the theory of value and distribution.

There are subtle differences among the various authors, and the resulting confusion has blurred the demarcation line between the natural and the market price of labour. The first and most significant thread to disentangle is that of the Malthusian theory of population, on which both Ricardo and his successors rely heavily.

It is important to trace the way in which Smith's vague and general proposition, stating that the population eventually finds a check in the scarcity of natural resources, is transformed into the 'iron law of wages' which functions as the adjustment mechanism of the capitalist labour market.[1] Ricardo is partly responsible for this degeneration, because of his use of the Malthusian theory of population, but he is not to blame for the analytical muddle created by his successors when they introduced, as a general case, a flexible demand-determined wage.

Smith's remark was transformed by Malthus into a general law, complete with rates of increase of population and production.[2] The relationship between these rates – geometrical and arithmetical respectively – not only supported the general idea of inherent scarcity; it also offered an oscillatory mechanism to be used as the equilibrating process in supply-and-demand theories of prices. I shall come back later to the methodological implications of the Malthusian theory; it is important now to note that Ricardo's relationship between necessary consumption and production is quite different from the Malthusian population–production relationship. As a matter of fact, the distorting and misleading effect of the wages fund theory is based on the confusion between the two. The first step, therefore, is to clarify the differences between Malthus and Ricardo, and then the differences between Ricardo and the wages fund.

2.2 Malthus versus Ricardo

Ricardo used Malthus's (West's and Torrens's) theory of rent to develop his theory of distribution, in which class conflicts (i.e. the existing profit–rent conflict and the potential wage–profit conflict) find an analytical expression. In this case he used a Malthusian tool without being trapped in Malthus's theory of prices. The same thing happens in Ricardo's use of the theory of population. The concept of supply and demand as indicators of scarcities is limited, within the Ricardian framework, to the action of accidental, and generally not persistent, forces. As we have seen, in order for scarcity to be considered as non-systematic, labour has to be considered as a producible commodity. The Malthusian theory of population provided Ricardo with a convenient theory of reproduction which was not only fashionable and well established in his time, but allowed him to consider changes in market wages as self-correcting. The wide difference in growth rates of production and population guarantees convenient oscillations in the market price of labour. In fact, given the specificity of the labour commodity which can communicate consumption patterns and sediment them in persistent habits and tastes, a scarcity of labouring population could generally and persistently affect the natural price of labour. Thanks to the symmetric Malthusian mechanism, persistent and cumulative effects are generally not expected and the exogenous determination of the natural price of labour is analytically safe. Standards of living of the labouring population are given in time and space, by habits, social contract, and historical power relationships. They do not change with changes in levels of production; that is to say they do not automatically change when demand changes.

The fact that Ricardo does not consider the process of social reproduction of labour to be automatically affected by changes in the level of production, or by the process of allocation, does not imply a lessening of his interest in this process; on the contrary it offers the possibility for a more direct and powerful focus. Ricardo gave much attention to the costs of reproduction of the labour force in relation to the cost of production of wage goods. Actually he identifies the cost of reproduction of labour with the cost of production of these commodities. This means that all the work necessary to transform wage goods into a physical and psychological disposition to work is dismissed. One possible explanation of this can be found within the framework of his clear distinction between the production of value and the production of riches (Ricardo, 1951a (1817), chapter 20).

31

Once the process of reproduction of labour is taken as natural or as external to an exchange in the market, the work of reproduction can be excluded from the analysis of value.[3]

The problem here is not to speculate on Ricardo's idea of the process of reproduction of labour, but to see where he located it in his analysis and how it was displaced by his followers. The difference between the natural price of labour and the supply-and-demand price of labour is important in analytical terms and can be crucial in policy terms. In fact one may consider poverty deriving from low wages and unemployment as originating from the structural conditions of capitalist accumulation and from its distribution; alternatively, one may consider an excess in the quantity of population as the sole cause of poverty. Ricardo, who struggled to maintain a clear distinction in his analytical framework, supported policies which would increase the productive powers of capital, and did not consider a downward flexibility of wages as an adjustment mechanism. The supply-and-demand theorists, on the contrary, supported policies of 'checks', and considered low wages and starvation to be caused by the sin of overpopulation. In real terms the policies supported were the same even if argued along different lines: that is, the abolition of the Poor Laws or at least a drastic, although gradual, reduction in their application.

Ricardo did use Malthus's theory as an adjustment mechanism for the supply of labour, but he maintained a different analytical core. His followers were on the whole unable to grasp the significance of the difference between the natural and the market price of labour, and as a result they introduced fundamental changes into the Ricardian analytical framework.

Marx captures the differences and also vividly characterizes the persons responsible for the analytical deterioration.[4]

In the course of this investigation, we learned that capital is not a fixed magnitude . . . We saw further that, even when the magnitude of the capital at work is taken as fixed, the labour power, the science and the land . . . embodied in it constitute elastic potentialities of capital giving it, within certain limits, a field of action independent of its own magnitude . . . The classical economists have always been fond of considering social capital as a fixed magnitude possessing a fixed degree of efficiency. But this prejudice does not harden into a dogma until we come to the archphilistine, Jeremy Bentham, the insipid, pedantic, leathertongued oracle of the commonplace bourgeois intelligence of the nineteenth century . . . *Not only by Bentham himself, but also by Malthus, James Mill, McCulloch and others the dogma was used for apologetic purposes, especially in order to represent one portion of capital, namely variable capital or capital convertible into labour power, as a fixed magnitude, this meaning the mass of the means of subsistence . . . or the so-called wages fund, was mythically described as if it constituted a special part of social wealth cut off from the rest by insuperable natural barriers.* (Marx, 1969–72 (1861–63), pp. 670–2, italics added)

Before introducing the specific contributions of individual authors, it may be useful to outline the main results of the wages fund theory. As we saw in the previous chapter, Ricardo proposed that the exogenously given necessary consumption be considered capital. Necessary consumption was defined as the product of the natural wage (w) and the number of labourers employed in production (L), which was also a given magnitude determined historically by the level of production and technology. As a result the fund of wage goods (W) going to the labouring population was also given ($w\underline{L}=W$). The data were not given by nature but were the result of historical processes of production and reproduction; they were taken as given only in order to determine relative prices.

Ricardo's successors transformed the identity into a causal relationship which radically transformed the Ricardian theory of wages. They assumed the wages fund (W) as a datum, and consequently any change in wages would lead to changes, inversely related, in employment ($\overline{W}=wL$).

Within the Ricardian circle, wages began to be seen as systematically determined by supply and demand, relatively adjusting within a scarce wages fund. The scarcity of fertile land, according to Ricardo, could in the long run affect the determination and the distribution of surplus via the increasing value of agricultural wage goods and the increase of rent. Now this scarcity becomes a general persistent feature imposing on wages a downward flexibility which did not exist before. Wages become the residual of profit within a given production, and this is all that remains of the Ricardian theory of distribution.[5] The analytical difference between the natural/normal price of labour and its market price blurs. The forces in action in the labour market respond exclusively to supply and demand in a system which mechanically adjusts to universal, ahistorical 'laws'. Differences between theory and reality can only be explained in terms of population 'checks' and rigidities (Stephen, 1900). In this way, all the real complexities of the reproduction process of the capitalist system itself – i.e. the inherent potential conflict between the process of production and that of reproduction of the labouring population – are displaced from the analytical core of classical political economy.

The wages fund, while pretending to follow the lines of Ricardian political economy, by using the same terminology and covering the same issues, nevertheless introduced a different methodology for wages – which, it was agreed, represented the central issue of political economy. This may be clarified by looking at the progressive reduction of analytical scope which occurred between Smith and the wages fund. The relationship between population and natural resources was transformed into a

Social reproduction of labour

relationship between wages and population, which implies substantial changes.

Smith presented his relationship within the framework of his theory of the four stages of economic development, defined by the modes of subsistence (Meek and Skinner, 1973; Meek, 1971). His idea was that the relationship between population and natural resources was historically determined, and presented an evolutionary (progressive) pattern dependent on what in Marxist terminology could be called 'modes of production'. His vision was far from being static and far from focussing exclusively on the limitation of population (in whatever way) imposed by the scarcity of natural resources. He also stressed the historical structural conditions of production and reproduction, rather than treating them as mere quantitative endowments.[6]

While Smith presented the precapitalist progress towards the final commercial–capitalist stage, Ricardo focussed exclusively on the capitalist relationships of distribution. The key distributive relationship is between the reproduction of one specific section of population, i.e. the productive labouring population, and a very specific form of production, i.e. the production of commodities. Within the Physiocratic–Smithian tradition, he did call necessary consumption 'advances to labour' or 'wages fund', but the necessary consumption–production relationship was seen in the dynamic framework of capital accumulation. The wages fund was capital itself, and the existence of other forms of fixed capital, while it enormously complicated the issue of value, did not change his definitions of labour and of capitalist production. Growth would not remove potential class conflicts over the distribution of surplus. This conflict was expressed in the general theory of relative prices. The scarcity of land would only make the conflict more clear. Necessary consumption was given by the historical standards of living of a given level of labouring population at a given level of capitalist development in a given place. It was thus defined in relation to the general conditions of production and distribution as embodied in past historical processes, and not in relation to supply and demand. Any of the given data could change, but only through the action of the basic forces historically shaping production and distribution. It was not a matter of mere changes in relative numbers, and it was not only a matter of allocation of given scarce endowments.

The wages fund theorists introduced a further reduction of scope. The conflict was no longer between man and nature over natural resources (as in Smith), nor between wage and profit within the total given value (as in Ricardo), but between sections of the labouring population within a given fund. The process of social reproduction of labour was assumed to depend on a given rate of profit, and the conflict was internalized within the labouring population as a trade-off between quantity and standards. The wage fund theorists are Ricardians in that by population they mean labouring population (dependent on wages), though they do not state this very clearly. But they are not Ricardians when they do not refer exclusively to the productive labouring population, but include the subsistence of the unemployed and the unsupported wageless in the wages fund. This difference is quite important in policy terms, since an increase in poor relief would automatically reduce wages. The differences between them and Ricardo come out clearly on the issue of taxes on wages: Ricardo, consistent with his theory of distribution, would take the standards of living of the labouring population as generally fixed, while the wages fund theorists would allow them to be reduced through taxation.

2.3 James Mill

In his *Elements of Political Economy* written in 1821 as the result of teaching a course on Ricardian economic principles to his son John Stuart, James Mill opens the discussion of wages with a section entitled 'That the Rate of Wages depends on the Proportion between Population and Employment, in other words Capital'. Then he goes on to the next section, entitled 'Proof of the Tendency of Population to increase rapidly and Proof that Capital has less a Tendency than Population to increase'. The wages fund theory, and the consequent supply-and-demand determination of wages, emerges clearly from the headings of the sections alone.

Mill's support for the Malthusian law of population had already emerged, in a wages fund framework, in his 1817 article on 'Colonies' for the Supplement to the *Encyclopaedia Britannica*. In this article he acknowledged the difference between slavery and the wage system with regard to the handling of an excess of population: in slavery the costs of reproduction of the excess supply of labour had to be met by the land and slave owner; in the waged system the labourers had to meet them with lower living standards (Winch, 1966, p. 94).

The enthusiasm for Malthus's theory of population was rooted in the Utilitarian doctrines which Mill shared and helped to propagate – he was Bentham's closest friend and disciple for almost all his life (Bain, 1882; Halevy, 1972; Stephen, 1900; Winch, 1966).

Thomas Robert Malthus . . . was not one of the Utilitarian band. As a clergyman, he could not share their opinion of the Thirty-nine articles. Moreover he was a Whig, not a Radical; and he was even tainted with some economic heresy. Still, he became one of the prophets, if not the leading prophet, of the Utilitarians. Belief in the Malthusian theory of population was the most essential article of their faith. (Stephen, 1900, p. 138)

Malthus's *Essay on Population* had in fact an enormous role in shaping the political, historical and sociological theories of the first decades of the nineteenth century (Burrow, 1970; Himmelfarb, 1984; Jones, 1980). His success was not due to the soundness of his theory but to the fact that at the right moment, when the problems were most tragically evident, he offered at least a theoretical approach to the contradictions that were manifesting themselves at the level of social reproduction – increasing population, increasing public relief, unemployment, high corn prices, food riots, etc. The theory itself was heavily used as an ideological weapon in the debates on poverty, to deny the demands of the labouring population for higher standards of living, and to attempt to gain a political mandate from the middle classes.

Mill's close direct involvement with the Utilitarians reflects a sane tradition in the social sciences in which the study of society was not divided into self-contained disciplines, such as history, sociology, political science, anthropology, philosophy, ethics, etc. as in modern practice. Mill's *magnum opus*, the *History of British India* (James Mill, 1817b) is in the tradition of the Scottish Enlightenment which was his original cultural background (Winch, 1966, pp. 383–4). Mill was the intermediary between the Utilitarians and Ricardo, who in his parliamentary activity passed for an 'ultrareformer and visionary' (Winch, 1966, p. 187) and declared himself 'a disciple of Bentham and Mill's school' (Ricardo, 1951b (1817), p. 52).

Returning to the analytical framework of the wages fund theory, it is worth following Mill's arguments more closely:

Production is performed by labour . . . The labourer has neither raw material nor tools. These requisites are provided for him by the capitalists . . . the commodity belongs to the labourer and capitalists together . . . The reward to both must be derived from the commodity, and the reward of both makes up the whole of the commodity . . . Instead of waiting till the commodity is produced . . . it has been found to suit much better the convenience of the labourers to receive their share in advance . . . It is very evident that the share of the two parties is the subject of a bargain between them . . . All bargains made in freedom are determined by competition and the terms alter according to the state of the supply and demand. (James Mill, 1965 (1821), pp. 40–2)

While Mill apparently attempts to maintain his loyalty to the theory of value and residual distribution, he introduces a flexible wage and finds himself suggesting a definition of profit in terms of interest, which provoked Marx angrily to defend Ricardo against his closest followers. The following passage from Marx is a very clear presentation of the displacement effect of the wages fund theory:

36

The wages fund

The value of labour, that is, the labour-time required by the worker for his own reproduction, is a definite magnitude; it is determined by the sale of his labour power to the capitalist. This virtually determines his share of the product as well. It does not happen the other way round, that his share of the product is determined first, and as a result the amount or value of his wages. This is precisely one of Ricardo's most important and most emphasised propositions, for otherwise the price of labour would determine the prices of the commodities it produces, whereas, according to Ricardo, the price of labour determines nothing but *the rate of profit*. (Marx, 1969–72 (1861–63), p. 94)

Mill's scientific proof of the fact that population increases faster than capital lies in the very existence of poverty.

That population has a tendency to increase faster . . . is proved, incontestably, by the conditions of the population in most parts of the globe. In almost all countries the condition of the great body of the people is poor and miserable. This would have been impossible, if capital had increased faster than population. (James Mill, 1965 (1821), p. 45)

Excess of population is never seen as unemployment, rooted in the very increase of capital and hence characteristic of capitalist systems, but as a natural phenomenon related, for instance, to the physiological constitution of women.

The facts respecting the physiological constitution of the human female are well ascertained, and are indubitable grounds of conclusion . . . The facts, which are fully ascertained in regard to the female of the human species, and the inferences which the science of physiology and comparative anatomy enable us to derive from the analogy of other animals . . . afford the means of very satisfactory conclusions on the subject . . . We can conclude, therefore, that in the most favourable circumstances, ten births are the measure of fecundity in the female of the human species. (pp. 46–8)

The wage–profit relationship is thus reduced to a problem of quantitative relationships; no scope is left for material historical processes of production and reproduction, or for power relationships which according to Smith and Ricardo did shape economic systems in historical time. Nothing is left of the Ricardian lucidity on the specific characteristics of the capitalist system. The result is: free labourers bargaining with free employers in a labour market ultimately regulated by demography. Instead of deepening the analysis so as to see how demography itself was linked to the structural conditions of the labour market, the wages fund allowed the issue of the social reproduction of labour to be circumscribed within very narrow naturalistic limits.

While Mill helped to narrow the analytical scope of classical political economy, at the same time he recognized that the social reproduction of the labouring population is the foundation on which government rests. His *Essay on Government* (1820) for the *Encyclopaedia Britannica* was based on the conviction that the 'primary cause of Government' is 'the necessity of labour for obtaining the means of subsistence' (James Mill, 1937 (1820), p. 3). Mill's *Essay* had a great impact on the public debate which led to the 1832 Reform Bill. Its role was to channel the social unrest of the times toward an institutional reform which would guarantee the leadership of the middle classes (Hamburger, 1963). In order to do that, he had to raise working-class expectations for higher standards of living, and then kill them under the hammer of a 'scientifically proven' powerlessness. This was the role of the wages fund theory. In a context of wider political representation of the working classes, the living standards of the labouring population were to be disciplined by the market with its supply and demand adjustment mechanisms. The naivety and arrogance that clearly emerge from the next quotation could not be expressed so baldly today, though they are far from extinct in modern thinkers and rulers.

Another proposition may be stated, with a perfect confidence of the concurrence of all those men who have attentively considered . . . the principles of human nature in general. It is that the opinions of that class of the people, who are below the middle rank, are formed, and their minds are directed by that intelligent and virtuous rank . . . to whom they fly for advice and assistance in all their numerous difficulties, upon whom they feel an immediate and daily dependence, in health and in sickness, in infancy and in old age; to whom their children look up as models for their imitation, whose opinions they hear daily repeated, and account it their honour to adopt. There can be no doubt that the middle rank, which gives to science, to art and to legislation itself, their most distinguished ornaments, the chief source of all that has exalted and refined human nature, is that portion of the community of which, if the basis of Representation were ever so extended, the opinion would ultimately decide. (James Mill, 1937 (1820), p. 72)

At this point we cannot but note that although women's reproductive capacity was implicitly taken as the main adjustment mechanism of the labour market (with a scientific dignity appropriate for a cattle market), in Mill's radical proposal women were excluded from suffrage. This open discrimination was not justified even in Mill's time and provoked the publication, in 1825, by another economist, William Thompson, of the *Appeal of one Half of the Human Race, Women, against the Pretensions of the other Half, Men, to retain them in Political and hence in Civil and*

Domestic Slavery (W. Thompson, 1825).

James Mill solved the problem of the relation between labour and subsistence in a peculiar way;

The principal thing, which, with a view to the conclusions of Political Economy, it is necessary to remark, in regard to Labour, considered as a distinct portion of a composite whole, and apart from Capital, is the necessity of subsistence to the labourer. *In the idea of labour, the idea of subsistence is included* . . . *By pure labour, we mean the consumption and operations of the labourer, taken conjunctly* . . . The idea of his subsistence is necessarily included, as that of the action of his muscles, or his life. (James Mill, 1965 (1821), pp. 8–9, 10, italics added)

The consumption of the labourer which constituted the value of labour is identified with his use value – action of muscles – which is embodied in the commodities produced. Mill, as Marx notices, transforms into an identity the basic problem of the value of labour which cannot be solved in the Ricardian framework without an unequal exchange, since the value embodied in wage goods is, necessarily for the survival of the capitalist system, lower than the value of commodities produced (Marx, 1969–72 (1861–3), pp. 89–90). This confusion relates back to the problem of the exogenously given rate of profit, which is then explained as interest on the advances for wages (p. 91). Marx finds an explanation for the root of the unequal exchange in the process of surplus creation by labour in the production of commodities. But if we focus directly on the process of reproduction of labour we can bring out the work and the institutional mechanisms that help to keep the consumption of the labouring classes within the limits imposed by capitalist accumulation and thus determine the rate of profit.

James Mill was well aware of the importance and difficulties of the relationship between production and consumption when he opened the *Elements of Political Economy* by saying:

Political Economy is to the State what domestic economy is to the family . . . Domestic economy has, therefore, two grand objects; the consumption and supply of the family. The consumption being a quantity always indefinite, for there is no end to the desire of enjoyment, the grand concern is to increase supply. (James Mill, 1965 (1821), p. 1)

Unfortunately, Mill fails to notice that the state does not represent an egalitarian society. The 'supply' is produced through the exploitation of labourers, and the limits on consumption and enjoyment hold only for the labouring classes. Thus we begin to see how domestic economy serves the political economy of the capitalist state.

2.4 Robert Torrens

The contribution of Torrens to the theory of the wages fund is less dogmatic than James Mill's, which he criticizes. His main idea is that wages are generally determined by supply and demand, but this operates between maximum and minimum levels which are, respectively, a so-called 'moral rate of profit' and the historical standards of living of the labourers. The supply-and-demand determination of wages is not added to the normal and exogenous distribution, but replaces it along a certain range of the profit–wage curve, with the result that the theory of wages as costs of production becomes simply a downward rigidity of the market price of labour, and the rate of profit is no longer a residuum but is given independently from wages.

The limit to the increase of wages is no longer the whole product (however measured) given by the production process but a certain part of it which remains to be defined (though Torrens decides not to do so).

In the vast majority of actual cases, the capitalist, in addition to the replacement of all his advances, will reserve a portion of the produce of industry as his profit, and though there will exist no physical, yet there will be a moral impossibility, that wages should exceed that which remains after the capitalist's other advances have been replaced, with the lowest rate of increase, for the sake of which he will carry his business. This, then, we may call the moral maximum of wages . . .

The rate of increase . . . varies, from causes which it is not necessary here to explain. (Torrens, 1834, pp. 8–9)

Torrens stresses the fact, already anticipated by Mill, that wages become the residual. This might possibly be logically consistent with the Ricardian framework, as Sraffa showed, but it has significant implications for the analysis of the historical processes and forces which are considered dominant in the process of reproduction of labour.[7]

Torrens rightly criticizes Mill for his loose use of words such as capital, wages and subsistence:

It is sometimes said, that 'in the idea of labour, the idea of subsistence is included' . . . Labour is one thing; the subsistence which supports the labourer is another, and a very different thing; and confounding these two different things under one common term, can only lead to ambiguity, misconception, and error. (Torrens, 1834, p. 4)

Mill attempted to change the meaning of capital: that is to say, he transformed the distinction between fixed capital and variable capital into a distinction between capital and labour. Then he treated wages and profit as incomes derived from separate contributions to production. This did not escape the notice of Torrens, who followed the Ricardian formulation that

the term wages is the specific term, marking that particular portion of the capitalist's advances which is given to the labourer for his labour . . . To call seed, material and machinery, wages, is a confounding of terms; to call the wages of that non-entity, accumulated labour, is still worse. (Torrens, 1834, p. 7)[8]

Torrens's wages fund theory has more sophisticated results than Mill's because he argues in terms of rates rather than quantities. This makes the wage–profit conflict appear less dramatic.

The general rule that actual wages settle is regulated by the proportion which exists between the number of labourers to be maintained, and the quantity of those ingredients of capital which are destined for their maintenance . . . It is but one out of the several causes by which wages are governed. (Torrens, 1834, p. 21)

According to Torrens, the use of less fertile land and the increase of labour productivity can in fact decrease or increase wages even when population and capital 'constantly preserve the same ratio'. The rate of profit is maintained at a constant level even if wages change when the general conditions of production change.[9] While a static wages fund implies a reduction of wages if the moral rate of profit increases, its dynamic form allows for an increase of both wages and profit (pp. 20–7).

One famous aspect of Torrens's theory of wages concerns the effect of combinations on distribution (Martineau, 1834; Robbins, 1958; Taussig, 1896). With regard to the combination of workers, Torrens is less sympathetic than is usually thought (Robbins, 1958, p. 49), since the regulation of the quantity of labour supplied is the ultimate means of adjustment of the labour market.

From all that has been said, it must be evident that the important power of increasing, or of diminishing, the reward of labour, is, by the essential order of society, placed in the hands of the labourers themselves. Irregularities in the seasons bring on scarcity and famine, foreign incursions, or domestic commotions, destroying property, or suspending production by rendering it insecure, may sometimes occasion a depression of wages, which no prudence on the part of the labouring classes can avert or mitigate. But under all ordinary circumstances, when the usual course of nature is preserved, and when law and order are maintained, it depends upon the labouring classes themselves whether wages shall ascend to the ultimate maximum or sink to the extreme minimum. By duly regulating their numbers . . . (Torrens, 1834, p. 26)

Once again Torrens is more sophisticated than Mill. He does not get involved in complicated calculations regarding the reproductive capacity of women, and he does not accept the Malthusian conclusion that capital necessarily increases less than population. He says excess population is caused by bad laws which encourage idleness and early marriages and penalize prudence. In an old well-populated country with scarce land, 'the unmarried labourer finds himself in much more affluent circumstances than the married labourer' (p. 30). Hence there would be no incentive to marry. Note that the consumption of the labourer's family is no longer an addition to be included in necessary consumption as for Ricardo, but is a further deduction from the given wages fund. Given the circumstances, labourers are forced to compete for scarce food resources not only among themselves but also with the future generations, and, according to Torrens, also with other labouring animals (horses). They will therefore keep the numbers down and 'the tendency in every civilised community is not for population to increase faster than capital, but for capital to increase faster than population' (p. 31). In policy terms, this means that Torrens did not change his early idea that emigration would be the real solution for excess supply. Public benefits, instead of being used for relief inside or outside the workhouses, could much more cheaply finance emigration schemes, which could provide for differentials in treatment between deserving soldiers and idle vagrants (Torrens, 1837).

The same conclusions, suggesting the impossibility of permanent wage increases, are reached when the issues of foreign trade and machinery are taken into account. This kind of reasoning was also applied to the increase in the costs of labour arising from the proposal by Mr Fielden, and by the 'benevolent monomaniac' Owen, to reduce the working day to eight hours. According to Torrens the exogenous constraints of the moral rate of profit, working at an international level, and of the scarcity of land, made workers' organization impotent: because close scientific reasoning, based on the wages fund theory, showed that wage increases were impossible.

No candid man can deny that Mr Fielden is, in intention, the friend of the working people; but no lover of truth, acquainted with the causes which regulate the amount of wages, will hesitate to say that, in practice, the plan which he has proposed for their adoption would lead them to destruction. (Torrens, 1834, p. 98)

In this case the positive policy perspective suggested was the abolition of the Corn Laws, which would allow the exploitation of the 'greater quantity of work which an Englishman performs in a day or year and the greater cheapness of machinery, of fuel and of carriage' at lower costs of wage goods and hence at higher profits.

The wages fund

2.5 J. R. McCulloch

Finally we come to McCulloch, whose role was to popularize the theory of the wages fund. His *Treatise on the Circumstances which Determine the Rate of Wages and the Condition of the Labouring Classes* poses the question of wages in precise terms, as he states in the first lines of his introduction:

We have attempted in the following treatise, to resolve the most important of all economic problems – that is, to trace and exhibit the circumstances which determine the rate of Wages and the condition of the labouring classes. (McCulloch, 1854, p. iii)

McCulloch's treatise is the latest of the works examined, as a revised edition of it is dated 1854. Its purpose is mainly political, as he aims to teach the workers that their interests are 'intimately connected with and . . . indeed inseparable from, the prosperity of the other classes' (p. iv). According to McCulloch, the conflict between wages and profits can be resolved by educating the working classes on the principles of political economy, which will show them that there is no reason for conflict.

The more indeed, that this knowledge is diffused, the more will the lasting and real interests of both classes be seen to correspond and the fewer will be the chances of peace and good order of society being disturbed by jealousies and disagreements between the masters and those in their service. (McCulloch, 1854, p. iv)

One way of easing the conflict is to define labour broadly enough to include, as McCulloch does, the Prime Minister, the professions, and anybody whose services are exchanged 'for valuable considerations of one sort or other' (McCulloch, 1854, p. 1). He even includes property owners on the assumption that 'the duties and obligations which property brings along with it are not a little onerous' (p. 1). So, if Mill thought that profit could be called the wages of hoarded labour, McCulloch dilutes the definition of wages from another direction – that is, by including the work of ruling and the insecurity of ownership. Within such a broad definition he then draws the distinction between those 'who work with their hands and those who work with their heads'. To explain the social conflict between these two sections would have required a sophisticated sociological enquiry that was not at all necessary in Ricardo's analysis. Ricardo gave immediate evidence of a much deeper conflict: he located the wage–profit conflict at the core of his analytical scheme and did not spend much energy in describing it.

43

His follower, having lost all the analytical clarity about labour and profit, confuses the fluctuations and accidental scarcities in the labour market (McCulloch, 1854, p. 3), with normal and persistent phenomena, which he lumps together within the supply-and-demand framework of the wages fund. Thus the focus is easily shifted from the normal and structural aspects of the capitalist system to its accidental features. Once attention is displaced from the fundamental problem of the capitalist system, i.e. the wage–profit conflict, McCulloch is ready to provide solutions for the labour market. On the whole, his solutions tend to shift the analysis of wages from the sphere of the reproduction and distribution to that of allocation. The wages fund becomes more and more a pretext for distracting analytical attention from the structural conditions of capital accumulation, on which the 'great dynamics' of classical political economy was founded. Simple arithmetic is used as a substitute for analytical interpretation:

The average amount of subsistence falling to each labourer, or the rate of wages, wholly depends on the proportion between capital and population . . . This principle is so very plain as hardly to require or admit of illustration . . . Now this case is not peculiar to this or that country, but it is of universal application. Labourers are everywhere the divisor, capital the dividend. (McCulloch, 1854, pp. 4–5)

The analytical simplicity of the wages fund, which is nothing but the truism of a ratio, is used to introduce a normal flexibility into standards of living and into the modes of organization of the process of social reproduction, breaking the classical relationship between real wages (estimated in commodities) and collective and average behaviour:

And to prevent misconception, it may be right to state at the outset, that the condition and well being of the labouring classes cannot in any case be correctly measured by, or inferred from, the wages they receive. It depends to great extent on their conduct and habits, more especially on the description and cost of articles used by them, and on their frugality and forethought . . . And, therefore, though the rate of wages, whether estimated in money or in commodities, depends on the proportion between capital and labour, the condition of the labourer is not determined by that rate only, but partly by it, and partly also, and perhaps principally, by the mode in which they expend their wages, that is by their peculiar tastes and habits in regard to necessaries, conveniences and amusements. (McCulloch, 1854, pp. 6–7)

This is how Ricardo's theory of wages is turned upside down. Wages are given but standards of living are not. Self-reliance will help when reliance on capital is not possible. No space is left anyway for long-term hope, since the Malthusian dogma finds in McCulloch another great disciple; mathematics is used to impose universal and automatic behaviour as if the power of logic could become a power over history. Nature is the force which disciplines the standards of living of the labouring population, and mathematics provides the fitting metaphor for its regularities.

> The principle of instinct which impels man to propagate his species has appeared in all ages and countries so nearly the same that it may, in the language of mathematicians, be considered as a *constant quantity*. However rapidly the means of subsistence have occasionally been increasing, population has seldom failed to keep pace with them. (McCulloch, 1854, p. 13)

The apologetic aspect of the wages fund theory comes out very clearly in its naivety. Nature is ultimately responsible for poverty, and the labourers are left alone in their struggle against it.

> The condition of the bulk of every people must usually depend much more on their own conduct than on that of their rulers . . . The lazy, the unskilful, and the improvident workman, whether he belongs to Australia or China, England or Russia, will always be poor and miserable. (McCulloch, 1854, pp. 16, 18)

Poverty was taken as the evidence of moral and social misconduct and as such it justified repression. Instead of being explained and related to the conditions of accumulation, it was taken as the indicator of the soundness of the natural and universal laws of population as described by Malthus. For McCulloch, as well as for James Mill, the standards of living of the labouring population were taken as the indicator of the capital–population ratio. But while for Mill poverty, given a fixed capital, indicated overpopulation, for McCulloch, given the standards of living and the rate of increase of population, it could be used to speculate on the unknown dynamics of the quantity of capital:

> It is not possible to obtain any accurate estimates of the quantities of capital in countries at different periods; but the capacity of that capital to feed and employ labourers and the rate of its increase, may, notwithstanding, be learned with sufficient accuracy for our purpose, by referring to the progress of population, and the habits of the bulk of the people . . . Whenever, therefore, we find the people of a country increasing, without any, or with but little variation taking place in their condition, we may conclude that its capital is increasing in the same, or nearly the same, proportion. (McCulloch, 1854, p. 8)

Mathematical logic may be safe, but the causal explanations of political and economic relationships drawn from this transposing of terms are both confused and confusing. The wages fund, at least in its dynamics, emerges as a vague entity which nonetheless serves, together with a deterministic theory of population, as the basis for general laws for the determination of wages and living standards of the labouring population. In spite of all the vagueness, the relationship between the two given quantities of capital and population is assumed as an 'iron law'; nothing can affect it, least of all governments and workers' organizations. As regards the government's role, McCulloch, like all the other wages fund theorists, explicitly excludes any scope for intervention in the relations between capital and the labouring population. The government's only role is to guarantee property and personal freedom in the exchange of labour and other commodities. Any direct involvement in welfare policies would prove ineffective or negative. It was considered a dangerous legacy of the eighteenth century that government administration had centred on the problem of welfare, as Steuart so clearly expresses it:

What economy is in a family, political economy is in a state . . .

The great art therefore of political economy is, first to adapt the different operations of it to the spirit, manners, habits, and customs of the people: and afterwards to model these circumstances so as to be able to introduce a set of new and more useful institutions.

The principal object of this science is to secure a certain fund of subsistence for all the inhabitants to obviate every circumstance which may render it precarious: to provide everything necessary for supplying the wants of the society, and to employ the inhabitants. (Steuart, 1966 (1767), vol. 1, pp. 16–17)

McCulloch was writing in a period of liberalism, and he shared the nineteenth-century myth of self-reliance.

Where Government has secured the property and the rights of individuals, and has given that freedom to industry which is essential, it has done nearly all it can do to promote the increase of capital . . . The reliance of individuals on their own efforts, and their desire to advance themselves, are the only principles on which any dependence can be safely placed . . .

It is nugatory, therefore, to expect any advantageous results from the efforts of the Government to increase capital or the demand of labour . . . And, if it attempt to set up national workshops for the employment of the poor, it will increase the poverty it seeks to relieve, disturb all the usual channels of industry, and become a potent instrument of evil. (McCulloch, 1854, pp. 23–4)

For McCulloch, as for Torrens, the only viable adjustment mechanism of the labour market is the quantity of population; and, if the Malthusian moral and demographic checks do not operate quickly and efficiently, emigration is the key policy. If wages and standards of living are low any decrease in population is considered positive, even if it is caused by mass starvation. In the revised edition of his treatise McCulloch had the opportunity to test his theories, and his cynicism, in the light of the recent dramatic Irish events. Both emerge unscathed.[10]

During the last seven years Ireland has been subjected to the joint influence of a scarcity and a very extensive emigration. The ravages of famine and disease, occasioned by the potato rot of 1846–47, combined with the efforts of many landlords to clear their estates . . . had such an effect upon the population, that it fell off, between 1845 and 1851, from about 8,000,000 to 6,515,794 . . . Enough has already transpired to satisfy everyone that this is the case in which the benevolent wisdom of Providence will educe real good out of apparent evil. (McCulloch, 1854, p. 22)

Nor does McCulloch question the belief that the flexibility of the supply of labour, in quantitative and qualitative terms, is the basic adjustment mechanism of the labour market, although he does recognize that the relationship between wages and quantity of labour supply is not clear-cut and positive. Changes in the structure of labour (work of women and children) and in the modes of reproduction can lead to some short-term rigidities in the adjustment process. But they do not permanently affect the basic relationship determining the supply of labour, which is now assumed as a mechanical relationship between two magnitudes, and no longer between two historical production processes. The arithmetic of the wages fund becomes the law which is assumed to regulate the most delicate and troublesome aspect (in analytical and historical terms) of the capitalist system, i.e. the labour market; and the analysis of processes and power relationships is wiped out of the general analytical picture. In such an impoverished framework workers' historical organizations can affect wages only in the short term, since the market forces of capitalist competition will automatically set the 'natural and proper' rate of wages. On the one hand workers' combinations are useless; on the other there is no need for legislation to forbid them. The defeat of the coal miners' strike of 1844 (when 40,000 miners were on strike for five months), is used by McCulloch as proof of the uselessness and the injurious effects of the Combination Laws. These laws had in fact helped to expose class conflicts when market forces would have dealt with them in a more disguised and politically less dangerous way.

The great evil of the combination laws consisted . . . in the mistaken notions respecting their influence which they generated in the minds both of workmen and masters. They taught them to believe that there was one measure of justice for the rich, and another for the poor. They consequently set the interests and the feelings of these two great classes in direct opposition to each other, and did more to engender hatred between the different orders of society – to render the masters despotic and capricious, and the workmen idle and turbulent. (McCulloch, 1854, pp. 90–1)

As we have seen, the wages fund theory aims to hide the class conflict and to internalize it within sections of the labouring classes and individual behaviour. 'Industry and frugality' and self-reliance on the part of the workers are the keys to the welfare of the labouring population. The Ricardian wage–profit conflict is either denied or mitigated in the name of common political interests:

It is true, that when wages are increased, profits are at the same time most commonly reduced . . . The rate of profit, how important so ever, is not the only thing to which they [capitalists] have to look. Security and tranquillity are still more indispensable than high profits to the successful prosecution of industrious undertakings. (McCulloch, 1854, p. 49)

According to McCulloch, the wages fund is not necessarily a theory of low wages. Wages in fact start to be linked to productivity: an increase in productivity allows for an increase in wages (in real terms) without a diminution of the wages fund. In McCulloch the increase in productivity removes a constraint; but this is not yet posed as a new theory of wages, though his confusion of terms begins to suggest it. Moreover, McCulloch is convinced, along Smith's lines, that high wages are desirable as incentives to industry and as the basis for the security of some sections of the working classes, such as those which can rely on thrift and on contributions to friendly societies.

McCulloch maintains the difference between the natural and the market price of labour, and he presents it apparently very much along Ricardo's lines – so much so that it has been difficult to rescue Ricardo from his companionship. First of all McCulloch inverts the order of presentation. In the first chapter of his treatise, he introduces the market price of labour in the form of the wages fund; and only in the third chapter does he introduce the concept of the natural price of labour. McCulloch also alters the meanings of the terms, since his whole treatment of wages is actually based on the wages fund supply-and-demand determination. As a matter of fact, he introduces the 'Natural or Necessary Rate of Wages' as a downward rigidity which is a special case of supply-and-demand wages, as in Torrens. It is only in the wording that he is more Ricardian and hence more misleading.

> It has been seen . . . that the market or current rate of wages in any country, at any period, depends on the magnitude of its capital appropriated to the payment of wages, compared with the number of its labourers. And it has also been seen, that in the event of the labouring population being increased more rapidly than capital, the rate of wages is inevitably reduced. But there are limits, however difficult it may be to specify them, to the extent to which a reduction of wages can be carried. The cost of producing labour, like that of producing other articles, must be paid by the purchaser. Work-people must, at all events, obtain a sufficient quantity of food, and of the other articles required for their support, and that of their families. This is the lowest amount to which the rate of wages can be permanently reduced; and it is for this reason that it has been called their *natural* or *necessary* rate. The market rate of wages may sink to the level of this necessary rate, but it is impossible it should continue below it. (McCulloch, 1854, pp. 26–7)

Actually, it is hard to see the difference between such sinking and the gravitating of the market price of labour to its natural price, but it is important to keep Ricardo's clarity on the issue of distribution. This is possible only if the natural price of labour is given as exogenous as the general case, and not only as a lower limit. As I have specified in the first chapter, in Ricardo 'natural and necessary' means given and exogenous from the determination of relative prices. A distinction must be made between a downward rigidity and a determination of wages which is exogenous from supply and demand. The wages fund theory obscures this distinction, and this is a great loss for the analytical methodology of political economy.

Given the necessary rate of wages and rent, Ricardo was in a position to determine profit as part of the surplus. As Marx pointed out, he was not able to make the process of the formation of profit explicit, but he did maintain the definition of profit as surplus. Even the difficulties encountered with regard to the measure of value did not discourage his conviction that the basic capitalist relationship is between the physical process of reproduction of labour and the physical process of production of other commodities. Ricardo was not able (or willing) to exploit his insight completely, because he could not explain the unequal exchange in the labour market between the labour value embodied in wage goods and the labour value embodied in the commodities produced. But he did hold his ground with regard to the specificity of labour, the price of which is not determined simultaneously with other prices; with regard to the basic assumption of class conflict as a general and persistent case and also with regard to the ranking of physical processes as more important than allocation in determining values for all commodities, labour included.

49

McCulloch reduces the scope of Ricardo's insight and uses his definitions, such as the natural price of labour, and distorts his analysis. This was done before the radical attacks on the theory of value and profit; it began with the theory of wages.

In a subtle and quite interesting way McCulloch introduces the element of time in his distinction between the natural and the market price of labour.

> The opinion of those who contend that the rate of wages is in no degree influenced by the cost of the articles consumed by the labourers, has obviously originated in their confounding the principles which determine the current or market rate of wages with those which determine their natural or necessary rate. Nothing can be more true, than that the market rate of wages at any given moment, is exclusively determined by the proportion between capital and population. But in every enquiry of this nature we should refer not only to particular points of time, but also to periods of some five, seven, or ten years' duration; and if we do this we shall immediately perceive that the *average* rate of wages does not depend wholly on this proportion. (McCulloch, 1854, p. 28)

It is worth noting how McCulloch expresses the process by which market prices gravitate towards the natural price of labour. The reduction of scope and significance is clear, although the qualitative difference in the forces determining the respective prices is maintained, since time may help the persistent forces to emerge. The next passage shows how time can also be used to introduce a certain degree of dependence of the natural price of labour on the market price. Rigidities in the adjustment of population can in fact produce persistent effects on habits and standards of living, and hence on the forces that determine the natural price of labour.

> The natural or necessary rate of wages is not, therefore, fixed and unvarying. It has a tendency to rise when the market rate rises, and to fall when it falls. The reason is that the supply of labourers in the market can neither be speedily increased when wages rise, nor speedily diminished when they fall. When wages rise, a period of eighteen or twenty years must elapse before the stimulus which the rise gives to the principle of population can be felt in the market. And during all this period, the labourers have a greater command over necessaries and conveniences . . . the natural and necessary rate of wages is gradually augmented. (McCulloch, 1854, p. 34)

McCulloch's observation is pertinent and significant, as it relates to the specificity of the process of reproduction of labour. Labour is in fact the only commodity which acquires habits, which sediments past experiences and uses them as a basis for improvement. The recognition that the production line of labour does not speed up so easily is also obviously significant, as everybody, including Ricardo, would agree. But from these descriptive observations on the rigidity of the reproduction process of the labour commodity it does not follow that the habits and standards of living of the labouring population must normally be considered flexible in responding to supply-and-demand changes. Nor does it follow that, if market wages depend on the demand for labour, workers share the same interests as their employers.

Of course Ricardo was not entirely an innocent victim, since he did use the Malthusian theory of population as a theory of reproduction; but it can be argued that he did this in order to concentrate on the conflictual aspects of capitalist distribution and on the primary importance of physical processes of production relative to allocation.[11]

His disciples used Malthus's theory of population to cover the conflictual nature of the relationship between necessary consumption (reproduction of labour) and production of commodities, which is the core of the capitalist system. This is why, from the wages fund onward, political economy acquired a 'vulgar' apologetic nature, which has been dressed up with sophisticated formalisms, but has by no means disappeared from the supply-and-demand theories of wages and distribution.

An interesting critique of the wages fund was developed at the end of the sixties by Francis Longe (1866) and William Thomas Thornton (1869). Both of them challenged the accepted version of the wages fund, which was that of John Stuart Mill, in his own version of the *Principles* and in Fawcett's popularization. The arguments advanced by Longe and Thornton are significant for any debate on supply-and-demand determination of prices. Their challenge was effective, and it forced Mill into a famous rejection of the most rigid aspects of the wages fund. Both economists had contributed to the critique, but only Thornton was honoured with recognition by Mill in his refutation, 'Thornton on Labour and Its Claims' (1869).[12]

The most interesting aspects of Longe's analysis are his critical attack on the notion of the wages fund as capital, on the general use of the abstract principle of supply and demand, and on a concept of labour which does not take into consideration the labouring population as a whole (Longe, 1903 (1866), pp. 2–27). Longe summarizes the main reasons for his discontent as follows:

The theory however is altogether false even as an abstract principle, and for these reasons – (1) Because the capital or wealth applicable to the payment of the wages of labour in a country, in any time or during any period, does not consist of a definite fund 'distinct from its general wealth', nor of a fund which is 'destined' for the purchase of labour. (2) Because the dependent or labouring population in a country, at any time or during any period, does not constitute a supply of labour or body of labourers, among whom the aggregate wage–fund or capital of a country could be distributed by competition. (3) Because the supposition that such a wage–fund would be all distributed among the labourers or (if they could be treated as 'general' labourers, capable of competing with each other) by the competition of the buyers and sellers of labour, if allowed free competition, involves an erroneous notion of the supply-and-demand principle. (Longe, 1903, p. 27)

Moreover, Longe criticizes in general the idea of systematic supply-and-demand relationships between prices and quantities, and in particular the use of such relationships in the case of the commodity labour.[13]

Thornton follows the same line and considers supply-and-demand determination of prices as a special case which has to be specifically verified with regard to continuity and direction (Mirowsky, 1990, p. 75). For instance, while it is perhaps true that the price falls in the case of excess supply, it is not usually true that demand rises if the price falls. Price flexibility does not function as an adjustment mechanism between quantities demanded and supplied; this is particularly true in the case of labour.

If the best possible answers of these momentous questions be not furnished by the experience of the 'law' of supply and demand it is only because that 'law', instead of containing merely one stray element of error, is almost entirely made up of error; because instead of being but one situation in which it must break down, there is but one solitary situation in which it can hold good. (Thornton, 1869, p. 69)

Mill recognizes the soundness of the critical remarks with regard to the constancy of the wages fund but he maintains his trust in the 'laws' of supply and demand. In fact, he adopts his critics' suggestion that the constraints on wages could be removed by increasing production and productivity, a conviction which was shared by many economists (for instance Senior and Fawcett) and also by union leaders. Mill used it to open the ground analytically for more progressive policies.[14]

Unfortunately the new link between wages and productivity was to lead to a new theory of wages, where production determines wages, formulated by Walker in *The Wages Question* (1876). The ground was thus prepared for a new theory of distribution based on supply and demand and on productivity of 'capital and labour'. All the interesting critical insights on supply and demand did not lose their significance but they lost the attention of an unsympathetic academic audience which had assigned a new paradigmatic role to supply and demand.

2.6 Conclusions

The removal of the concept of the natural price of labour from the core of the Ricardian theory of distribution had major effects at various levels. First of all it displaced the social conflict from the profit–wage relationship to a trade-off between size of population and standards of living, to be contained within the labouring population through internal struggles. The competitive model of the capital market became the pattern for analysing working-class internal relationships. While the concept of social reproduction and subsistence could easily embody an idea of equality, solidarity and collective cooperation for survival and progress, competition of large numbers of workers for access to a limited wages fund implies destructive struggles within the labouring population, in the family, the community and the work place. Amid widespread Malthusian cynicism, it was taken for granted that the weak sections of the social structure would be defeated and obediently fade away; indeed this idea was adopted by Darwin as a starting point for his theory of evolution.

Given the unrest of the working classes and the open conflict with the middle classes, the Ricardian framework had proved to be too candid in showing the basic characteristics of the capitalist system (Meek, 1967a). Words such as 'labour' changed meaning; adjustment mechanisms changed from structural and institutional adjustments of production and distribution to simple mechanisms for allocating physical quantities. The new analytical method expressed a new view of the world. A broad social and historical analysis was replaced by a simplistic mechanical framework in which specific historical processes were homogenized by universal laws, and social conflicts were mystified by theories of technical and natural constraints (Burrow, 1970; Jones, 1980). The significant aspects of the real world could be considered only as *ad hoc* rigidities and 'checks' in the functioning of the universal laws.

It might seem exaggerated to lay such a heavy burden on a single definition, but the concept of an exogenously given wage – within a context of labour value and of exogenous distribution – was a way to express the fact that labour is a very peculiar commodity. Its peculiarity lies in the fact that it produces surplus value, eats and struggles. All these aspects are interrelated: it produces because it eats and it produces a surplus because it eats less than it produces. It is also the only commodity which socializes collectively with its similars, which embodies historical progress and can organize for more. These aspects are common to all forms of labour, slave labour included. But the main characteristic of waged labour is that the process of reproduction of the labouring population is not under direct control of the owners of the means of production. This makes the control over the supply of labour a very specific and difficult question, as is partly acknowledged in the analytical exogeneity of the natural price of labour.

The regressive cynicism of the Malthusian theory of population was used by the supply-and-demand theorists of the wages fund to introduce the idea of mechanically determined wages. This had the effect not only of impoverishing and narrowing the scope of the analysis of the labour market, but also of helping to kill the great visions of universal progress of the French Revolution (Meek, 1953).

The Newtonian mechanical scientific method, of which Malthus was so proud (Flew, 1957), and which still rules in economics, is inappropriate for the social problems related to the social reproduction of labour; indeed it is also out of date for the methodology of natural and physical sciences, which economists always try to emulate (Mirowsky, 1989). Tools and methodologies have to be chosen with regard to the problems under scientific scrutiny. If the problem is the process of social reproduction of labour, as a fundamental component of the capitalist system, not only is a mechanistic approach inappropriate and misleading, but so also are biological evolutionary approaches. History shows that one characteristic of the human race is its capacity to protect its weak sections and the power of the weak sections to take collective action for their survival. Social selection is historically determined and depends on power relationships among the different sections of the population.[15]

The social reproduction of labour has to be analysed in the context of the economic framework of the capitalist system because it is related to the historical definition of labour and its market, to the distribution between wages and profits, to the structural historical processes of production of commodities and reproduction of the labouring population. As we have seen in the previous chapter, these aspects of the labour market could up to a certain point be located at the core of the analytical framework, via the definition of wages as costs of social reproduction. With the wages fund, however, these aspects were removed from the general and normal framework and displaced to other social sciences or treated as accidental rigidities of the economic system. This displacement, and the consequent loss of lucidity, also led to a split between the theory of the labour market and economic policy. The separation between theory and policy – usually seen as a distinction between science and art – was introduced when the theory started to take wages as endogenously determined by supply and demand – Sidgwick apparently attributed the separation to Senior and J. S. Mill (McNulty, 1980, p. 73). At any rate, it was totally alien to Smith and Ricardo, who did not distinguish between policy and theory.

The distinction was made necessary only when the theory of wages came to be based on a supply-and-demand determination of wages. At that point the real problems of the labour market, no longer compatible with the theory, were relegated, together with policy making, to a sphere outside the realm of 'true science'. Policy became an 'art', labour problems became 'history' and economics was transformed into 'a tight theoretical system, based on hypothetical premises and enjoying much of the supposed certainty of the physical sciences but clearly demarcated from the pressing issues of the day' (McNulty, 1980, p. 74).

As will be shown in the next chapter, however, the real world imposes itself – in spite of the efforts of economists to discipline it – through the systematic failure of policies. This happened to the wages fund-based policies of the Poor Law Act of 1834: 'It was, in fact, discovered that those who failed in the struggle of existence were not necessarily or even usually "eliminated" as "unfit"' (Webb and Webb, 1963, p. 551).

The link between the wages fund theory and the 1834 Poor Law policies is Senior, who as Professor of Political Economy was a member of the 1832 Royal Commission and provided the basic analysis of the labour market. According to Senior, there is no possibility of alliance between wages and profit against rent. As he says in the preface to the new edition of his *Three Lectures on Wages*, the 'age of tranquillity' is over. The social conflict which was only potential in the Ricardian framework, is now open. The political context has changed:

Have sufficient pains been taken even to expose the absurdity of what appears so obvious to the populace – that the landlords ought to reduce their rents and the clergy their tithes, and then the farmer would give better wages? If the farmer had his land for nothing, still it would not be his interest to give any man more wages for a day's work than his day's work was worth. He could better afford it, no doubt, to be paid as a tax. (Senior, 1831, pp. xii–xiii)

What the work is worth is now the productivity of labour at the work place: the family and the costs of reproduction have nothing to do with the determination of wages:

As marriage has no tendency to increase the value of his [the freeman's] labour, it has no tendency to increase his remuneration. (Senior, 1831, p. viii)

Thus the value of labour is no longer determined by the physical and social process of reproduction, but by technological relationships between quantities of capital and quantities of labour. Moreover, when substitution of machines for labour is taken as general and systematic, the labour market – given the proper flexibility of wages – is seen as a clearing market.

When the analysis of the labour market changed, and the natural price of labour – understood as the cost of social reproduction – gave place to the market price as the sole determinant of wages, in reality major changes in the structure of the labour market had occurred. In a developed industrial and urban context, subsistence in fact came to depend more and more on wages: both because subsistence goods are commodities sold on the market, and because the general form of access to subsistence is waged labour. The insecurity of workers' access to means of subsistence is a historical phenomenon, not a natural or technical one; from now on this aspect disappears from the analysis.

Control over labour becomes impersonal, but impersonal does not mean natural and objective – though economic theory tends to give that impression. In reality the mechanisms by which the modes of reproduction adjust to the requirements of the labour market are social and not automatic. In the following chapters I shall try to throw light on the various adjustment mechanisms of the labour market which involve intervention by the state and the functioning of the family.

In this chapter I have tried to bring out the way the view of the labour market changed when the concept of the natural price of labour changed its meaning.[16] With the wages fund theory the way in which the production–reproduction relationship was seen underwent a complete reversal: wages were no longer taken as a reflection of the exogenous modes of reproduction, but reproduction – in quantity and standards – was seen as depending on wages determined by the allocation of quantities of capital and population. Up to now this reversal has not been corrected, or indeed even questioned. It is still the foundation of the modern approach to the question of population and development.[17]

The reality of the capitalist system tends progressively to increase the dependence of subsistence on the market. But the forms of dependence, while impersonal, are not uncontrollable and still less automatic: they reflect decisions made by responsible agents. The first step towards regaining a clear view of the real mechanisms operating in the labour market is to recover the long-dismissed concept of wages as a cost of reproduction, exogenous from other prices. A wages fund understood as a quantity of capital cannot be determined without a previous specification of the wage–profit distribution, which is exogenous and not technically given.

3

The role of the state in the labour market, i.e. social insecurity

If no body did Want no body would work; but the greatest Hardships are look'd upon as solid Pleasures, when they keep a Man from Starving.

From what has been said it is manifest, that in a free Nation where Slaves are not allow'd of, the surest Wealth consists in a Multitude of laborious Poor; for besides that they are the never-failing Nursery of Fleets and Armies, without them there could be no Enjoyment, and no Product of any Country could be valuable.

Mandeville
Fable of the Bees

So that they have nothing to stir them up to be serviceable but their Wants, which it is Prudence to relieve, but Folly to cure. The only thing then that can render the labouring Man industrious, is a moderate quantity of Money; for as too little will, according as his Temper is, either dispirit or make him Desperate, so too much will make him Insolent and Lazy.

Mandeville
Fable of the Bees

3.1 Starting from the bottom

The theory of the wages fund managed to hide the structural problems of the labour market by shifting them out of the analysis of the normal determination of wages; but it could not find any solution to them. The implementation of the policies of the 1834 Act made it necessary to face those problems, which in reality proved to be persistent and general although they were dismissed by theorists as marginal and accidental. In this chapter and the next I shall introduce some historical evidence of the real contradictions inherent in the separation of production and reproduction.

Social reproduction of labour

I chose a Poor Law Report as a source of information on the assumption that a specific focus on the social insecurity of the poorest sections of the labouring population could help bring to light the structure of the labour market. For the poorest classes, in fact, the problems of reproduction are always explicit; this helps to make the whole historical process of social reproduction more transparent, and to expose the main tool of capitalist command over labour: that is to say, the general insecurity over the means of reproduction at individual and collective level.[1] The poor necessarily disclose the real difficulties of reproduction inherent in low standards and insecurity.

This fact is generally recognized in theories of wages which consider subsistence as a downward rigidity to otherwise flexible wages. This rigidity is considered to represent only a limited case for the number of people involved. But the material process of reproduction, its historical and cultural aspects, power relationships between classes and within classes, and the general insecurity over the means of reproduction, link the poorest sections of the labouring population to those which enjoy greater security. This brings out some fundamental characteristics of the whole system.

By focussing on the process of social reproduction of labour we also obtain a clearer picture of some historical functions of the state. Conflicts arise from the fact that the entire process of reproduction involves a huge amount of labour, a complex division of labour and enormous resources. This means that a great deal of social control is required. The recurrent failure of social policy to limit state intervention in support of reproduction to a residuum, shows that it is not so easy to impose constraints on the process of social reproduction of labour.

State institutions often prove inadequate at times of instability of employment and structural changes in the process of reproduction. The state is forced to intervene on new terms and to modify its role significantly. This was the case, for example, in the latter part of the nineteenth and the early twentieth century, when the whole system of poor relief established in Great Britain with the 1834 Poor Law Act proved to be totally inadequate and a new public initiative was needed. Some of the problems and tensions underlying the state's changing role found their expression in the Poor Law Report of 1909.

A number of reasons prompted me to focus on the 1909 Report of the Royal Commission on the Poor Laws: (a) it represents a change from the so-called free market policies formulated in the previous Report of 1834; (b) it constitutes a very articulate and sound enquiry which focusses directly on the problems of standards of living, the family, health and education, low wages, and unemployment; (c) it represents a monumental

58

research effort, sponsored by the state itself, to clarify the basic structure of the labour market, to survey its own practices, and to find new lines of intervention at a time when the structural mismatch between supply and demand for labour, i.e. between production and reproduction, was evident.

The historical background of the Report itself, at the turn of the century, was complex and involved some major social developments: increasing unemployment in industry, due to the restructuring of various important productive sectors (Beveridge, 1909; Deane and Cole, 1962; Hunt, 1981); important changes in pension schemes, unemployment insurance, health service, children's and women's work, education and working hours (Bruce, 1961; Fraser, 1976; Gough, 1979; Hay, 1975; Webb and Webb, 1963); a decrease in birth rates, a general concern for standards of living, and an increasing institutional representation of the working classes through the broadening of the franchise and the foundation of the Independent Labour Party (1893); and a change in the scientific and ethical views of society after Darwin (Soffer, 1978). Last but not least, nineteenth-century industrialization and urbanization had greatly affected the structure of the family, and a massive women's movement was challenging the state on the issue of suffrage.

3.2 The Royal Commission on the Poor Laws and Distress, 1905–9

Two Reports – Majority and Minority – for England and Wales, separate Reports for Scotland and Ireland, and several volumes of appendices (all printed in folio by HMSO on about 20,000 pages) were the result of three years of assiduous meetings of the Royal Commission appointed in December 1905 by Balfour at the very end of his mandate. Among the members were prominent representatives of the COS (Charity Organization Society), members of LGBs (Local Government Boards), a professor of political economy (Smart), representatives of the Church, social investigators such as Booth and Beatrice Webb, and two labour representatives – George Lansbury and Francis Chandler. The head of the Commission was Lord Hamilton, a conservative.

Goodwill and genuine commitment were common features among the members, yet this was not sufficient to mediate the conflicts. Three basic policy lines were at stake (Hamilton, 1910). The conservatives, aiming to maintain the 1834 deterrent policies, still rested their hopes on a natural disappearance of poverty, or at any rate on the endurance of the labouring population. The moderates, while accepting the necessity of changing the 1834 approach (based on the assumption of moral weakness of the poor as the main cause of poverty) emphasized the responsibility of the state to prevent destitution, but were not willing to go beyond the Poor Law policy of limited assistance to a marginal social residuum. The progressive policy was based on the perspective of 'breaking up' the Poor Law institutional framework and dividing state intervention according to functional criteria. Prevention of destitution was to operate at a 'universal' level, through general support of minimum standards of living by unemployment relief schemes, minimum wages, benefits and services – especially health and education – measures aiming to support the family throughout the social structure. The fundamental conflict was over the role of the state and over the forms and degrees of its intervention in the labour market. The real confrontation was between those who wanted the state to take direct responsibility for poverty and unemployment, and those who thought that the administration of poverty and the prevention of destitution should remain mainly in private hands or at least under a limited Destitution Authority.[2]

The Royal Commission coordinated a huge research effort based on questionnaires, interviews and *ad hoc* memoranda of economists, union leaders, doctors, philanthropists, social officers, employers, civil servants, trade boards, etc. Booth and Beatrice Webb were both determined to improve the methods and scientific standards of research, which in their opinion were usually poor.[3] This was not the only government intervention in the field of the labour market, and specifically in the social reproduction of labour. Around the second half of the nineteenth century and at the turn of the new century, numerous formal actions were undertaken by the various governments on matters related to the living conditions of the labouring population. Factory Acts, the Health and Town Bill, Public Health Acts, Vaccination Acts, Contagious Diseases Acts, the Working Class Housing Act, the Royal Commission on Housing of the Working Classes; and, in the new century, the Interdepartmental Committee on Physical Deterioration (1904), the Education Act (1905) and the Provision of Meals Act (1906) were the most important. This intense public activity shows the complexity of the process that the state had to go through to find its way, in a very pragmatic fashion, towards viable adjustment mechanisms. The research work could no longer be left to the COS officers or to private researchers with limited access to the relevant institutions and personalities (K. Williams, 1981). The state itself had to sponsor the effort and to mobilize all the sources of information, providing direct access to all the pertinent participants in the functioning of the labour market.

The leading people involved in the Report, as members of the Royal Commission or as experts, often had experience in common, experience gathered in connection with the 'colonization', 'moralization' and the anthropological study of East End London (Beveridge, 1953; Stedman Jones, 1971; B. Webb, 1926; Freeden, 1986). Their relationships with the working classes remained elitist and detached, with a diffuse feeling of guilt, strongly expressed by Toynbee in the following passage.

We – the middle classes, I mean, not merely the very rich – we have neglected you; instead of justice we have offered you charity, and instead of sympathy we have offered you hard and unreal advice; but I think we are changing. If you would only believe it and trust us. I think that many of us would spend our lives in your service. (quoted in B. Webb, 1926, pp. 182–3)

The positive characteristic of this generation was a deep and widespread feeling of trust in change and progress. Scientific methods for social research and the state would provide the tools for change. Needless to say, the whole political and cultural environment was not homogeneous, and there was no conscious and explicit plan for social control. What did exist were some open problems in the labour market (explicitly related to conditions of social reproduction of labour and unemployment), some vested interests, changing power relationships, and a fertile progressive mood. The results were extremely interesting and had many seminal effects for the future Welfare State. The breadth and the nature of the problems dealt with in the 1909 Report made its immediate legislative use impossible. It took two world wars, with the pragmatic use of state machinery for massive intervention in the economy and social environment, to clear the ground for the Welfare State, and, unfortunately, also to kill the optimistic progressive mood (Carr, 1951; Winter, 1975; Freeden, 1986).

The major event in the work of the Royal Commission of 1909 was a radical split among the commissioners which led to the publication of two separate final Reports, although a basic agreement was reached on the data collected and on the failure of the free market policies embodied in the 1834 Report (Webb and Webb, 1909, Part I, p. ix). Differences emerged on the diagnosis of the failure. The majority attributed it to incompetence and corruption of the 24,000 guardians involved in the administration of the Poor Law, while the minority attributed it to structural changes in the social context and to overlapping policies within the Public Administration (Webb and Webb, 1909, Part I, pp. x–xi). The chief cause of the split was the attempt, perpetrated by the majority, to step backward by supporting a 'Public Assistance Authority' against the proposal of specialized institutions providing services and social benefits on a universal basis; the handling of involuntary unemployment within the Poor Laws was considered particularly unacceptable.

In order to grasp the novelty of the policy perspectives in the 1909 Report it is necessary to look back at the 1834 Report on the Poor Law, to which it explicitly refers.

3.3 The 1834 Poor Law

The 1834 Report and the immediate Act of Parliament which enforced its policies, were based on the economic theories of the wages fund and intended to free the labour market from state intervention on the matter of wages, mobility and standards of living of the labouring population. The analytical framework adopted by Senior, a member of the Royal Commission, was that of a market supply-and-demand adjustment mechanism which would guarantee a clearing labour market and the adjustment of living standards of the labouring population to flexible wages. Economic theory was used as an ideological device to justify imposing a double obligation on the labourers: to accept work at whatever wage rate was offered and to adapt their standards of living to the market rate of wages. Unemployment was explained in terms of workers' inability or unwillingness to work. The economic policies of the 1834 Act were explicitly dependent on established economic theories; in contrast, the 1909 policies were rooted in the pragmatic behaviour of public institutions.

For the nineteenth-century legislators and policy-makers, the liberalization of the labour market was essentially meant to free the state from any responsibility towards the labouring population, or at least to limit very strictly the cases of public relief. The labourer and the labouring population as a whole were to be made totally dependent on wages. The social insecurity inherent in wages thus was strengthened as the basic force for disciplining work, both outside and inside the family.

The fundamental aim of the 1834 Act was to transfer resources, as quickly as possible, from public expenditure to profit accumulation. All the costs arising from the instability of the process of reproduction were to be laid on the shoulders of the labouring population. Homogeneity in public relief within each section of destitution was to be reached by guidelines designed to counteract corruption, inefficiency and favouritism on the part of parish overseers – which were apparently the main causes of discontent that led to the appointment of the Royal Commission in 1832. This implied a major restructuring process, leading to the agglomeration of parishes into unions, and later on to the establishment of Poor Law Boards of Guardians (Nicholls, 1898). The policy was enforced by strong deterrents such as the workhouse (with its inherent logic of punishment and criminalization), reduced 'eligibility' (public works had to be less remunerative and less attractive than market jobs), and deprivation of civil rights.

The 1834 Report is based on the distinction between the able-bodied and the non-able-bodied. What is really implied in this partition is that for some sections dependence on somebody else's wage is taken for granted as the normal case. The state intervenes only in certain cases when there is no wage to depend on: children, old people (before the introduction of pensions), the sick and the disabled. At first glance the distinction between the able-bodied and the non-able-bodied seems to imply a physical difference but that is a mystification: from a capitalist point of view the distinction is between the waged and the wageless sections of labouring population. The non-able-bodied are in fact defined as the residual sections of the waged population. Physical and biological differences are used as a pretext for social segmentations which in reality depend on power relationships.[4] Although the distinction between able-bodied and non-able-bodied was far from precise, it was considered clear enough to serve as a basis for extremely repressive policies against the able-bodied males who were the main target of the 1834 commissioners. Unemployment was in fact considered their fault, and it was thought that relief would only encourage, or even induce, vicious idleness.

The 1909 Report provided information on the failures of the 1834 policies which not only brings out the unclarity of the definition of able-bodied person, but also exposes its mystifications. The distinction was used as the basis for a 'surplus labour' theory of the labour market:

We have seen that the Royal Commission of 1832 considered the great problem before them to be the reduction of able-bodied pauperism. In this most difficult part of their task they were constantly confronted by a cry with which we have recently become very familiar – the cry of 'surplus labour'. The argument is very plausible; there is only a certain amount of work to be done and the fact that men are out of work shows that there are enough workers without them. There is a surplus of labour, and, since the surplus labourers cannot keep themselves, the community must keep them out of the rates. The line taken by the Commissioners was, that it depended very largely upon the man himself whether there is work for him to do or not; that if the services he offered were worthless to everyone, then he would be 'surplus' but that ability and industry were pretty certain to find a market, if not in one place, then in other. (House of Commons, 1909, p. 201)

According to the wages fund theory, given a certain amount of capital the worker can always adapt to market conditions by increasing his mobility and accepting the downward flexibility of wages; in this context only physical and moral inabilities can cause a rigidity in the labour market. Increasing and persistent unemployment and poverty showed that not all the able-bodied willing to work had a wage, and that not all the employed able-bodied had adequate wages.

The theory that only physical incapacity or moral weakness could cause dependence on public assistance was contradicted by facts, but the distinction between able-bodied and non-able-bodied continued to be used to introduce forms of social segmentation. Every effort was made to separate the deserving from the undeserving. Protection of some sections – such as widows of soldiers and deserving workers – went hand in hand with the exclusion of others such as idlers, vagrants, prostitutes, etc. The core of the labour market was basically defined as sober, hard-working, able-bodied males. Workers were classified according to criteria based on health and morals, health being defined as the ability to work and morality as the disposition to work.[5]

While the recipients of relief were divided between able-bodied and non-able-bodied, deserving and undeserving, the forms of assistance were divided into indoor and outdoor relief. Indoor relief (the workhouse) was forced on the able-bodied in order to discipline them. Outdoor relief, less repressive and much less costly for the state, was generally given to the non-able-bodied: single mothers, children and aged people. Towards the end of the century the number of able-bodied males on indoor and outdoor relief in urban areas had greatly increased (House of Commons, 1909, pp. 42–6).[6]

The 1834 Act was extremely cynical and brutally repressive towards poverty, and thereby provoked strong reactions. From the start the 1834 policies were resisted, especially in the North, with massive struggles that were later absorbed into the Chartist Movement which specifically attacked the new Poor Law and maintained a direct confrontation with the state.[7] Deterrent policies were never strong enough to avoid favouritism and inequalities, which were mainly due to different power relationships between the relieved population and the guardians. Moreover, the problem of outdoor relief for unemployed able-bodied males, while presenting itself in new forms, was far from disappearing. To deal with it required new modes of intervention and the modification of old ones. The administrative machinery was continuously disrupted by changes in unemployment rates, mobility, and new social demands such as health and education. The wages fund theory had provided an ideological scheme by which to define and marginalize 'surplus' population which was supposed to function as a safety valve for the labour market. This residuum was defined by the lack of access (direct or indirect) to stable and adequate wages. The residual population was expected to disappear from public concern (possibly emigrating), especially if comprised of unemployed males.

In practice the implementation of the principles of the 1834 Act had been changing quite a lot during the nineteenth century. Changes had occurred both in outdoor and indoor relief. Towards the end of the century relief was losing part of its deterrent nature, especially in the case of unsupported mothers, the aged, the sick and children. Forms of outdoor relief for able-bodied males remained in use. These involved disfranchisement and maintained certain deterrent aspects, but were less repulsive than the workhouse (Fraser, 1976), whose running costs for the state were meanwhile increasing with new buildings and the introduction of waged social workers (K. Williams, 1981; House of Commons, 1909, pp. 28–30).

The relief of the sick played a very important role in both outdoor and indoor relief, activating a slow movement towards universal provisions which undermined the principle of deterrence. The 1834 Act had not dealt specifically with the problem of health, but this sector of intervention became very important politically and very significant in terms of expenditure (B. Webb, 1910). Health conditions led to the distribution of relief among the different sections in a less rigid way and with milder deterrent features.[8]

Living conditions of the labouring population were seen mainly in terms of health standards. The medical profession thus gained a tremendous social influence. The top levels of the profession, while continuing to treat the upper classes, had the power to shape sanitary policies and to control the growing medical schools and infirmaries. To the lower levels of this very hierarchical profession the increasing demand for sanitary services for the labourers offered a new market for professional activity. Apothecaries and general practitioners worked first for 'sick societies' and fraternities and then for the state in Poor Law infirmaries (Navarro, 1978).[9] The workhouse, although on the whole maintaining its very repressive features, was transforming the mixed workhouse (containing all sections of the population on relief) into more specialized institutions serving the purposes of efficiency and social discipline (K. Williams, 1981). Poor Law infirmaries were transformed in the course of time into public hospitals.

3.4 The failure of the 1834 policies

It is impossible here to give proper consideration to all the information provided by the Reports (Majority and Minority) on the implementation of the 1834 policies during the long time span before the 1905–9 Royal Commission. However, it is important to analyse their major failures: (a) the persistence of the mixed workhouses and of outdoor relief for the able-bodied, (b) the increased numbers of people on relief, (c) the overlapping of other state provisions which undermined the policy of deterrence, implementing the tendency towards normalizing and extending state intervention in the labour market.

The persistence of the mixed workhouse shows the failure of the 1834 policies which had strongly opposed it. The reasons for the inefficiency of the mixed workhouse are numerous. The family model of organization was not tenable because of the large size of some of the workhouses (800–1,000 inmates) and the fact that without the discipline of the wage and its inherent insecurity, it was very difficult to achieve discipline on purely ideological or physically repressive grounds. Thus the amount of work done in the workhouse depended explicitly on the power relationships between the inmates and the overseers. It became even more difficult to discipline services to adults, children and the sick, than to discipline work in the workyard. Waged nurses, teachers and overseers had to be enrolled to provide for services and control.

Another major reason for the failure of the 1834 policies was the persistence with which the social residuum of the wageless sections required increasing state provisions. The residuum was not disappearing and its costs of reproduction, inside as well as outside public institutions, were increasing. Public expenditure for social transfers and services within the Poor Law increased from 7 million pounds in 1834 to 20 million in 1909. Indeed, if provisions outside of the Poor Law are taken into account as well, expenditure added up to 60 million pounds (House of Commons, 1909, p. 52).[10]

As time went on it became impossible to separate the population into rigid sections with regard to education and health, housing, etc.[11] So, in the second half of the nineteenth century, the state showed a tendency to turn into a permanent and general agency of support for subsistence. The administrators of the Poor Law were caught in an insoluble dilemma: either to create new destitution by repressing the poor, or to prevent it, thereby undermining the very foundations of the 1834 Act. The dilemma was indeed not soluble by the 24,000 guardians; they had been appointed to deal with limited and temporary cases of destitution and idleness, and could not be expected to solve, or even to hide, the fundamental problems of the labour market arising from the fact that labour is not a commodity easily produced, disciplined and disposed of. To some extent guardians and social workers found ways to escape frustration through inefficiency, corruption or missionary effort in support of the poor; but ultimately, the state itself had to change its policies, and started to experiment on different lines inside and outside the context of the Poor Law. Hence what really undermined the 1834 policies was the state itself, through conflicting actions undertaken by various state agencies dealing with the problems caused by unemployment and poor living standards of the working classes.

Among the major steps undertaken by the state in the labour market at the beginning of the twentieth century were the Unemployed Workmen Act of 1905 and the Old Age Pension of 1908 (Bailward, 1912, p. 542). These important pieces of legislation actually had the effect of 'breaking up' the Poor Law: they relaxed the social stigma, took open responsibility for social distress, intervened with specialized provisions, and moved towards establishing a right of security rather than a punishment for poverty.

More specialized and flexible institutions developed within the Poor Law as well. The Able Test Work House was intended exclusively for the able-bodied, so that work discipline could be implemented without having to make concessions as a result of giving more generous treatment to children, the sick and the aged. The 'Poplar' workhouse in London was an exemplary establishment of this kind, so effective in repression that more than once the magistrates had to intervene to soften it (Webb and Webb, 1909, Part II, pp. 44–5). Different institutions were used for different kinds of workers, according to their character, wages and employment segmentation. Classification of workers was an instrument used by the state to assess power relationships between classes and different sections of the working classes, inside and outside public institutions. But the history of the implementation of the repressive policies of 1834 shows that the social classifications are not easily controllable. For instance, many able-bodied workers were listed under other categories on relief, such as young people, single mothers, vagrants, aged men who could not find new jobs, etc. Even among the ever-increasing number of people on health relief there were some disguised able-bodied people who tried to avoid the unpleasant deterrent practices of the workhouse.

In 1909 the inability of the majority commissioners to abandon the theory of voluntary unemployment and/or physical and moral inabilities led them to make some very pessimistic comments on the effects of the social policies of 1834. They could not cope with the fact that public benefits, far from disappearing, had started to become part of a social wage which had nothing to do with physical and moral criteria, and that the deterrent policies of the Poor Laws had become outdated and powerless, even if officially still in use.

The consideration of these statistics leads to the conclusion that it is in regard to the able-bodied that least progress has been made. Indeed it would appear that there has recently been a considerable retrogression in this branch of the Poor Law. Either the urban population is becoming less fitted for maintaining their independence, or the facility with which relief may be obtained and the immunity to labour which it confers are enticing a larger number of persons to avail themselves of Poor Relief. (House of Commons, 1909, p. 43)

The commissioners also had to recognize that the preventive policies of increasing expenditure for education and health, which ought to have reduced destitution if it were due to physical or moral causes, were not successful.

It is very unpleasant to record that, notwithstanding our assumed moral and material progress, and notwithstanding the enormous annual expenditure, amounting to nearly sixty millions a year, upon poor relief, education, and public health, we still have a vast army of persons quartered upon us unable to support themselves, and an army which in numbers has recently shown signs of increase rather than decrease. To what is the retrogression due? It can not be attributed to lack of expenditure. Is this costly and elaborate machinery we have established defective, and if so where does it fail to accomplish its end? (House of Commons, 1909, p. 52)

Forms of social insurance were also provided by 'friendly societies' and by the unions, but they covered only the stronger sections of the working class, as they were based on regular contributions and played a complementary role with respect to the Poor Law (Thane, 1978b; Wilson, 1979). Employers provided some welfare benefits within the firm, although private welfare was distributed mainly as contributions to charities and generally at local level. As a matter of fact, private charities did provide the great bulk of poor relief in the nineteenth century. For London, in 1860, the annual budget for charities amounted roughly to the Poor Law expenditure for England and Wales combined (Hunt, 1981, p. 126). As we have seen above, one of the aims of the Royal Commission was to survey private charities, and the authors of the Minority Report were convinced that 'without State action private charity and Voluntary Agencies nowhere fit the need – they are in most places and for most purposes demoralisingly superabundant' (Webb and Webb, 1909, Part I, p. 507).

3.5 The Minority Report

The Minority Report of 1909 is divided into two parts: (i) the destitution of the non-able-bodied, (ii) the destitution of the able-bodied. The same partition appears under different headings in the edition of the Report which Sidney and Beatrice Webb published under their own names and used to campaign for the 'break-up' of the Poor Law (Hamilton, 1932, pp. 185–208). In this version, the sections are given as: (i) the break-up of the Poor Law, and (ii) the public organization of the labour market.

The new partition avoids the physical connotations, but it maintains the political and economic implications of the distinction between the waged and wageless sections of the labouring population. The most problematic groups are the involuntary unemployed and women engaged in housework, who proved to be an embarrassing case with single mothers treated basically as incapable labourers. The impossibility of earning a wage is dealt with as an incapacity for work. Dependence, which is the real social handicap to which the partitions of both the 1834 and 1909 Reports refer, implies different degrees of insecurity, as the insecurity of dependence has to be added to the general insecurity of wages. According to the experts and policy-makers of the Minority Report, state intervention has to be auxiliary; it cannot replace the two poles that sustain the whole structure of the capitalist labour market, the wage and the family.

The first part of the Minority Report deals with the following sections: infants and children of school age, the sick, the mentally defective, and the aged and infirm. For these sections the Report recommends 'breaking up' the Poor Law into specialized and independent Education, Health, Asylums and Pension Committees (Webb and Webb, 1909, Part I, p. 599). The second and better-known part of the Report deals with the able-bodied, i.e. with the problems of unemployment, low wages, casual work and generally of disguised unemployment. Women, as we shall see in the next chapter, in a sense represent the 'missing link' between the able-bodied and the sections which are considered physically or mentally incapable of work. This problem is implicitly recognized in the extraordinary question which titles a section of the first chapter: 'Are Women Able-Bodied?'

The Minority Report expressed a radical change at the level of principles. The individual moral responsibility of the poor was supplemented by a collective and state responsibility for prevention of destitution. The state thus became a fundamental official adjustment mechanism for mediating between the process of production and that of reproduction. In practice it had always been so, but the political recognition of this fact had to wait until 1909 and for the cooptation into Parliament of some sections of the working class and its historical organizations. The recognition was also induced by struggles and various forms of resistance against the repressive aspects of the Poor Law, waged at collective and at individual level and by the broadly progressive ideas held, at the time, by middle-class parties such as the Liberal Party (Freeden, 1986).

The distinction between able-bodied and non-able-bodied kept its fundamental role in the Report, as its organization clearly shows. The distinction between deserving and undeserving was also fully maintained. The state's continuous efforts to classify the labouring population by dividing it into sections did not cease. On the one hand, such classifications were determined by functional requirements; on the other, they were designed, and used, as a tool of social control in the distribution of relief (K. Williams, 1981).

With regard to the non-able-bodied, the policy perspectives put forward by the Minority Report generally ratify practices which had already been tested within and outside the Poor Law – as in the case of old-age pensions – stressing the universal character of public provisions within sections and services.

As far as the able-bodied workers are concerned, the Minority Report moves straight along the lines of the policies advanced in the Unemployed Workmen Act. As we have seen, it was the progressive members' strong support for these policies that led to the split in the Royal Commission. In contrast to their nineteenth-century predecessors, the Minority members of the Royal Commission did not assume any gross population adjustment mechanism, nor did they expect the market to automatically clear or settle at an adequate wage level. They adopted the progressive perspective of an open state support for the family and for wages, as they thought that in the long run the prevention of destitution would cost less, both financially and politically, than its repressive disciplining. In their view no private charity organization could fulfil the role of an adjustment mechanism for the labour market – indeed private charities might even be dangerous, as they confused the issues and implemented wrong classifications and policies. It was only with regard to emigration and character building that the role of the religious associations, such as the Salvation Army, was given credit.

The second part of the Minority Report, 'The Public Organization of the Labour Market', aims at removing the relief of the unemployed from the Poor Law administration. This avenue was opened by Chamberlain in 1886 in a circular which offered a new basis for public work programmes. Chamberlain's circular concluded as follows:

The Law exists for securing the assistance of the community at large in aid of their destitute members; and where the necessity has arisen from no fault of the persons concerned, there ought to be no idea of degradation connected with such assistance. (Webb and Webb, 1909, Part II, p. 116)

The circular offered an opportunity for experimenting with public works projects designed for the 'deserving' – as designated by the guardians – at a wage lower than the market rate. The circular was re-issued many times and other local authorities, 'responding to the perpetual pleadings and threatenings of deputations of unemployed workmen', followed the same path; but the idea of offering lower wages had to be abandoned because of riots and disturbances (Webb and Webb, 1909, Part II, p. 118).

The circular was originally issued to deal with the problem of qualified silversmiths and electroplate workers in Birmingham, and it was meant to exclude casual workers. In order to keep the work offered by municipal authorities less attractive than the open-market opportunities, the period of employment was shortened. This had negative effects on the tasks performed, as people with different skills were not given training on the job. The high social utility in terms of conflict absorption, mental health and income maintenance had to balance the high cost in terms of low productivity (Webb and Webb, 1909, Part II, p. 123). Once again the problem was the heterogeneity of the labour force, in spite of drastic selection from the start.

The Unemployed, as statistics will show, are usually men of the most varied occupations; and it may fairly be presumed that some of them are not the most thrifty, thoughtful workmen, or men particularly handy at their respective trades. (Webb and Webb, 1909, Part II, p. 125)

One of the aims of the Royal Commission had been to survey the extent of unemployment. The results were very worrying, though the worst was yet to come and chronic underemployment had to be added to structural and cyclical unemployment (p. 130). In fact, unemployment and distress were endemic, and public works were just a drop in the ocean (Brown, 1971; Garside, 1980; Harris, 1972). The failure of municipal employment was caused mainly by the fact that the public works schemes were designed to meet emergencies and the needs of limited sections, whereas in fact they encountered a bottomless situation of distress of the waged workers.

The Unemployed Workmen Act of 1905 had run into the same kind of inadequacy.

The Unemployed Workmen Act embodied the policy of Mr. Chamberlain's circular of 1886 – that respectable men, temporarily unemployed, should not be cast on the Poor Law, but should be assisted by the Municipal Authority of the district in which they were resident. The casual labourers were expressly excluded. 'We proposed' said Mr. Gerald Balfour 'to deal with the elite of the Unemployed.' (Webb and Webb, 1909, Part II, p. 134)

The Unemployed Workmen Act failed for lack of funds, which proved to cover little more than the machinery built up to administer the public works schemes. But it also failed because these schemes were not economically productive.

The evidence we have collected seems conclusive that relief works are economically useless. Either ordinary work is undertaken . . . which . . . throws out of employment the men who are in the more or less regular employment of

71

the councils or else it is sham work which we believe to be even more deteriorating than direct relief. (Webb and Webb, 1909, Part II, p. 138)

The Royal Commission supported Beveridge's idea of the labour exchanges with the objective of increasing the mobility of the workforce and creating an observatory on the labour market at a national level. Information could be collected and made available to the workers and, more importantly, this information could be used by the state to implement some kind of anticyclical policies when unemployment figures were rising. The jobs passing through the labour exchange would keep all the open-market qualifications and no personal information would be used as a condition of employment. The social stigmatization of the Poor Law had to be abandoned. An experiment with the labour exchange in London had proved a notable success: in one year 30,000 jobs had been allocated of which 20,000 were permanent. In spite of this encouraging success, the Minority Report does not show great confidence in the potential for job creation by the labour exchanges. Much more interest was shown with regard to the possibility of using them to introduce demand-management policies. The Minority Report's role as a forerunner of Keynes's effective demand policies emerges clearly from the following passage.[12]

For (what is usually forgotten) capital is unemployed and Underemployed to at least as great an extent as labour. It is in the lean years of the trade cycle, when business is depressed, that most capital is Unemployed, and the Bank rate is at its lowest. It is, accordingly, just in the years that Government works are needed in order to keep up the National Demand for Labour that Government can borrow at the cheapest rate. (Webb and Webb, 1909, Part II, p. 286)

Since 1909 public expenditure policies have shown that on the one hand the labour market cannot rely on any automatic or endogenous mechanisms of adjustment, while on the other hand the role of the state as an adjustment mechanism is a very difficult one: plans to control the reproduction of labour like the production of other commodities have never succeeded. The whole process of social reproduction of labour involves forces and agents whose power has never been fully understood.

The 1909 commissioners openly denounced free labour-market policies and tried more reformist ways of coping with the labour market. They introduced an open support for the family and for the wage. Reforms aimed at a rational adjustment of the labour market in order to reduce the violent shocks imposed by free trade policies. They were put forward for fear of social conflict, for humanitarian reasons, through trust in scientific social engineering; their basic aim was to control public expenditure and to reduce it. Classification and segmentation were the main tools of social engineering; however, the boundaries continued to shift and public expenditure for the support of the social reproduction of the labouring population increased, as shown historically by the increasing weight of transfers and benefits (Peacock and Wiseman, 1961).

While the reformist commissioners offered important insights on the nature of unemployment and on the role of the state as a structural agent in the labour market, they did not closely analyse the link between the first and the second part of the Minority Report: i.e. the link between the insecurity of the waged and the insecurity of the wageless sections of the labouring population. The policies of 1834 had kept separate from the normal structure of the labour market all the segments included in the social residuum. The repressive policies aimed to reduce and limit the surplus population. Everything possible was done to segregate the social surplus from the core, which means that the social surplus had to absorb the instability and insecurity of the core without challenging the labour market and its functioning. In this respect, by recognizing the existence of involuntary unemployment, the necessity for universal policies of intervention in support of wages and the services of reproduction, the Minority Report undermined a fundamental aspect of nineteenth-century social policies and anticipated the Welfare State.

Nonetheless, in the Report the family–wage relationship remains unquestioned and the labour market is considered able to function once the state has guaranteed its supportive and auxiliary role. Its main focus on unemployment, minimum wages, effective demand and fluidity in the labour market, and its secondary focus (even if much more stressed than in current approaches) on the process of social reproduction of the labouring population as a whole, undermines some of its potentialities.

4

Women and the Poor Law

One important truth sufficiently impressed upon your mind
will materially assist in this desirable consummation [to be
satisfied in marriage] – it is the superiority of your husband,
simply as a man . . . For want of a satisfactory settlement of
this point before marriage, how many disputes and
misunderstandings have ensued, filling, as with the elements
of discord and strife, that world of existence which ought to
be a smiling Eden of perpetual flowers.

Sarah Stikney Ellis, *The Wives of England* (1850)

4.1 Victorian and Edwardian housework

Before discussing the position of women within the 1909 Poor Law
Reports, it will be useful to provide some historical background regarding
women in society in the second half of the nineteenth century and at the
beginning of the new century. Women's position in the family and in the
labour market can be understood only in terms of the increasing separation
between the processes of production and reproduction. This separation
affected cultural and personal attitudes and social relationships. It also
introduced a marked distinction between the private and the public spheres
which affected family members in different ways according to sex and
age.

In pre-industrial society, when production was organized together with
reproduction within the family, the conflicts involved in the division of
labour could be considered as inherent in the household economy; class
and gender relationships were conditioned by ownership of land and by
patriarchy. With the development of the industrialized capitalist system,
production and reproduction were divided into separate spheres. This in
time led to different work places, different ideologies, different perceptions
of time and different social and political relations.

The developing industrial mode of production within the capitalist logic
of accumulation created a general insecurity of access to the means of
reproduction that could serve as a lever of command over work both in
production and in reproduction, disciplining both houseworkers and waged
workers to adapt to the needs of the accumulation of capital. For all
workers this meant control over bodies, minds and emotions; but it
imposed on women new modes of reproduction in which they were

expected to function more and more as reproductive workers instead of as persons. Women had to reproduce waged workers, the basic capitalist commodity. In order to do this they too had to become capitalist workers, although as they received no wage for their work this fact was effectively hidden. Not only was their work made invisible, but their bodies and feelings were controlled by powerful and specific forms of repression – necessary because giving birth and emotional nourishment are essential elements in the process of reproduction of labour.

The specific capitalist relationship between production and reproduction processes shaped the relationship between the work of production and the work of reproduction and therefore between production workers and reproduction workers. And just as the capitalist mode of production alienates the relationship between the worker and his product, in the case of women, the capitalist need for control alienates the relationship with their children and lovers, with much graver consequences for their personal identity. The failures of the social policies of the 1834 Act show in fact that the family, and women within and outside it, did not function smoothly as an adjusting mechanism between production and reproduction, for in spite of social engineering they did not absorb all the shocks of the industrial capitalist labour market.

In the second half of the nineteenth century, with the takeoff of the industrial system and the great acceleration of urbanization, production and reproduction were fully established as separate processes. Forms of production such as 'putting out' and agriculture were losing weight in the economic structure. Factories and offices were absorbing an increasing proportion of the labour force (Levine, 1985; Tilly and Scott, 1978; Stedman Jones, 1971). In this period the lack of adjustment mechanisms between the demand and the supply of labour, and at a deeper level between the production and reproduction processes, become obvious. A number of structural changes in living conditions called the state into action. For instance, conditions in the cities were so appalling as to become a matter of public concern (Briggs, 1968; Dyos and Wolff, 1973).

Men and women were affected in different ways and degrees by environmental conditions.

Man's life in crowded towns was bad, but woman's was infinitely worse; it was the housewife who suffered most from the misery of defective sanitary arrangements, and from the constant struggle with dirt. (Hammond and Hammond, 1966, p. 103)

The employers left to speculators the task of providing houses (Hammond and Hammond, 1966, pp. 52–4) and to the housewife the task of organizing life in houses and streets where crowding, lack of water, insects, the impossibility of storing food and lack of play space, not to mention distress caused by recent urbanization, made housework (in terms of hours and effort) a very hard job indeed. Women's bodies were marked by the violence of the environment, by poor health, scanty diets, and a fair amount of battering. The effects on their health were so noticeable that doctors, police and public reports had to acknowledge them (Thane, 1978a, p. 34; Hunt, 1981). Moreover, various inquiries into the sanitary conditions of the working classes, the low physical standards of conscripts and the appalling conditions of the urban environment, made the state aware of how much housework was worth.

The media of the times were campaigning on the role of the family. Health tracts for household consumption were widely circulated, while health officers were asked to train and check on housework.

To provide district or missionary nurses for the poor . . . relieves an amount of suffering most intense in its character, and capable of alleviation to a great extent, by a proportionately small expenditure. It does more than this; it teaches the people to nurse their own sick, and by introducing a knowledge of sanitary laws among the working classes, tends to prevent illness and strengthen health . . . The district nurse must be trained . . . But she must just do many things herself, such as clean a disorderly grate, dirty windows, etc. . . . and so show them how to do it. (F. Nightingale, quoted in Hollis, 1979, pp. 250–1)

Social services were used to set the standards for domestic services, and provided a network of social workers who entered homes with the aim of training and checking on the domestic performance of housewives (Thane, 1978b). Housewives, in fact, were the real instrument of reform. An ideological campaign exalting the family represented housework as a labour of love for the Family, the Nation and the Empire (Ehrenreich and English, 1979). In the last decades of the century a sharp decrease of birth rates created public anxiety for the future of the 'imperial race' (Davin, 1978; B. Webb, 1907). The fall in birth rates was interpreted as a parents' revolt against the burden of parenthood (Titmuss and Titmuss, 1942). Women were the pillar of the social security system for the rest of the labouring population. They provided security (or at least the illusion of security) at low social costs, to the employed, the unemployed, the children, the aged and the sick. Women had to be generous to the point of heroism, providing services to all sections of the community. Nobody ever complained – not even Beatrice Webb – that the family was in fact a 'mixed workhouse'.

One part of Victorian housework was getting the family members to conform to certain norms of behaviour (Vicinus, 1977). These norms followed the lines of behaviour set by middle-class families where higher incomes, servants and better housing made the organization of housework less burdensome. For the working-class family of the nineteenth century, these norms imposed a great many changes. For instance, sexual life was intended to be limited to marriage, with specific repression of widespread forms of cohabitation; working-class sexual habits were disciplined through norms of morality, health and religion (Walkowitz, 1980). The family was by no means homogeneous across classes or sections of the same class. In the first part of the nineteenth century sexual behaviour, rates and ages of marriage, and the care of children, all depended to a large extent on community and occupational patterns – this was especially true of the working class (Anderson, 1980; Goody, 1983; Hareven, 1976; Laslett, 1972; Rapp, Ross and Bridenthal, 1983; Levine, 1985). Later on, urbanization and organization of production at factory level implied a corresponding level of homogeneity in living conditions, which facilitated interpersonal communication in the community and at work. Crowded districts, collective means of transport, and public institutions, required a certain homogeneity in social conventions. The family was the basic institution whose task was to provide that homogeneity; and social policies, including the Poor Laws, counted heavily on women's efforts to educate family members to conform to the new social norms.

Apparently, according to Lytton Strachey's literary biography, even Queen Victoria was coopted to the family engineering of the ruling middle classes.

A few aristocrats might sniff or titter; but with the nation at large the Queen was . . . extremely popular. The middle classes, in particular, were pleased. They liked a love-match; they liked a household which combined the advantages of royalty and virtue, and in which they seemed to see, reflected as in one resplendent looking glass, the ideal image of the very lives they led themselves . . . The last vestige of the eighteenth century had disappeared; cynicism and subtlety were shrivelled into powder; and duty, industry, morality and domesticity triumphed over them. Even the very chairs and tables had assumed, with a singular responsiveness, the forms of prim solidity. The Victorian Age was in full swing. (Strachey, 1921, pp. 123–4)

If the Queen was behaving well, other women were not. The building of the new family went hand in hand with a continuous process of ostracizing those women who for various reasons located themselves outside the family. All women who practised some form of autonomy or independence from men, for instance single women, were considered objects of pity or repression (Hollis, 1979; Vicinus, 1977). Prostitutes were particularly repressed. But the barriers between casual workers, immigrants, housewives and prostitutes were not as rigid and clear as the state and some moralists would have liked. Women could pass from one section to the other depending on circumstances, and other women were not keen to discriminate against prostitutes (Walkowitz, 1980). Women knew very well that even within the family – with the sanctification of the church and the control of the state – they were often forced to exchange sexual services for subsistence (Ramelson, 1967). Prostitution simply made the material nature of this exchange more transparent, since the commercial transaction was more explicit (Walkowitz, 1980).

The new relationship between the social processes of production and reproduction also structured the women's labour market. Changing and increasing needs for reproductive services on the part of the urban industrial workers, public policies, legislation, public opinion, and women's resistance to working extra shifts ouside the home for very little money, all contributed to the structuring of a female labour market. In the 1851 Census, the number of 'unoccupied' women was much higher than the total occupied women (Table 4.1). The same pattern was maintained in the 1901 Census. Unoccupied women, which in the language of statisticians means housewives, reached the figure of over 5 million in 1851 and over 10 million in 1901.

In the nineteenth century housework was a basis for class divisions among women. Part of the housework of middle-class women was to control servants; they shared class interests with social policy-makers and experts, and they could protect their children within middle-class boundaries (Donzelot, 1980, p. 36). Voluntary social work by middle-class women outside the home did not have the same destructive effect on women's lives as did work in factories, offices, shops, and on the streets (Hollis, 1979; Vicinus, 1977). The sanctification of motherhood for the sake of the nation meant that the process of reshaping, building and controlling interpersonal relationships – so as to breed the right race and the right kind of labour force – was more oppressive for working-class women. Middle-class women could ease their housework burden with the help of servants; they could buy water which was supplied from tanks or have water pipes installed.

The great number of servants (often including single middle-class women) can in itself serve as a rough indicator of the large amount of housework required in an urban environment with very low standards of public facilities and services. The classification of servants indicates how labour for the reproduction of middle-class families could be divided. The following list, from the front page of Mrs Beeton's famous household handbook (published in 1861) shows the possibilities of domestic division of labour: mistress, housekeeper, cook, kitchen maid, butler, footman, coachman, valet, upper and under housemaids, lady's maid, maids-of-all-work, laundry maid, nurse and nursemaid, monthly wet and sick nurses, etc. The statistics of the domestic service sector, presented in Table 4.1, are also a significant indicator of the amount of domestic work involved in the process of reproduction, although of course they refer only to the reproduction of the middle classes. Housework in working-class homes, being wageless, disappeared from statistical evidence.

Table 4.1: Women's employment (GB)

	1851	1901
domestic service, laundry	1,135,000	2,003,000
agriculture	229,000	86,000
mining, quarrying	11,000	6,000
metal work	36,000	84,000
wood, furniture	8,000	30,000
bricks, cement, pottery, glass	15,000	37,000
chemicals, soap, etc.	4,000	31,000
skins, leather, hair, feathers	5,000	27,000
paper, printing	16,000	111,000
textiles	635,000	795,000
clothing (sewing, gloves, shoes)	491,000	792,000
food, drink, tobacco	53,000	216,000
professional	106,000	429,000
others	88,000	104,000
TOTAL occupied women	2,832,000	4,751,000
unoccupied women	5,294,000	10,229,000
occupied workforce (male and female)	9,377,000	16,220,000

Source: Hollis, 1979, p. 53.

The structure of the female labour market basically did not change in the fifty-year period considered – a period, by the way, that was very important in the development of the British capitalist system.[1] Simple calculations on the data show that the proportion of unoccupied to occupied women increases from 1.9 to 2.1, while that of occupied women to the total workforce was respectively 0.30 and 0.29. Finally, the proportion of unoccupied women (housewives) to the total workforce increased from 0.56 to 0.63. If we consider the women occupied in the traditional female sectors – domestic service, textiles, clothing, food, professional – it can be seen that these industries included 85 and 89 per cent of the total occupied women in 1851 and 1901 respectively. Moreover, the new professional jobs opened to women towards the end of the century were predominantly subordinate service jobs (Hunt, 1981).[2]

The link between the conditions of reproduction and waged work in the case of women is clear and persistent. Women are historically assumed to be dependent upon someone else's wages and not to have dependants of their own; hence they do not need a full wage or a family wage. Their wages are also substandard because the training necessary for housework is not recognized, because housework is taken to be 'natural' and hence unskilled. Moreover, women's subordination at home also affects their power relationships with employers (private and public).[3]

4.2 Women and poverty

The analysis of women's condition under the Poor Laws brings out the structural features of social insecurity. Because of their wageless work, women are the most exposed workers; moreover, it is part of their housework to absorb the insecurity of the other sections of the labouring population – waged, unemployed and wageless.

Women's poverty historically presents specific characteristics (Thane, 1978a; Titmuss, 1963; Wilson, 1979; Zopf, 1989). According to the statistical information of the 1909 Report, they form the majority of the recipients of poor relief. Table 4.2, for instance, shows that in 1908, in the day account, adult women constituted 43 per cent of the persons relieved by the Poor Law (men were 27 per cent and children 29 per cent), and that women's rate of pauperism – per 1,000 of estimated population for each section – was around 28, which means that almost 3 per cent of female population was pauperized. Moreover, women stayed on relief longer than other sections (House of Commons, p. 16), and they were the great majority of outdoor relief recipients (p. 19).

The higher rates of women's pauperism are a general and persistent feature in the history of the Poor Laws, although women's insecurity takes different forms over time. For instance, the problem of widows presented different features: in the eighteenth century the widows of deserving soldiers more than once made it necessary to change the rules for outdoor relief (Nicholls, 1898, pp. 135–6). In the nineteenth century widows of deserving workers needed public relief. This was no minor problem in a period when about 4,000 people were killed in industrial accidents per

80

Table 4.2: Number of adults and children relieved on
1 January 1908, and excess of female pauperism

	Number	Percentage of total number of persons relieved	Per 1,000 of estim. population in each group
Men	221,022	27.6	19.8
Women	343,825	43.0	27.8
Children under 16	234,792	29.4	20.6
TOTAL	798,898*	100.0	22.9

* Deducting persons who are counted twice by reason of being reckoned for various reasons both as indoor and outdoor paupers.
Source: House of Commons, 1909, p. 16.

year – in the industries covered by the Factory Acts alone – according to the statistics of the last decades of the nineteenth century (Department of Employment and Productivity, 1971, p. 399).

In order to understand the persistence of women's poverty, it is important to see the structural specificity of women as wageless houseworkers, and their consequent peculiar position in the waged labour market. The unfavourable differences are persistent – which does not mean static – with regard to employment, wages, poverty and, most of all, work loads in the process of social reproduction (Hunt, 1981, Tilly and Scott, 1978). Male–female differences in figures and policies have to be seen in the light of the relationship between production and reproduction. The separation of these processes leads to certain ambiguities with regard to the position of women, which for quite a long time created difficulties for the statisticians collecting census data. In the first decades of the nineteenth century, women were lumped together with men and were listed under the profession of the head of the family. Later the statistics for men and women were separated.

The separation of the two economic spheres was a long process. In the nineteenth century putting-out production and living-in domestic services were used on a large scale, and in the mining industry gangs of workers were commonly formed on a family basis (Humphries, 1981). In the Poor Law administration some forms of identification of women with the head of the family were practised until the twentieth century. The whole family would enter the workhouse together with the head, and its members would be listed as able-bodied or non-able-bodied according to his position – although, as commonly happened in the Poor Law administration, this practice was not consistent. Waged labour meant the separation of production from reproduction, but it also meant a clear distinction between the waged and the wageless sections of the population. This part of the story became clear at a general level only with the industrialization and urbanization of the nineteenth century, and it posed the problem of where to classify women and how to analyse their work.

Women have always worked both in the process of social reproduction and in that of production (Pinchbeck, 1930), but, in an industrial system they have to do it in different places, and one job is waged while the other is not. In the analysis of women's work both sides of the labour market must be kept simultaneously under scrutiny, to see how they mutually interact in the reproduction of the economic system as a whole.

The fundamental capitalist division between the waged and the wageless was stressed in the 1909 Report, though still disguised under physical criteria:

It is, in our judgment, of the highest importance to complete without delay the process begun under that Act, and to remove the remaining sections of the Able-bodied, once for all, from any connection with the Local Authorities dealing with the Children, the Sick, the Mentally Defective, and the Aged and Infirm. (Webb and Webb, 1909, Part II, p. 333)

Housewives, being wageless, were excluded from the able-bodied to receive Home Aliment, which was much lower than minimum wages and subject to strong moral overtones. An enormous amount of housework was still required from women as the voluntary and natural labour of love (Beveridge, 1942; Fleming, 1986; McNicol, 1980; Rathbone, 1917, 1947 (1924); Wilson, 1979); its destructive capacity was directly proportional to the high cost savings for employers and the state. The Poor Law found a sort of answer to the differentiation of waged and wageless work, although this was mystified by a supposed physical distinction. Economic theory not only failed to find the answers, but even lost the question and the analytical tools for dealing with it. As Eleanor Rathbone vividly puts it:

In the work of still more recent economists, the family sank out of sight altogether. The subsistence theory of wages was superseded by theories in which wives and children appear only occasionally, together with butchers' meat and alcohol and tobacco, as part of the 'comforts and decencies' which make up the British workman's standard of life and enable him to stand out against the lowering of his wage. I would not think it would be an exaggeration to say that, if the population of Great Britain consisted entirely of adult self-propagating bachelors and spinsters, nearly the whole output of writers on economic theory during the past fifty years might remain as it was written, except for a paragraph or phrase here and there, and those unessential to the main argument. (Rathbone, 1947 (1924), p. 10)

While the problems inherent in the new social organization were removed from the scientific analysis of the economic system, they deeply affected women's lives. The separation between production and reproduction carried special consequences for women. Insecurity, dependence, and sexual division of labour, already well known to women in agrarian patriarchal systems, took new forms directly related to the new forms of surplus creation and accumulation of capital. For instance, insecurity took the specific form of limited access to money and wage goods, mediated by indirect access to the already insecure wages of the head of the family.

In the new context of the capitalist waged labour market, the state tended to take on the role of supervising the process of social reproduction, making it compatible with the process of capitalist accumulation and consistent with the reproduction of free waged labourers. This role required repression or mediation according to historical necessities and conflicts; it also required a particular control over women's work and their bodies.[4]

Thus a very specific relationship was established between women and the state. Poor Law Reports and public inquiries explicitly refer to housework as the keystone of social reproduction. Moreover, 'Domestic ignorance and incapacity on the part of women' is listed among the main causes of poverty and destitution (House of Commons, 1909, pp. 226–7).

It is interesting to note that while on the one hand this work is presented as natural, on the other it is usually recognized that it needs proper and specific training. Training of working-class women in the houses of the propertied classes was often suggested, and training in the workhouses imposed: 'The first object was to bring all the inmates to more industrious habits . . . so that these young women might learn household work, and form useful domestic habits, instead of bad habits and immorality' (Checkland and Checkland, 1974, p. 433). Even the progressive Sidney Webb, when questioned by the Poor Law Royal Commission on the issue of unemployment, with regard to young women had nothing more to suggest than housework training:

I have so far said nothing about the girls. But their problem is an analogous one. They all need the training of body and brain, hand and eye; they all need the instruction in the use of the household implements and tools; they all need the technical education that is necessary to produce competent housewives and mothers . . . An extension of the half-time clauses of the Factory Acts up to 18 would benefit girls no less than boys. (S. Webb, 1910, p. 184)

While housework is the object of careful scrutiny inside and outside the workhouse, its effects on women's lives are not questioned. The only recognition women get is to be classified as non-able-bodied persons.

So far as we can discover from the official statistics, there were in England and Wales alone, on January 1, 1907, 62,240 healthy Able-bodied adult persons . . . simultaneously in receipt of Outdoor Relief on that day. Of these only 2,528 were men, and no fewer than 59,712 women . . . The vast majority . . . are not free to engage in industrial employment, because they are occupied by the care of young children dependent upon them. To rank these in any sense with the Able-bodied is only to obscure the problem. The Scottish Poor Law, more logical than the English classification, while prohibiting any form of relief to the Able-bodied, does not include as Able-bodied any women, however physically and mentally competent, who have young children dependent on them. (Webb and Webb, 1909, Part II, pp. 18–19)

Women's insecurity in the capitalist system takes two forms: dependence on somebody else's wage, and lower wages relative to men. The two aspects are linked and cannot be studied separately: because women reproduce the labour force they work more, and for the same reason they earn less money. This is a persistent feature of the labour market, acknowledged in the Minority Report.

when women engage in industry their wages are habitually fixed at rates calculated to support themselves alone, without a family of children. If, by some mischance, the husband and father is withdrawn from the family group, the wife and mother is, with regard to self support, under a double impossibility. She cannot, consistently with her legal obligation to rear her children properly, give her time and strength to wage earning to the extent that modern competitive industry demands; and even if she could do so, she finds the woman's remuneration fixed on the basis of supporting one person and not several. Hence it becomes practically indispensable, as it is only equitable, that there should be afforded to the mother bereft of the man upon whom she had been encouraged to depend suitable public assistance, not so much for herself, as to enable her to bring up the children whom the community, though the breadwinner is withdrawn, still expects her to rear. (pp. 19–20)

While the repressive policies of 1834 based the control of women's housework mainly on the insecurity of the free labour market and on the repression of every form of dependence on the state, the progressive policy perspectives of 1909 recognized a certain degree of responsibility of the state as subsidiary 'head of the family'. This recognition did not challenge the basic insecurity of women as houseworkers and of waged work in general. The state may intervene by supporting the process of social reproduction when it is undermined by high unemployment and low wages. However, it has no interest in changing the social organization based on a division of labour between waged work and wageless housework and between men and women. Savings on the costs of reproduction are so crucial that wages for the work of reproduction are avoided wherever possible, with consequent gains in social control because of the greater insecurity inherent in women's wageless condition within the family. Moreover, the historical experience of the Poor Laws shows that costs of replacing wageless family housework with institutionalized reproductive work, although low paid and even voluntary, were quite high. Increasing costs of provisions in public institutions proved that collective organization was very expensive. Fostering poor children, even if the foster-mothers had to be paid, cost less than keeping them in the workhouse. The same was true for the sick and the aged, and indoor assistance was much more expensive than outdoor relief (K. Williams, 1981).

In both the 1834 and the 1909 Reports, women's dependence on the family was taken for granted and used as a fundamental instrument of policy. In 1909 the family had to be rescued from the hardship imposed by the 1834 Act, for it could induce a destitution trap in which different sections of the labouring population would end up at the lowest level of health and discipline. Wageless housework was the general means of reproduction and had to be protected not only for the sake of children, the aged and the sick, but also for the sake of the able-bodied males. The Minority Report was quite explicit on the content of women's implicit social contract.

As we have already said in Part I of this Report, we have chosen so to organise our industry that it is to the man that is paid the income necessary for the support of the family, on the assumption that the work of the woman is to care for the home and the children . . . When the breadwinner is withdrawn by death or desertion, or is, from illness or unemployment, unable to earn the family maintenance, the bargain which the community virtually made with the woman on her marriage – that the maintenance of the home should come through the man – is broken. (Webb and Webb, 1909, Part II, p. 211)

The terms for the proposed new deal for women were stated in the concluding proposals:

16. That for able-bodied women, without husband or dependent children, who may be found in distress from want of employment, there should be exactly the same sort of provision as for men. That for widows or other mothers in distress, having the care of young children, residing in homes not below the National Minimum of sanitation, and being themselves not adjudged unworthy to have children entrusted to them, there should be granted adequate Home Aliment on condition of their devoting their whole time and energy to the care of the children. *That for the childless wives of able-bodied men in attendance at a Training Establishment, adequate Home Aliment be granted, conditional on their devoting their time to such further training in Domestic Economy as may be prescribed for them.* (Webb and Webb, 1909, Part II, p. 329, italics added)

Hence nineteenth-century privatization of the family was to be followed by its twentieth-century institutionalization. The private and violent hardship of the previous century cannot be an object of nostalgia.[5] It should be noted, however, that both the Reports (Majority and Minority), once again took it for granted that women would be willing to exchange for subsistence – with men and the state – a huge amount of work and control over their bodies and feelings.

State intervention was seen not as a substitute for the family, but as its safety net. The prevention of destitution, via income maintenance for the waged, would ultimately bring a reduction of public expenditure by allowing the family to function at its greatest efficiency. With the family in general good health, the marginal sections would be reduced to a residuum with small economic and political impact. The reformist proposals of the Minority Report rationalized state responsibility in the process of social reproduction. The Victorian family presented some cracks but it could be reinforced with generalized state support.

4.3 'Are women able bodied?'

The failure of economic analysis to grasp the functional separation between production and reproduction, waged and wageless work, waged and wageless labouring population, leads to confusing policies with regard to women's employment. The attention given to women's waged employment in the Poor Law is very limited if compared with the focus on their housework and on male employment and wages. The 1834 Poor Law Report which argued aggressively against outdoor relief for the able-bodied male workers was much more vague with regard to able-bodied women.[6] This was partly because of the difficulty of separating women's position from that of the head of the family. As Beatrice Webb noted in a Memorandum to the Royal Commission on the History of the Poor Law:

neither the 'principles of 1834' nor the enactment of Parliament had prescribed the policies to be pursued with regard to women; except that it was implied or assumed that wives were to follow their husbands exactly as if they were infants. With regard to the widow, the deserted wife, the wife of the absentee soldier and sailor, the wife of an husband resident in another parish or another country – above all, with regard to the independent able-bodied woman – the Central Authority had either to let the existing practice of outdoor relief continue, or to discover a policy for itself. (B. Webb, 1910, p. 131)

Women were the object of a long series of exceptional measures which departed from the general rules. On the whole, the exceptions were made necessary by a few simple facts: that women were not men; that they were wageless but not workless; that they were economically dependent, but at the same time supported the rest of the labouring population. Exceptions to the general rules, based on the male population, were necessary because those rules failed to take account of the real position of women's work in the operation of the labour market and of the amount of women's work that waged workers embodied.

In 1909 the state was still mainly concerned with housework, and attention to women's employment was again limited. The progressive aspects of the new policies were related to the normalization of state intervention in supporting the family; they did not represent a change in the social norm. Women were expected to look after children and other dependent members of the family. This was also stated in one of the recommendations of Mrs J. R. MacDonald, representative of the Women's Industrial Council, to the Royal Commission:

As our last word we wish most strongly to urge that widows with young children, and wives with sick husbands and perhaps young children dependent on their care, should not be driven to neglect their charge by going out to earn money to keep themselves and their dependants. Such women have useful work to occupy them in caring for young or helpless citizens, and the state should enable them to perform that service fully, by giving them adequate monetary support for themselves and those dependent on them. (MacDonald, 1910, p. 231)

It was also generally acknowledged that housework was necessary to maintain the standards (physical and moral) of male workers. Beveridge expressed this basic feature of the capitalist labour market very clearly:

The great majority of married women are occupied on work which is vital though unpaid, without which their husbands could not do their paid work and without which the nation could not continue. (Beveridge, 1942, quoted in H. Rose, 1978, p. 524)

Social reproduction of labour

The fact that housework's contribution was omitted from statistics was one of the points made by Pigou in his memorandum on the assessment of public policies presented to the Royal Commission:

> some contributions are made to the dividend that are not represented in income. All work put forth by a mother in the care of her children is such a contribution. So is the service of all savings which a man invests in the education or training of his children. These contributions are very large and important. The essential point, however, is not their magnitude, but the fact that they are in a measure alternative to other contributions. If for instance the Poor Law encourages a widow to earn more wages . . . , the extra wages she earns mean a much less proportionate addition to the dividend, because a large part of the work she does for them is merely diverted from the non-wage-yielding occupation of tending her child. (Pigou, 1910, p. 990)

The correct calculation of housework in the statistics of the national product would perhaps not change the power relationships which set relative incomes, but it would show the enormity of the amount of work involved.

The recognition that the strength of male workers and of the nation derives from housewives and their housework, should expose the myth that women can achieve equality in the waged labour market without a radical challenge to the basic structure of the capitalist system. What makes women different is that they do not have wives. In the case of the female labour market, the fact that the norm for the determination of wages is not set by supply and demand is often recognized, although typically as an exception. Women's specificity is interpreted as an exception to the general rule instead of being considered crucial in the shaping of the general rule. In the classical approach, as seen in previous chapters, the social reproduction of the labouring population was seen as a fundamental aspect of the economic system at several levels: at the level of production, because labour is considered a basic commodity; at the level of distribution, because savings on the costs of social reproduction of the labouring population lead to higher profits; at the level of circulation, because the consumption of wage goods is the largest component of the aggregate demand. It is also important at the institutional level, because insecurity of access to the means of reproduction is the fundamental source of command over work processes; and at the political level, because the process of social reproduction implies a radical conflict (not always open) between profit and the living standards of the whole labouring population.

The enormous amount of housework embodied in labour as a commodity has major implications for all of these aspects. We have also seen in chapter 2 that in a competitive supply-and-demand analytical framework the picture changes radically. The proponents of the wages fund tried, at least in theory, to shift the burden of the costs of reproduction and its inherent conflicts onto the labouring population. In this analytical perspective, wages and standards of living were assumed to be flexible; the flexibility of wages and employment was expected to be absorbed by the family, which had to adapt in terms of numbers and living standards. Individual self-reliance, in reality, meant reliance on the family, and this was explicitly recognized in social policies and legislation (Crowther, 1982).

In this context the head of the family became the major agent of control of the process of reproduction, and conflicts were internalized within the family. Social policies sometimes aimed to protect wageless housework, by limiting women's waged work and by giving money benefits to single mothers, treating them as non-able-bodied. Protective policies were necessary to relieve some of women's burden, but they were not sufficient because they did not question the structural causes of women's heavy work loads and their deep social insecurity. Of course men, as heads of the family, found no difficulty in performing a role which had been theirs since agrarian times and was blessed by religions, ratified by law and regarded as natural by social scientists. Men, as the state, used 'protection' to control women's work, and when protection did not suffice they often used direct and indirect violence, to the point where sometimes even the state had to intrude into the men's free territory to protect women. This happened, for example, in 1909 with the passing of the Cruelty to Women Bill, which applied the penalties for cruelty to children to assaults upon wives.[7]

In the second part of the nineteenth century, the male workers and their organizations maintained the idea of a family wage as a point of reference in their struggles (Land, 1980; Tarling and Wilkinson, 1982). The problem was that they had an extremely biased idea of what the real costs of reproduction were and how they were distributed within the family (M. Young, 1955; Wilson, 1979; Zweig, 1975). Moreover, bargaining over the dynamics of wages was generally argued in terms of productivity and supply-and-demand conditions of the labour market.[8] The male core of the working class assumed that the best and only way to defend the living standards of the labouring population was to struggle over the head-of-the-family wage (Humphries, 1977, 1981). In doing so they apparently disregarded the fact that not all families had a waged head, and thus helped to perpetuate the dependence of the wageless sections within and outside the family. While there is no doubt that the working class used the family to 'protect the individual from the harshness of the capitalist labour market' (Humphries and Rubery, 1984, p. 341), there is some question as to which individual was protected. The question of the relative insecurity associated with differences in sex, age, race, and nationality of individuals within the family and the community was generally not posed.

According to the wages fund theory, in its static version, which was often supported by labour organizations, the only way to increase wages was a reduction of the quantity of labour supplied. Women were directly affected by this reduction, not only in the case of changes in birth rates, but also in the case of emigration, whose traumatic effects on the whole organization of the process of reproduction had to be absorbed within the family. Moreover, by the logic of supply and demand, the withdrawal of women from the labour market and consequent reduction in the supply of labour was supposed to bring about an increase in the wages of the head of the family (Humphries, 1977). As the classical political economists recognized, the relationship between the quantity of labour supplied and its price is not systematic and needs to be seen in its historical context.

The demand relationship between prices and quantities is not a clear-cut one. A continuous and systematic inverse function is not empirically based, and it was in fact questioned in the Minority Report. The case of women is used once again for wider generalization.

The example of women disposes, we think, of the suggestion which has been quite seriously made to us, that *Unemployment might be prevented if only the workers would accept lower wages!* The docility of women, and their lack of organisation, has led them to take this course; but although women's wages are as low as any one could conceive possible, this does not prevent them to stand idle, probably to an even greater extent than men, at each recurring slack season. (Webb and Webb, 1909, Part II, p. 208)

The supply-and-demand theories of wages are misleading for wages in general and for women's wages in particular. In case of women's wages the distinction between natural and market prices becomes crucial. What is most relevant for the analysis of women's wages is the distinction between the quality of the forces at work in the determination of normal wages, and those which are assumed to determine market prices of labour. As we saw in the first chapter, the forces acting on the normal determination of wages are forces of material and physical processes of reproduction, cultural habits and tastes, and power relationships between classes and within sections of the same class.

For women's wages this analytical distinction bears crucial political implications with regard to a realistic struggle for equality, as Marx reminds us:

To clamour for equal and equitable retribution on the basis of the wages system is the same as to clamour for freedom on the basis of the slavery system. What you think just or equitable is out of the question. The question is: what is necessary and unavoidable with a given system of production. After what has been said, it will be seen that the value of the labouring power is determined by the value of the necessaries required to produce, develop, maintain, and perpetuate the labouring power. (Marx, 1975 (1865), p. 46)

If for every commodity the basic determinant of prices is the process of production, for the labour commodity this is even more so, since to define given physical processes we must analyse historical cultural and political relationships as well. In the nineteenth century, as well as in the twentieth, women have been and are the keystone of the process of reproduction and the guardians of social norms (Hollis, 1979, p. 299). In order to control the reproduction of labour, necessary for capital accumulation, it is fundamental to control women. In order to maintain social control, it is crucial to control women. In the case of women any struggle for equality in the waged labour market has to include a struggle over the conditions of work and over security in the process of social reproduction. Otherwise equality, like protection, can be used to maintain the status quo in the organization of that process, hiding a specific exploitative process.

While the perspective of social reproduction is present in conservative policies and analysis – since historically the 'right' aims to control and maintain the status quo in the family – it is quite alien to radical debates. Egalitarian perspectives distrust any policy which grants political and/or material recognition to housework. Nineteenth-century radicals – as well as modern ones – usually waged their struggles in terms of equality, while conservatives showed great interest in controlling the process of social reproduction (Rossi Doria, 1985). The control of the sector of reproduction, including birth, socializing and nurturing, is crucial because labour is a basic commodity whose production is not directly in the capitalists' hands, and it is a very peculiar commodity which cannot function well without love and affection (H. Rose, 1983).

Workers, including houseworkers, are capable of resistance and their choices affect the shaping of the social system. This explains why the policing of families was difficult both in 1834 and in 1909. Stuctural characteristics of the economic system can be general and persistent but they are never static. All workers are aware of the power stemming from their work and express this power at different levels, material, cultural and symbolic. The problem of social theorists is to trace specific forms, moments and structures where changes take place, for instance with regard to power relationships among sections of the population and in the relationship between production and reproduction.

The Poor Laws, with their specific focus on women's relation to the family, the state and the labour market, offer a good case study to bring out structural relationships and their inherent potential conflicts. The process of reproduction is extremely costly, and therefore a huge amount of resources is needed to restructure the capitalist relationship between production and reproduction and between waged and wageless work. This does not necessarily mean that the costs are prohibitive: the definition of what is possible is historically given. Experience shows that in social systems where resources are generally producible – the kind of world Smith was talking about – constraints which seemed impossible to move have always been moved. For example, the charges of Utopianism made against the reformers of the beginning of the century were answered on the basis of past experience, and the example of education is put forward in the following passage of the Minority Report.

Could there have been anything more 'Utopian' in 1860 than a picture of what to-day we take as a matter of course, the 7,000,000 children emerging every morning, washed and brushed, from 5,000,000 or 6,000,000 homes, in every part of the Kingdom, traversing street and road and lonely woodland, going o'er fell and moor, to present themselves at a given hour at their 30,000 schools, where each of the 7,000,000 finds his or her own individual place, with books and blackboard and teacher provided? (Webb and Webb, 1909, Part II, p. 325)

The extent to which public budget constraints were removed in order to finance the massive destructions of two world wars in the first half of the twentieth century provides an example of how modest the Utopian aspects of welfare schemes were if compared with warfare schemes.

The use of scarcity as a general case, to introduce a fixed constraint on the consumption of the labouring population as a whole, has the same analytical basis as the wages fund theory of wages. The classical analytical framework may be used to separate the problems of distribution of income and of the relationship between production and reproduction, from an analytical perspective based on the notion that scarcity is the only force structuring markets, including the labour market. But once the historical processes of production and reproduction and political power relationships are located at the centre of the analysis, recognizing the historical determination of the basic data, the specific character of labour as a capitalist commodity can be fruitfully approached. A greater analytical visibility of the process of social reproduction of labour can contribute to a more direct and powerful grasp of the role of women's work of reproduction in the economic system. This will make houseworkers more visible as potential political subjects.

The autonomy and the dynamics of the sector of social reproduction is closely related to the struggles of women who, like everybody else, bargain and make choices with regard to their material condition and political representation. The attention paid by policy-makers in 1909 to the process of social reproduction, recognizing a direct state responsibility in support of the family, can itself be seen partly as a result of the struggles women had waged in direct confrontation with the state during the whole nineteenth century: women were massively involved in the Reform movement, in the strong protests against the 1834 Act and in its Chartist developments, in the campaign for the repeal of the Contagious Diseases Acts, and of course in the battle for suffrage (Ramelson, 1967). They were also active in the labour market, for example with the famous strikes of the London match girls (Hollis, 1979, pp. 115–17) and the feminist demands of some women in the unions (Hollis, 1979; Ramelson, 1967). Women had also fought for access to education and positions in public administration, including the Poor Law administration. They had resisted Poor Law officials and their meanness, in and out of the workhouse (Digby, 1978). In the nineteenth century the state administration was very reluctant to employ women as waged workers in public offices. The struggle for professional paid nurses, led by Florence Nightingale, and women's struggles to enter the medical profession, are just a few of the many examples of resistance (Hollis 1979: Ramelson, 1967). In order to escape the confines of their homes, women had flocked into voluntary social work (Hollis, 1979; B. Webb, 1926). The Poor Law administration was no exception with regard to discriminatory practices. The Royal Commission of 1909 was presented with a formal request, put forward by the Women's Local Government Society, to employ women in order to reduce women's dissatisfaction with the practices of male Poor Law officers.

It is interesting to note that although the reformist members of the Royal Commission all had to cope with the social changes induced by women's struggles, they did not share common views on the issue of women's suffrage. While Landsbury was a convinced suffragist, Beatrice Webb was quite reluctant in acknowledging women's political autonomy. In this regard, it is revealing that Beatrice Webb signed 'an appeal against female suffrage', worded in very clear terms:

We, the undersigned, wish to appeal to the common sense of the educated thought of the men and women of England against the proposed extension of the Parliamentary suffrage to women.

1. While desiring the fullest possible development of the powers, energies, and education of women, we believe that their work for the state and their responsibilities towards it, must always differ essentially from those of men, and

that therefore their share in the work of the state machinery should be different from that assigned to men . . . Therefore it is not just to give to women direct power of deciding questions of Parliamentary policy, of war, of foreign or colonial affairs, of commerce and finance equal to that possessed by men. We hold that they already possess an influence on political matters fully proportioned to the possible share of women in the political activities of England. (Hollis, 1979, p. 322)[9]

The 1834 policies failed because they treated some of the basic and permanent features of the labour market as exceptional, limited and temporary. The Minority Report had the great merit of showing, with ample historical evidence, that unemployment, casual employment and low wages are structural, and that the process of social reproduction of labour does not conform to mechanical or naturalistic models. The process of social reproduction had shown a high degree of autonomy from the allocative market mechanisms of supply and demand – an autonomy that was based mainly on the 'animal spirits' of the whole labouring population, always alert in defence of its standards of living. In other words it was based on class struggle broadly defined. The progressive members of the Royal Commission fought to keep the ground open for new social policies but they assumed that on the whole the family would continue to function as the basic reproductive unit for the waged labour market, without ever questioning the specific capitalist relationship between production and reproduction.

5

Women's work
at the core of the labour market

5.1 The work of reproduction

In the women's labour market certain basic features have remained surprisingly constant: (a) the substantial number of women without paid work; (b) the amount of housework done by waged women; (c) job segregation; (d) the large proportion of women in poverty.

The persistence of these facts despite radical changes in social and productive structures can be seen in a new light if one takes account of the relation between production and reproduction. For example the figures on activity rates,[1] while they do show changes in level and composition (e.g. large increases for married women and women with children), still present features similar to those brought out in the last chapter and in Table 4.1. The percentage of women without paid jobs remains similar to that of the end of the last century (Table 5.1), despite major changes in birth control (which led to a reduction of fertility rates), family structures and educational levels – all factors usually held responsible for determining women's entry into the labour market (Hartmann and Reskin, 1986).[2]

To understand all of this we must look at the dark, hidden side of women's work – housework. If we begin with the female labour market we can never bring out the true magnitude and importance of the problems involved. One reason for this limitation is that the question of housework has been squeezed into analytical models of the labour market which marginalize and conceal the whole process of reproduction. In this chapter, therefore, I shall define housework and try to quantify it in its present dimension, using some statistical data.

When the relationship between production and reproduction disappeared from the context of economic analysis the concrete work of reproduction was hidden from view, and houseworkers became invisible social subjects even though they represent a large section of the labouring population. More precisely, what is hidden is not housework and houseworkers, but the capitalist relationship between production and reproduction. That is how the central problem for any economic system comes to be seen as a narrow and peripheral women's issue.

Table 5.1: Working population* and employment, 1987

Countries	Eur 12	West Germany	France	Italy	UK
Activity rates					
female	33.3	34.7	35.9	29.4	39.4
male	55.2	58.5	51.0	55.2	59.1
Part time**					
female	28.6	29.0	22.5	8.7	44.5
male	3.4	1.3	3.3	2.6	5.0
Unemployment rates (annual average)					
female	13.2	8.0	13.5	17.3	10.1
male	8.9	5.3	8.3	7.4	11.0

*   The working population comprises all persons in employment and the unemployed

**   Percentage of part-time employees on total employment

Source: EUROSTAT, 1989, pp. 99–182, 223.

It is true that recently definitions of work have been broadened to include the unwaged work of reproduction (Gershuny and Jones, 1986; R.L. Pahl, 1984); and in empirical studies on the use of time, housework and waged labour are usually summed together in calculating the total work load. This is a necessary step towards equity but not towards clarity: what is important in the case of women's work is not to broaden the meaning of the term work, but to specify the production–reproduction relationship.

The nature of this relationship becomes evident in the context of a surplus approach to profit. Housework is the *production* of labour as a commodity, while waged work is the *exchange* of labour. To be exchanged, labour must be produced; and to be used in the production of other commodities, labour must be produced and exchanged. This is not a question merely of time sequences, but one of functional relationships between processes. While wages are a cost of production, housework as unpaid labour is a deduction from costs. Needless to say, housework itself has its costs (the subsistence of the houseworker), but the relationship is such as to guarantee a high surplus. This is not directly obvious because labour is not sold by capitalists: the surplus is realized by capitalists not in selling labour but in buying it.[3]

This is why Smith recognized, as we saw in the first chapter, that a well fed and well clothed high-waged worker costs his employer less than a badly fed, poorly clothed slave. He explained this paradox by pointing out the fact that the administration of the labourer's reproduction had passed from the employer's responsibility to that of the labourer himself. The paradox of the value of labour – i.e the fact that the more labour is embodied in its reproduction the less it costs the employer – can be explained only in terms of the separation of the process of production from that of reproduction, the capitalist distinction between waged and unwaged work, and the subordination of social reproduction to the needs of capital accumulation. What is paradoxical for the theory of value becomes tragic for women as the system's contradictions and conflicts materialize in their personal lives.

Sociologists concentrate, at an international and local level, on the use of time. A considerable amount of information emerges from the rather diffuse empirical studies of the complex social interactions between the family and the labour market, and between housework and waged work (Gershuny and Jones, 1986; R.L. Pahl, 1984; Roy, 1989; Saraceno, 1987). What we need now is an analytic framework for the new awareness, if only to be sure of making full use of the new data. This need is felt, for example, by Gershuny and Jones who are doing valuable work in collecting use-of-time archives at the Dublin-based European Foundation for the Improvement of Living and Working Conditions:

> This is a rather large body of empirical work, and considering the fundamental and comprehensive nature of the data it yields, it ought to have had a substantial effect on social science. In fact its impact has been less than impressive. With a few honourable exceptions, the publications that emerge as a result of time budget research are blandly descriptive and theoretically uninformed and uninformative. There are two connected reasons for this: the practical complications of time budget analysis – and the almost complete absence of appropriate theory . . .
>
> We have as yet no adequate theorising about the determination of time use patterns; the elegant and ever-more-sophisticated models produced by economists, which seek to explain cross-sectional differences and historical changes in time use patterns by wage differentials (e.g. Becker 1965, Gronau 1977), while internally consistent, bear little relation to the intricate patterns of behaviour exhibited by the data. (Gershuny and Jones, 1986, pp. 3–4)

Housework is not merely a combination of tasks necessary for the daily reproduction of households and for the physical and psychological life of their members. Housework's job is to restore a relation between production and reproduction that makes sense from the point of view of the people involved. It is expected that within the family, through women and their housework, the alienated relation that structures the system of production and the social system will be reversed and its conflicts absorbed. Housework serves the well-being of people, whereas the production of commodities is geared to the accumulation of capital. Accumulation uses people as commodities, and the task of housework is to produce and restore them as people within the constraint of reproducing them as commodities. That is what makes this work so endless in spite of all the changes which have occurred in the household and in the technological and occupational structure of the waged labour market. The family, however defined and composed, functions as an alternator: in the outside world the direction of energy is from the reproduction of persons to production of commodities (capital accumulation), while in the family this direction has to be reversed – at least apparently – in favour of a more human process whereby the reproduction of persons is the goal and commodity production is the means.

The family has to offer a space, physical and psychological, in which individuals feel themselves to be the primary objects of attention, the final objective of social activity. The more alienated is the relation between persons and the system of production, the more burdensome and difficult housework becomes. And the more burdensome housework is, the more unequal is its distribution within the family between men and women (Maurin, 1989; Saraceno, 1987).

Within the work of reproduction performed by women in the family, it is impossible to distinguish between material tasks and the psychological care of persons (Finch and Groves, 1983). Women's love in the family is expressed and demanded in terms of work. The difference in gender is reflected in this enormous mass of energy which women pour into others, to make them feel like human beings in a system that treats them as commodities (whether in current use, to be used, or out of use). Historically the work of material reproduction and reassurance of personal identity – including that of adult males – has been delegated to women. This means women have to compensate for inadequate public services and for the destructive effects of the labour market. The more these effects are concealed, the more the family becomes a place where the tensions and insecurities of all its members are discharged.

5.2 Some empirical evidence

The marked difference in the work done by women and men in the family, the persistence of an enormous quantity of housework, the close dependence of men's and women's family behaviour on historically given social norms – all these are well known from daily experience, and it might seem pointless to insist on them further. But as a matter of fact, the transposition of direct experience from the sphere of common knowledge to that of academic research involves changes in perspective and in the subjects and objects of research:

Every knowing (*wissen*) has its own style of thought with its specific tradition and education. Out of the almost infinite multitude of possibilities, every way of knowing selects different questions, connects them according to different rules and to different purposes. (Fleck, 1986, p. 49)[4]

In this transposition from common to scientific knowledge important aspects of common experience often become less directly visible and appear less important. This loss of focus results not only from the process of abstraction: it also reflects the power relationships between social subjects, in society and in the scientific profession. In the case of housework the problem is related not only to the fact that women have less power in social institutions, and specifically in scientific communities but to the fact that the prevailing analysis of the economy usually conceals the process of social reproduction of labour.

Available statistics help to illuminate the dimensions of this question. Let us start with the cases of Italy and France, and then go on to compare some historical trends in different countries. Table 5.2 gives a quantitative idea of the unequal distribution of housework between men and women in Italy. A comparison of the overall figures shows that the average total number of hours per week is 5.5 for men and 36.3 for women. But what is most interesting is that men in couples do only half the amount of housework done by single men; the other half is transferred to women. The fact that women do more hours of housework than men when they are living alone, due to their upbringing and lack of money for market services, does not explain why they work more and men work less when they are in a couple. Thus women living in couples do more housework than single women, and that difference exceeds the increase caused by further additions to the family. For example, the birth of the first child in the age group 25–44 brings an increase of about 8 hours of housework per week for women and a slight decrease for men. This explodes the myth that children are the sole cause of women's excess burden of housework. Another interesting surprise in the table is the fact that when the number

Table 5.2: Italy, weekly average number of hours of
housework, according to sex, age, family members

Age	Family members						Total
	1	2	3	4	5	6 +	
MALES							
14–24	8.3	4.5	3.0	2.7	2.8	2.7	2.9
25–44	9.5	5.8	5.6	5.2	5.1	3.8	5.4
45–64	15.1	7.8	6.3	5.3	5.2	5.4	6.3
65 +	17.1	8.5	7.7	6.3	8.0	5.5	8.7
TOTAL	14.1	7.4	5.6	4.6	4.4	3.9	5.5
FEMALES							
14–24	24.4	29.1	26.0	16.9	15.6	18.1	19.5
25–44	21.6	30.9	38.6	44.9	45.8	45.7	41.8
45–64	32.3	41.7	45.8	48.0	47.5	46.9	44.6
65 +	29.2	35.7	33.1	25.2	25.6	26.0	31.3
TOTAL	29.5	36.9	38.3	37.9	34.8	33.4	36.3

Source: ISTAT, 1985, p. 73.

of children increases, the amount of housework done by men aged
between 25 and 45 actually decreases from 9.5 to 3.8 hours, while for
women it passes from 21.6 to 45.7.

Among women in couples without children, the number of housewives
is not very much smaller than that of employed women: evidently the
mere fact of being in a couple strongly affects the rates of employment.
This supports the view that there is a solid core of housework which has
nothing to do with the number of children, and that for 36.6 per cent of
women living in couples the presence of a mate acts as a deterrent to
entry into the waged labour market. The proportion of housewives
increases with the number of children until it reaches 65 per cent (Fadiga
Zanatta, 1988, p. 291). Thus in Italy even today a very significant
percentage of women of all ages have housework as their only occupation,

although this does not mean that the same women are permanently housewives.

Housework, of course, is not done by housewives alone, however many they may be. It is also performed by women with jobs: from 27.2 hours a week for women without children to 34.5 hours for women with 3 children (Table 5.3). The same table also shows that the 'double load' is a purely female phenomenon. The very few hours of housework done by men do not increase either with greater numbers of children or in response to the waged work of their wives.

Table 5.3: Italy, weekly average number of hours of housework done by couples, according to number of children and woman's employment

Number of children	Family unit with woman employed		Family unit with woman not employed		Total
	Female	Male	Female	Male	
No children	27.2	6.4	43.1	7.6	23.2
1 child	31.7	6.6	52.1	6.1	25.2
2 children	33.4	6.2	56.0	5.2	27.0
3 children	34.5	6.0	57.1	5.0	28.0
4 children	32.1	4.8	57.6	5.3	28.1
5 or more children	36.1	5.9	55.5	4.2	28.6
TOTAL	31.7	6.3	51.5	6.1	25.7

Source: ISTAT, 1985, p. 74.

The case of Italy is less provincial than one might expect. France, for instance, presents the same kind of pattern as that which appears in some very interesting studies on the allocation of time for work and life activities. Table 5.4 confirms the distribution of working time between the sexes (disaggregated by number of children) which we have already seen for Italy in table 5.3. If we add up the so-called 'constrained times' (i.e. paid and unpaid working times) we see that among the various sections of the working population it is employed women who bear the heaviest burden of work (averaging over 10 hours a day). Next come employed men, and then women without paid jobs – who, however, work as many hours as men if they have three children. In France too, men's housework

101

Table 5.4: France, use of time according to the number of children and women's occupation, 1981

Time used in	Men with employed wives			Men with housewives			Women employed			Women housewives		
	1 child	2 children	3 or more	1 child	2 children	3 or more	1 child	2 children	3 or more	1 child	2 children	3 or more
Paid work	6h 30	6h 40	7h 25	6h 50	6h 50	6h 35	5h 30	4h 40	4h 40	–	–	–
Housework	2h 10	2h 05	1h 40	1h 35	1h 40	1h 45	4h 35	5h 15	5h 45	7h 30	8h 10	9h 00
Constrained times	8h 40	8h 45	9h 05	8h 25	8h 30	8h 20	10h 05	9h 55	10h 25	7h 30	8h 10	9h 00
Physical needs	11h	11h 00	10h 55	11h 00	11h 00	11h 30	10h 55	11h 00	10h 40	11h 30	11h 15	11h 15
Leisure	4h 20	4h 15	4h	4h 45	4h 30	4h 10	3h 00	3h 05	2h 55	5h 00	4h 35	3h 45

Source: Roy, 1982, p. 60.

decreases as the number of children increases, even in cases where the woman holds a paid job.

Having sketched a picture for Italy and France indicating the amount of housework and the glaring differences in its distribution between the sexes, we can now try to see whether the hours of housework tend historically to decrease, whether the phenomenon is geographically limited, and whether the gender differences are narrowing. We have some data available for the USA and a comparison, over time, between different countries.

The trend of housework in the USA is effectively illustrated by the data published by Vaneck (1980).[5] The results serve to deflate some widespread optimistic views on the relation between economic growth and the reduction of housework. It emerges that in the period between 1926 and 1964, despite the enormous changes in types of houses, consumer goods (durable and non-durable) and family structures, the amount of housework did not decrease but increased: for housewives it rose from 51 to 56 hours a week. In an urban situation, with running water, better health services and electric appliances, the reduction in the time used for food preparation was more than compensated by the increase in time devoted to care of the house, shopping, coping with bureaucracy, and child care (Vaneck, 1980, pp. 82–7).

A. Szalai (1975) compares the working hours of housewives to those of women with paid jobs. In very different institutional and productive contexts, the results show that if housework is divided according to tasks, for employed women and housewives, the overall amount of work does not diminish over time and the differences tend to decrease. The daily totals for housewives are 6.1 hours in 1926 and 6.2 hours in 1969, while for employed women they are respectively 3.8 in 1952 and 4.5 in 1969 (A. Szalai, 1975, p. 393).[6]

Robinson and Converse (1972) after standardizing the samples – for example by eliminating differences owing to the fact that women without jobs have more children – conclude that the disparity between employed women and housewives does not arise from a greater use of household technology or outside services, or from more help given by employed women's husbands (Vaneck, 1980, pp. 87–8). The standards of home and child care prove similar for the two categories; hence the differences are apparently due to a more efficient organization of the work. Actually Vaneck seems to endorse Szalai's opinion that housewives work as much as men purely in order to feel (and to show) that they are earning their living. This ideological interpretation does not explain why employed women do long hours of housework as well.

Social reproduction of labour

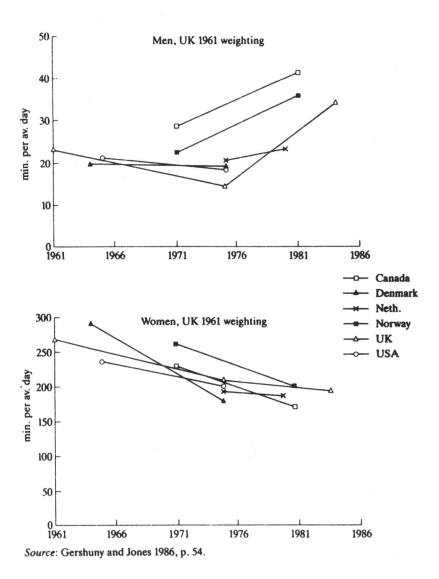

Source: Gershuny and Jones 1986, p. 54.

Marked differences between women's and men's work emerge also from the data collected by Gershuny and Jones (1986). These data enable us to make some comparisons between different countries – the United States, the United Kingdom, Denmark, Canada, the Netherlands and Norway – for the period 1961–85. As in the cases of Italy and France, there is evidence that the structure of the family, while it heavily influences both the waged and the unwaged work of women, leaves men practically unaffected (Gershuny and Jones, 1986, p. 30).[7]

The differences in work loads are such that the figures representing them often use different scales for men and women. Men's working time is mostly measured in ten-minute segments, while that of women is expressed in hundreds of minutes (Figure 5.1). There is no question about the size and persistence of the gender difference, but the data do show a reduction in women's housework and a slight increase in that done by men. The reduction of time for women's housework is mainly due to the increased number of women in paid employment. As in the previous case, the differences in time spent on housework by housewives and employed women mainly reflect different rhythms of work rather than different responsibilities and duties. All women must, and generally do, perform the same jobs; but they organize them in different ways. In fact, a marked ideological difference would be most unlikely as almost all women have paid jobs at various times in their lives; few remain exclusively 'housewives'. The differences in habits and social norms are mainly linked to differences in generation, class and educational level. For men, however, the increase seems attributable to a change in social attitudes during the seventies (Gershuny and Jones, 1986, p. 77).

In the case of child care the absolute differences between men and women are very marked, and again this is common to all the countries (Gershuny and Jones, 1986 p. 55). Times devoted to shopping generally increase within persistent differences between men and women (p. 56). Men and women shop together for durable consumer goods, while shopping for daily consumption is still mainly women's job. The time spent on personal care is remarkably equal between the sexes (p. 58); this is the category which includes personal services, sleep and rest, and meals. However, if we bear in mind women's responsibility for cooking and child care, it is fairly clear that mealtimes have different connotations for men and women – for example, men are usually served at table. Even sleep may not be equally protected: uniformity in the times of going to bed and getting up does not always mean equal hours of sleep, especially if there are small children or old people in the family, or if someone is ill.

105

5.3 Becker's 'home-economics'

Becker (1960, 1981, 1986) provides a systematic attempt to deal with the economics of the family. He defines the family as a firm in which the time of its members is allocated on the basis of traditional neoclassical criteria of maximization of utility (in this case collective) at the margin, under given constraints of time and income.

The data presented in the previous section do not confirm Becker's hypothesis of a systematic interchangeability between housework and waged work. As we have seen, for women the two kinds of work are generally added together rather than substituted. Even the interchange between machines and housework does not take place in the way expected by the neoclassical theory, which proposes a marginal substitution based on the opportunity cost of time, whereby the more women are paid for their labour the more they will supposedly substitute machines for housework. Instead, the introduction of household technology depends on social patterns of consumption which in turn are determined by habits, tastes, and cultural contexts. Given the social coordinates, 'housewives' and 'employed women' use the same appliances and services.

Nor can the view of the family as a firm be justified in terms of a maximization of collective utility under given constraints. As in the case of machines, the interchangeability between women's waged work and men's housework depends on cultural factors rather than on relative wages. In fact, between men and women there is no exchange of domestic responsibilities (beyond those set by convention) even when the woman's wage is higher than that of her partner. What does prove important in determining the relation between housework and waged work is the context of social norms, habits, tastes, power relationships, etc. Becker's model has nothing to say about these factors, since he reduces the analysis to a problem of allocation of scarce endowments tending towards equilibrium and hence staticity. Moreover, the logical requirements of the model are such that variations in prices and quantities (wages and times) cannot affect the parameters of their systematic functional relationships. In reality, the parameters themselves are precisely the most important element in the analysis because they reflect the fundamental structure of the labour market and because they may be affected by changes in prices and quantities.

The basic relations between modes of production and modes of social reproduction cannot be reduced to the distinction between historical parameters of general and ahistorical price–quantity functions. The way quantities are measured in terms of prices always depends on social structures and power relationships which can change in time and space (this has been proved by the critique of the neoclassical theory of capital).

Moreover, with regard to the adjustment mechanisms of the labour market, the flexibility of the system depends not on the elasticity of wages, but rather on the flexible nature of historically given institutions like the family. What we have to acknowledge therefore, is an institutional flexibility and not an elasticity of price–quantity functions.

Some of Becker's observations are quite reasonable, and they were already brilliantly expressed by Smith: for example, the fact that the structure of the family is affected by (among other things) economic factors that determine relations between the sexes and the number of children. What one cannot accept in Becker are the tools and the methodological approach used to express these aspects of reality. The picture of the family as a firm accentuates the worst defects of neoclassical reductivism. The use of time, relations between the sexes and the decision to have or not have children, are seen as systematically dependent on wages, in such a deterministic way that they become not only repugnant from the ethical point of view but also useless from the point of view of analysis.

Willis (1987), in his survey of the 'Economics of the Family', provides an example of where calculations on intertemporal utilities can lead economists. We might call this a 'Dynasty Model of Optimal Investment in Children':

parental preferences can be represented within the overlapping generations framework by a 'dynastic utility function' if parents' utility is equal to the sum of their own utility from consumption and the lifetime utility of each of their children multiplied by a weight representing the degree of parental altruism. Because of recursivity, the parents' utility is equal to the sum of the levels of utility from own consumption of their children, grandchildren, and all subsequent generations in the dynasty discounted by the rate of altruism. Given such preferences, a child's level of lifetime utility (i.e. the weighted sum of his utility from consumption and the utility of his children) can be interpreted as a scalar measure of child quality.

Following this strategy, Becker and Nigel Tomes . . . address the determination of the optimal investment in children. Their analysis provides an explicit model of the role of the family in the finance of human capital. (Willis, 1987, p. 75)

Neoclassical economics is generally based on the denial of the specific nature of labour as a commodity – and in particular on the specificity of its process of reproduction and its political implications. Its theory of wages is based on the old wages-fund concept of wages as supply and demand, determined as a systematic relationship between the quantity of population and a quantity of capital. First the theory of wages as costs of social reproduction was rejected, thus removing the focus from the process of reproduction of labour; then followed the simultaneous determination of wages and relative prices of other commodities, with the rejection of the exogenous theory of distribution. In this context, if the reproduction of labour is re-introduced into the economic analysis, a desperate effort must be made to reconcile its problems with the reductive analytical methodology. Thus it is no accident that Becker, precisely when he speaks about problems of reproduction, stresses the ahistoricity of the neoclassical analysis. His theory has been used to explain the reproduction of all the social groups that now exist or have historically existed in the world. Every individual will rationalize his/her choices by maximizing the marginal utility as well as he/she can; the important thing is that every choice can be represented in a diagram of indifference curves under constraints of given resources.

Last but not least, the measurement of the huge contribution made to the national economy by women with their housework, calculated at between 30 and 40 per cent of the National Product depending on the methods of measurement used (Goldschmidt-Clermont, 1982), demonstrates the unrealistic character of the theory of wages as productivity of labour, used by neoclassical economists.

5.4 Two jobs for one wage

The experience of women's double work forces us to look again at the dichotomy between the family and the market, not only in connection with the female labour force but for the general analysis of the labour market.

The complexity of women's double load arises from the constant need to mediate deep conflicts as well as more superficial tensions. The deep conflicts are connected with the historical disparity of power between the sexes – expressed as control over women's reproductive labour – and the crucial contradiction in the social system between the processes of reproducing people and the process of capital accumulation. The superficial contradictions are those involving the continual and often lacerating conflicts arising from the separation between the times and places of the two processes. Women's identity, and their success in managing not merely to fit into the mould fixed by family and society but to escape from it, depends on their capacity to act within these conflictual relationships (Balbo, 1987). Women are in fact very dynamic and resourceful in finding ways of changing the conditions of their lives, but they face structural impediments which do not allow very much scope.

The 'double load' of women puts them in an ideal position to expose the trick whereby two jobs are performed for one wage. This remains essentially the same in the traditional context of a male breadwinner and a female housewife, in the more modern one where both men and women are breadwinners, and in the post-modern one where men eventually share housework. The nature of the capitalist trick can be exposed only through a radical change of analytical (and political) perspectives.

The uneasy relationship between the exchange of women's labour power on the market and the daily organization of the process of reproduction is amply reflected in the data on women's employment. The data show that just as there is a core of housework for working women, there is also a solid core of women who are unable or unwilling to enter the waged labour market, at least during certain periods of their lives. It should be noted that some women also combine housework and other jobs within the home – mainly in crafts, shopkeeping and agriculture. These women form a category adjacent to that of housewives because they do their jobs – often unpaid – within the family, but they are counted among the employed. They are not a marginal group; their labour, precisely because it is performed in a production unit defined by the family, involves a continuous interaction between work for the market and reproductive work: actually, such women usually enter their trade through marriage (Finch, 1983).

In terms of working hours, the influence of housework on waged work becomes still more obvious. At the international level, part-time work is mainly a female phenomenon (Beechey and Perkins, 1987; Walby, 1990). Other systems of time management (shifts, night work, flexible time, overtime, availability on call) are used differently by men and women; and the disparity is once again based on their different family responsibilities (Horrel, Rubery and Burchell, 1989). Women are prepared to work at various times of day, but they strongly resist indefinite and unpredictable schedules. The great variety of solutions offers employers a labour force which is flexible overall, though rigid for individual employees. The hours of work chosen by women, including those most disadvantaged, are always strongly determined by the needs of the family – an element which proves to have very little importance for men.

The increase in women's employment rates cannot be read as a continuous progress towards a mythical neutral worker, defined by an imaginary equality. The sense of frustration which women experience demonstrates the inadequacy of the solutions offered by the present system to the problems involved in the relation between production and social reproduction, which are by no means limited to women. By using women's experiences in both processes we can begin to move from a sacrificial perspective (inculcated in women at various ideological and symbolic levels, and not only by the political right) to one based on a social and political critique of the capitalist waged labour market.

In this respect housewives are no more passive and inert than waged women; they are merely made less noticeable by the ideologies surrounding work. There are two ways of making them politically invisible: one is to consider them as potential political subjects only if they become waged workers, and the other is to glorify their role and push it out of the economic and political sphere. Both these perspectives aim to neutralize housework as an issue for political negotiation.

5.5 Policy perspectives

Awareness of the qualitative and quantitative dimensions of the work of reproduction, and its proper location in the general analytical framework, have crucial implications for women's strategies. If policy is concerned only with waged labour, women are caught in the equality–protection dilemma. That is to say, they must either hide their work of reproduction so as to be equal to men in the work place, or acknowledge it and ask for 'protection'. But once the historical relationship between production and reproduction is made explicit, the functional link between waged work and housework becomes a general question rather than a women's issue. 'Protection' is exposed as a petty manoeuvre, 'equality' as a mirage; and both strategies are grossly inadequate for dealing with the problems of the conflictual relationship between production and reproduction under capitalism. Women see this clearly, but they are forced to accept either 'protective' measures such as part-time jobs, which undermine their wages and careers, or else to play Wonder Woman in pursuit of a spurious equality in the waged labour market. Wages hide not only women's double load but, more insidiously, the huge amount of women's energy which their male colleagues absorb in order to cope with their own problems.

Under present circumstances the idea of a more equal distribution of the work of reproduction between men and women seems more like wishful thinking than a realistic perspective. First of all, historically sedimented chauvinism, so persistent and general that it cannot be ignored, interacts with the structure of the labour market. Secondly, men are too aware of their own historical struggles for higher real wages and less work to accept an increased work load with no other compensation than reduced feelings of guilt. A redistribution of housework can be made possible only by a massive redistribution of resources in favour of the reproduction of the labouring population. This redistribution might take many different forms of 'wages for housework' – money benefits, paid leaves, paid reduction of work hours, public services, etc. – and it would certainly favour both men and women – but in any case it has to be massive and it must challenge the modes of production.

In the past few decades the women's labour market has greatly changed. Women have fewer children and an increasing part of their lives

110

is unregulated by the biological rhythms of childbearing. Thus they can stay longer in paid employment, though as we have seen this does not necessarily mean they do less housework. With looking after old and sick people, increased time spent in travel and shopping, bureaucratic commitments, children remaining at home longer, men having more insecure, flexible and stressful jobs, etc., women have little hope of a reduction of 'constrained time'.

Women's wages are now an essential component of the family income, and households have very different compositions. But this does not alter the relation between production and costs of reproduction of waged labour: it only means that the man's wage is no longer enough to provide for the historical living standards of the family. The relation between men's and women's wages and the real standard of living is still mediated by the separate organization of reproduction, and by the need to keep its costs low enough to allow the formation and accumulation of profits. For that purpose housework still carries out its task very well.

The empirical evidence seems to show that women do not buy more in order to work less; instead, they work more in order to buy more. The phenomenon is similar to the transformations that took place in the household economy in the eighteenth century, when independent farmers were induced in various ways to depend on the commodity market and the labour market for their subsistence.

Women generally use the labour market to escape from the forms of personal dependence inherent in patriarchal relationships; but they end up with a greater work load, and usually cannot manage to escape from the trap of low pay and poverty. In fact it happens that while on the one hand they gain some personal liberty through reducing the personal impositions that restrict their freedom of action, on the other hand women are under more pressure to sell themselves on the labour market owing to an historical increase in the general insecurity of workers' access to the means of subsistence.[8]

All this can be understood only if one analyses the nature of the labour market, which is apparently democratic (because it presupposes free choice on the part of the workers) but whose underlying features lead to such deep and widespread insecurity as to threaten individual freedom. By exposing the nature of the labour market, on which the commodity market is based, we can gain more clarity about the relation between production and reproduction that characterizes the capitalist economy.

For women this clarity is essential because it brings out the fact that their entry into the waged labour market, while it can undoubtedly solve many problems in their lives, cannot really 'liberate' them. In reality it does not even bring liberation from patriarchy, because the waged labour market, as we have seen, is based on a particular sexual division of labour in reproduction.

5.6 Women and the state

Housework is the basis for a certain relationship between women and the state. The state is the institution which regulates the adjustment between the process of accumulation and the process of social reproduction, as we saw in the third and fourth chapters. Modern states have the role of controlling the conflicts arising from waged work and the particular division of labour and resources it involves. Under capitalism the labour of reproduction takes the form of unwaged housework, whose function is to reproduce the population, especially waged workers. This arrangement enables the system to count on the continuity of the processes of production and reproduction, using the form of social command provided by the endemic insecurity of wages. An adequate proportional relationship between the two processes is the condition on which the continuity of the process of capitalist accumulation depends. As we have seen, the question of this proportion lies at the heart of political economy.

The insecurity of reproduction, inherent in the wage system, has induced the state to assume certain direct responsibilities for social groups such as low-waged workers, the unemployed, the wageless and people with no waged person to depend on. The state, however, has never been a neutral institution with regard to social classes; still less has it been so with regard to the gender division of labour in the process of reproduction. Control over women's work leads to control over the whole reproduction of the population.

The state, in fact, is far from passive with regard to the control of women's reproductive functions, in terms of both quantity and quality. For example, it has always tried to exercise control over abortion – repressively or permissively, according to need (Walby, 1990). It has also controlled the enforcement of the marriage contract, which imposes precise domestic and sexual obligations on women (Pateman, 1988). Moreover, it has tolerated as normal a certain degree of private violence against women, which partly explains the general reluctance to pass laws banning violence within the family; while this tolerance appears to contradict policies of equal rights for all citizens, it is quite efficient in controlling women's work and bodies. The state also tolerates the fact that compared to men women work more, are poorer and have less protection in terms of social security (Brocas, Cailloux and Oget, 1990).

When the state assumes direct responsibilities in connection with reproduction it never aims to replace housework, but only to supplement it. Women's domestic obligations are always tacitly taken for granted in

112

the formulation of social policies. Health services and schools could not function if they were not sustained by plenty of housework within the family. The bias is even more evident in the provision of services such as nurseries and kindergartens. It is always taken for granted, implicitly or explicitly, that places will be allocated to the children of employed mothers, thus reinforcing the specific responsibility of mothers rather than recognizing a general public responsibility for children. The allocation of public resources at various institutional levels is always based on the principle that it is basically the mother's job to solve problems connected with children. It is generally assumed that women's work and energy are unlimited and impose no constraints on social policy.

It must be noted that where there are high rates of female employment and widespread public services, as in the Scandinavian countries, the problem of women's relation with the state, based on the work of reproduction, has by no means been solved. Precisely because these countries are so advanced, they clearly show how difficult it is to overcome the idea of women as the primary instrument of social reproduction – in the family, in the labour market and in public institutions (Hernes, 1987). Only the widespread resistance of women at all levels, including institutional levels, can expose the costs which women are forced to bear, in terms of work and stress, because the responsibilities of reproduction are dumped on them by men and the state.

It is above all with the state that women have to negotiate the conditions of their reproductive work. They cannot win by bargaining privately in a labour market which ignores women's reproductive work in order to pay low wages to both women and men. Moreover, in almost all countries the state is now the largest employer of women, thus a successful struggle to modify conventions and power relationships in the public sector could well serve as a pattern for the private sector as well.

Only direct bargaining with the state over modes of reproduction can correct, at least partly, the abuses of a system of production that subordinates social reproduction to capital accumulation. The division of reproductive labour between the sexes is too deeply rooted in the structure of the social system to be transformed by a simple rationalization of individual working times. Women's bargaining with the state, however, does not eliminate the need to expose, and to act on, the deep, historically established conflict between men and women in the area of reproduction. The modern material basis of these conflicts is rooted in the unequal access to the means of subsistence, and the unequal work of reproduction, as well as in the general control over women's bodies and lives maintained by men through paternalism and/or harassment and violence.

5.7 A political subject

In the present situation women have become a social subject with a decisive influence. It is no accident that this has coincided with the opening of a new phase of conflict over historical modes of reproduction. The feminist movement of the seventies focussed directly on the question of reproduction: contraception, abortion, sexuality, the family, housework, health, services and living standards were the issues most vigorously debated (Rowbotham, 1990). During the eighties women's energies were mainly channelled into the creation and expansion of cultural instruments. Women's publishing houses, journals and bookshops, women's studies, conferences and cultural centres have contributed to the inclusion of women among the protagonists – as well as the issues – at the centre of today's cultural debates. In that decade women also established and consolidated relations with public institutions: local and governmental administrations, trade unions, the media, etc. And they also focussed attention on the fact that in public institutions their representation is still scandalously unequal.

Women's political and cultural activism has helped to establish the question of women's liberation as a central element in contemporary social dynamics. Since the beginnings of the feminist movement the question of liberation has been distinguished from, and counterposed to, the question of emancipation (understood as women's entry into the world of men and the effacement of differences between the sexes). Women's rejection of that kind of levelling has laid the foundations for a radical criticism of the social institutions in which we live. Those institutions are criticized not only because they impose barriers to entry, but because they themselves are based on women's subordination and inseparable from it. All this has led to an intense debate on the theoretical foundations of the social sciences, which are only apparently neutral: in essence they are based on purely male ways of looking at the world and at women (Braidotti, 1991; Pateman, 1988). Even in the physical sciences, institutions and methodological approaches have been challenged for the partiality of their research perspectives (Donini, 1990; Fox Keller, 1985; Harding, 1986).

The fact that women form a political subject does not mean that women are all equal or all have the same interests. They are deeply divided by differences of class, nationality and race as well as by their own individual histories. Obviously the social interactions between subjects with different levels of power are very complicated. But clarity on the specific question of reproduction may well facilitate new alliances. For example, until recent decades housework was a great source of division between classes, because paid domestic work was the employment sector most crowded with women. Today it is much less common for a woman to command another woman's housework directly through wages; moreover, standards of housework have to a great extent levelled out between women of different classes for various reasons – the spread of social norms, products and technologies, the media, social services, urbanization.

By adopting an analytical approach that focusses directly on reproduction and its historical conditions, we also find a common denominator for women's work in very different countries and economies (e.g. those of the northern and southern hemispheres). The multiplicity and specificity of the relations between production and reproduction are certainly reflected in radical differences between women of different countries. But giving these relations due recognition at the political level should encourage the building of alliances and solidarities with a potentiality to overcome, at least in part, the conflicts among women in different locations in the international system of capitalist accumulation. In this area women's organizations and women scholars have begun to create effective tools for a critical reassessment, at an international level, of the historically given relations between production and reproduction in each specific real context (Deere, 1976; K. Young, 1988; Brydon and Chant, 1989). Institutions like DAWN (Development Alternatives with Women for a New Era), WID (Women in Development) and the women's caucuses of the non-governmental organizations form an international network for alternative development policies (Sen and Grown, 1988).

5.8 Conclusions

In my analysis of the capitalist system, alongside the exploitation of labour in production, I have explicitly stressed the exploitation of labour in reproduction. To analyse this second form of exploitation we must focus centrally on the work of reproduction and the control of women to guarantee the quantity and quality of labour necessary for accumulation.

To understand both class exploitation and gender exploitation it is necessary to recognize the specific functional relationship between production and reproduction. This absolutely does not mean that the political organization of the conflict between the sexes can be confined within the narrow limits of the trade unions or other historical organizations of the labour movement. Those organizations are so patriarchal and chauvinistic that they allow very little space for the necessary manifestation of the conflict between the sexes – in fact, they are not even open to radical criticism of class exploitation. They take it for granted that women, with their housework, will absorb the insecurity of conditions of reproduction which is endemic in waged labour. The impotence of the unions affects not only women but men as well – it involves not only gender but also class. Nor do I imagine that the conflict between the sexes is purely a problem of capitalism, or of exploitation of work. The conflict is so rooted in the history of social development, and so disguised in the history of social thought, that it would be absurd to imagine that a mere change in the theoretical perspectives of political economy could trace its historical foundations, let alone resolve it.

With regard to the question of materialism and economism, I think this is usually posed in the wrong terms. Reproduction necessarily has a large material component. It has to do with bodies, nutrition, nativity, etc. But at the same time there is nothing more deeply symbolic than the body, food, birth, motherhood. The difference between the sexes is first of all biological; but its perception and expression are profoundly rooted in the structure of language and in myth. Its history goes so far back that current studies on women's anthropology and history have scarcely begun to scratch the surface.

My approach to political economy, therefore, is clearly materialistic but not necessarily economistic. I do not want economy as a specification of the subject under examination – i.e. the production, distribution and exchange of wealth – to be confused with economism, which has many reductive implications. When due attention is given to the process of reproduction of labour, the whole subject of political economy is necessarily seen as inherently social and political.

6

The supply of labour
as a process of social reproduction

6.1 Standards of living: the quality of labour

Up to this point, working at different levels and using a variety of tools, I have sought to recover the essential features of a question which played a fundamental role in the birth of political economy, but which is now practically excluded from economic analysis. This is the question of the social reproduction of labour and its relationship with the structure of the waged labour market.

It is now time to draw the threads of the study together and define an approach in which the labour supply figures as a social process that guarantees a certain size of population and a general disposition to enter the labour market. In this perspective the labour supply is determined by the combination of material, demographic, institutional and cultural elements sedimented over time – historically given elements which may form the basis for future changes.

The view of the supply of labour as the result of an historical process has its macroeconomic foundations in the classical surplus approach, where 'subsistence' was taken as one of the crucial aspects of the economic system. Let us recapitulate the basic aspects of the surplus theory of profit discussed in the first chapter of this book. They are: (a) the inverse relation between production and costs of production (i.e. especially costs of reproduction of labour); (b) the treatment of the price of the commodity labour separately from prices of other commodities; (c) the principle of exogenous distribution; and (d) the attention given to the normality of the system, focussing the analysis on its general and persistent aspects and distinguishing them from superficial, accidental and temporary phenomena. This is the analytical approach that comes closest to the questions I am most concerned with: the social reproduction of labour and its relationship with the structure of the waged labour market.

The supply of labour can be defined in terms of two dimensions: standards of living, and the number of labour units (however defined). Standards of living cannot be expressed in purely quantitative terms, though they are material and to a certain degree measurable. Even minimum living standards, though apparently dominated by biological and physical factors, have always proved difficult to evaluate. This was

Social reproduction of labour

realized by Booth and Rowntree, as well as Beveridge and the social policy-makers dealing with poverty and minimum wages in the post-war period. Atkinson, among others, acknowledges the problem and frames it within a classical context:

The basic problem is that, despite Rowntree's pioneering efforts, it is just not possible to define an absolute subsistence level as a basis for the poverty line. Even in the case of food, it is difficult to determine requirements with any precision, and rather than any absolute level of subsistence requirements, there is a broad range where physical efficiency declines with a falling intake of calories, proteins, etc.

It must be recognized that any subsistence standard is inevitably influenced by current living standards, and that we cannot define a poverty line in a vacuum but only in relation to the living standards of a particular society at a particular date – a point well appreciated by Adam Smith. (Atkinson, 1969, pp. 16–17)[1]

Recently, fresh attention has been given to the problem of defining historical standards of living and to their social structure (Sen, 1987). And the question is raised again in connection with the problem of defining the poverty line for policy purposes (Sen, 1983, 1985b; Atkinson 1989).

Standards of living of the labouring population are not a clearly definable concept: not only because there is no production function for labour (i.e. no systematic relationship between inputs and output), but also because in economic terms standards of living have a dual nature. On the one hand they represent the means of reproduction of the population; on the other hand they are costs of production for employers. Therefore they are influenced by two different perspectives: (1) the habits and expectations of the labourers regarding the conditions of reproduction of themselves and their families, and (2) the expectations of the employers and the state regarding the health, discipline, skills and training necessary for the work process and for a viable social system based on private property. These different viewpoints with regard to habits, expectations, attitudes and standards of living are a potential source of radical conflict between workers and employers, and between the whole labouring population and the state.

Reproductive needs and expectations can of course also lead to forms of social cooperation among classes and institutions, on the basis of implicit social contracts in areas of possible mutual interest. Rising material standards of living within an unequal social system based on private property, for instance, were seen by Smith as a possible basis for an alliance between the middle classes and the working class. The prospect of increasing standards of living for some sections of the population still underlies the implicit social contract which holds together

118

the social system of free market economies. But the capitalist social contract, although apparently thriving at the moment, cannot resolve the tensions inherent in the capitalist system between capital accumulation and social reproduction of the labouring population. There are social institutions that can mediate the conflicts, and techniques for disciplining them, but there are no final solutions which can free the system of its inherent conflicts. Moreover, although increasing consumption seems to have provided a vast ground for alliances, the increasing insecurity inherent in pressures for capital accumulation has made potential conflict more radical and pervasive. This is why economic analysis has to take wages into consideration not only as costs or as a major part of effective demand, but also as means of subsistence.

The contradictions inherent in the capitalist relation between production and reproduction emerge with particular clarity in certain cases. Problems arise when grave inequities become apparent in the functioning of the labour market as a filter of access to the means of subsistence. In certain historical moments it becomes clear that: (a) not all those who want to work for a wage can be employed; (b) not all those who work for a wage receive a wage sufficient to satisfy their historically given habits and tastes; and (c) not all work provides autonomous access to the means of subsistence.

These problems, which become politically prominent in particular historical moments, are in fact general and persistent because they are part of the system's basic structure. Economic theories and policies, seeking possible mediations, have confronted them in different ways.

From this point of view Keynes represents the highest level of mediation, both in theoretical terms and in terms of economic policies. His recognition of the possibility of involuntary unemployment, the role of wage-earners' consumption in the realization of profit and the institutional rigidity of money wages, and his advocacy of social policies involving the state as an adjustment mechanism between production and reproduction, make his analysis highly innovative by comparison with those of his predecessors. What Keynes does, in fact, is to put the problem of the relation between capitalist production and social reproduction in new terms.

But the Keynesian mediation, while it represents a progressive gain that must be defended, does not provide a solution to the underlying contradictions of the labour market. New perspectives can be found only through a process of social experimentation. A viable relationship between production and reproduction can exist only on the basis of concrete practice in which individuals and social groups react to manifest problems in terms of their needs, interests, objectives, views of the world and power balances.

The two contradictory aspects of living standards – rising expectations and costs of production – emphasize the specificity of the labour commodity.[2] While other commodities have no autonomous views about their costs, human lives become capital, i.e. means of production, through a process of adaptation the results of which depend on power relationships between classes and between sections of the labouring population. Living standards reflect conflicts within the population because consumption goods express relative social power (Douglas and Isherwood, 1979). Consumption patterns are conditioned by the selfishness of the ruling class on the one hand, and by the frustration of waged workers and houseworkers on the other.

The task of determining a standard of living is impractical, though some useful indicators can be developed empirically for specific purposes. I find it rather more useful to look at the way the provision of real standards of living is organized, and which social subjects are involved in this process.

In fact, the actual relationship between wages and real standards of living depends on the whole process of social reproduction of labour. The following table presents an outline of the process of reproduction, showing the social subjects active in the process, the places of production, and its components: the bundle of wage goods and services provided by different subjects in different places.

Table 6.1: The process of social reproduction of labour

Social subjects	Waged worker	Wageless house-worker	Public institutions
Place of production	Factory	Home	Hospitals, schools, etc.
Goods and services to the reproduction unit	Wage goods	Housework	Services and benefits

Table 6.1 shows the differentiation within the labouring population between waged and wageless workers, recognizing that the separation of productive functions historically leads to a separation of individuals, places of production and institutions. Most of all, as we have seen, it leads to a

120

separation between waged and unwaged work.

The structure of the whole process of course cannot be taken as constant. Changes can take place in working hours, attitudes to work, wage goods and services, according to the productive structure, the structure of the family, institutions, demographic patterns, and power relationships within and between classes and between genders. Housework and the wage bundle are closely interdependent, and so are the subjects who provide them. The providers of wage goods need housework because labour power is a joint product of wage goods and housework; and houseworkers need waged workers to get access to subsistence in a market economy.

Housework – which serves to close the gap between wages, public services and historically given standards of living – is seen as a residual category. The standards of living of the workers and their families do not fully correspond with costs of production for the employers. As we saw in the previous chapter, an increase in housework guarantees relatively higher standards of living, and hence a higher quality of labour, while the costs in terms of wage goods, and hence of wages, may be the same or even reduced. The complex structure of social reproduction shown in the table gives the system a high degree of flexibility. Various sections of the population are able to move in and out of the waged labour market precisely because the family provides services and alternative sources of subsistence. The family absorbs the costs of flexibility and internalizes its conflicts. As I have previously pointed out, this institutional flexibility is radically different from the concept of elasticity of the supply of labour seen as a systematic price–quantity relationship.

The capitalists' problem is to keep the costs of reproduction of labour in step with production so that profits will not be reduced. This can be achieved by various means. One is to keep the standards of living of the labouring population low in terms of level and composition; another is to reduce the cost of wage goods and services through high productivity. Still another is to transfer the costs of reproduction to the state. Last but not least, the costs of social reproduction can be reduced by shifting them on to the family, increasing women's burden of housework.

If the process of reproduction is not explicitly taken into account in economic analysis, the reproductive functions of the public sector are also left without any proper location: their role, in fact, is to mediate the separation between the sector of production and that of household reproduction. Thus without a clear picture of the role of the process of reproduction, and of the family within it, the role of the state in the labour market and the social system cannot be fully understood.

6.2 Inherent conflicts

The structure of the process of reproduction embodies various conflicts between waged workers and employers over wages, between wageless houseworkers and waged workers within the family, between wageless houseworkers and the state, between waged workers and the state, and indirectly between wageless houseworkers and employers.[3] These conflicts make the production–reproduction relationship changeable and at times unstable, in spite of its flexibility.

The conflict between waged workers and employers over wages, hours and working conditions is generally acknowledged by social scientists. I shall leave this aspect out of the present picture in order to concentrate on some other social relationships, and their inherent conflicts. A fundamental conflict within reproduction is between the waged worker and the unwaged houseworker, who depend on each other for subsistence and hence need to control each other. The deep social conflicts inherent in the separation between production and reproduction are not acknowledged as such; they are disguised as personal conflicts to be overcome by 'love' and 'sacrifice'. Moreover, the open and covert violence required to keep any form of labour under control takes on the character of domestic violence, in the privacy of the family, and hence appears as personal rather than social.

Another inherent potential conflict is between houseworkers and the state. Public institutions are notoriously unwilling to take over direct responsibility for services usually provided privately by housework. This resistance is due to the costs of those services and the distributive implications of switching from unwaged work to waged work financed by taxation.[4] Consequently, as we saw in the fourth chapter, public institutions exert special pressure to maintain the standards of services provided by the family.

Waged workers also confront the state over the conditions of social reproduction on the issue of the 'social wage', i.e. welfare and fiscal policies. Here their position is weakened by the fact that the confrontation generally involves only a restricted section of the labouring population, that of employed workers. The unions have often accepted strategies which concentrate on wages and conditions at the work place, disregarding the fact that the wageless sections of the labouring population are also political subjects who have the power, though in a different form, to resist and struggle to improve their standards of living by putting pressure on employers and public institutions.[5]

Struggles undertaken at community level are not easy to link with those at the work place. The reasons lie not only in substantial differences in the issues and the forms of organization, but also in the narrow approach of unions, and working-class organizations in general, to the whole question of social reproduction.[6] They have usually supported the dominance of the (male) wage earner in the family, and have chosen to ignore the repressive and often violent means of commanding housework, dismissing them as purely private matters.

The lack of an adequate perspective on the whole question of reproduction can be seen in the fact that unions have often endorsed policies that benefit only the core of the labour force, white adult male native-born workers with housewives behind them.[7] As a matter of fact the relative weights of wages, family and public services in the process of reproduction differ between sections of the population which have historically different habits and tastes and different power relationships with employers, state institutions and unions.

6.3 The quantity of labour

I have been using the term 'labouring population' in the classical sense, to include all the people who directly or indirectly depend on a wage for subsistence and who have no access to property as main source of income. The structure of population can be defined for a given period as the result of an historical process which, through conflicts, power balances and social behaviour, lays down the conditions for access to subsistence – which in a free market economy means access to money. The demographic endowment shown by census figures must therefore be divided into different classes depending on the source of income (property or labour). The distinction between the labouring population and the propertied classes implies different roles in production and different degrees of security and control over the means of reproduction.

The labouring population itself must be divided into different sections, for it is by no means homogeneous or rigid in time. Its structure reflects not simply demography or physical characteristics, but again power relationships based on different degrees of security in relation to the means of reproduction. Differences in access to the waged labour market and in relative wages, based on age, sex and nationality, have more to do with factors like the family and immigration than with demographic endowments or productivity.

Historically, the supply of labour has never been fixed and scarce in the long period or at a general level. Some sections may be scarce for periods of time, but in the long run immigration and social flexibility guarantee that the labour supply is not persistently and generally rigid. The result is a structural oversupply of labour which only apparently depends on demography: it has to do with social norms, segmentation in historical standards of living, and different power relationships within the family and the state.

This is even more true if hours rather than individuals are taken as the units of labour. The structure of the labour market includes customs and norms regulating the hours of work which can differ between segments of the population. The same thing holds, as we have seen in the previous section, for the relationship between standards of living and wages. As is shown in the first chapter, quantities of labour supplied and wages are thus definable only in historical terms; they are graphically expressible as points and not as functions, since no systematic relationship can be assumed. The whole structure of the process of reproduction reacts to changes in relative prices, wages and employment, in ways that are not systematic but historically given.

6.4 Supply and demand

An analysis of the labour market, if confined within the limits of the orthodox supply-and-demand theory of wages, leads to a limited view of the real forces acting in the labour market. On the contrary, with a radical and explicit change of analytical perspective we can take advantage of many observations on the real structure of the labour market – its institutions, power relationships and living standards – without being caught in the defensive game imposed by a supply-and-demand methodology where logical requirements rather than historical facts determine what is taken as systematic and what is taken as accidental.

This holds also with regard to the relationship between supply and demand themselves. In the neoclassical theory, supply and demand are price–quantity functions based on individual preferences and are assumed to be mutually independent. The classical economists had a different view: in the Physiocratic tradition, they represent both supply and demand as macro-founded on circular, material and institutional processes of production, distribution and exchange. This perspective is radically different from an approach to supply and demand founded on micro individual choices taken on the basis of relative prices and marginal utilities. The difference is crucial. Production and reproduction can be seen as the processes which determine, respectively, the demand for labour and the supply of labour. For given available technologies, the level of production sets the demand for labour. The historical process of social reproduction determines the supply of labour. Supply and demand are not seen as functions of prices, but as the result of production, distribution and the historical size of markets. Supply and demand do not need to be considered mutually independent. The problem, therefore, is not to 'reconstitute the supply side of the labour market' or to assess 'the relative autonomy of social reproduction' (Humphries and Rubery, 1984), but to step finally out of the neoclassical way of approaching supply and demand.

While the present study is not directly concerned with the demand for labour, what has been said about wages and the supply of labour does imply a definition of the economic system whereby production, distribution and exchange are linked in a circular flow. In this picture wages are costs of production, a major component of aggregate demand, and means of reproduction. The theoretical problems of political economy all spring from incompatibilities between these functions. This complexity is lost in the neoclassical perspective, where the allocation of quantitative endowments of 'factors of production' is motivated by changes in relative prices and based on the assumption of technical substitutibility between labour and capital, and wages are treated merely as costs of production. The shift of paradigm has important analytical implications not only for the labour supply, but also for the demand for labour.

The relationship between wages and employment can be considered more as a structural relationship between two sectors of production – production of commodities and reproduction of labour – than as an allocative relationship (Garegnani, 1978–9). The two processes are taken as exogenous in the determination of relative prices, but both are obviously fundamental components of the economic system and they usually interact. Although the theory does not allow any space for systematic and general relationships, the structure of production, the structure of class distribution and the habits and tastes of the population are the basic determinants of aggregate expenditure because the system is analysed as a circular flow. In the same way the levels of employment and wages may affect habits and tastes and attitudes to work.

This was noticed by Dobb who tried to use the peculiarity of the supply of labour as a basis for a critique of the neoclassical theory of distribution. The attempt was not successful although it is worth taking into consideration. Later on the critique of the neoclassical theory of distribution was successfully undertaken by Sraffa with regard to the measurement of heterogeneous aggregates; nonetheless, Dobb's remarks keep their importance with respect to the supply of labour.

As a Marxist Dobb was well aware of the methodological differences between the classical approach and the neoclassical one. He was also an economic historian who saw the development of the waged labour market as an essential feature of capitalism.[8] Moreover, he was convinced of the historical and institutional nature of the processes which shape the social system. After reading Sraffa's 1926 article on 'The Laws of Returns under Competitive Conditions', he questioned the relationship between functions and parameters and the assumption of independence between supply and demand functions of labour. We can follow his attempt, and then Keynes's subsequent acknowledgement of its importance. According to Dobb:

In the theory of distribution an attempt was made to carry over the same method of analysis and to apply it to the factors of production . . . And here again is the implicit assumption of the independence of the supply-and-demand curves required. By interdependence for this purpose it is necessary to mean that a change in one of them, through its effects on the price of labour or on any other prices, does not thereby produce a change in the other . . . An example where this assumption of independence would not hold in the case of a specific commodity was offered by Mr. Sraffa in his important article in the Economic Journal for December 1926 (to which I am personally indebted for providing this present train of thought). (Dobb, 1929, p. 509)

Dobb uses Sraffa's point on the interdependence between supply and demand to argue that in the case of labour – a basic factor in production – a change in price would affect supply and demand functions.[9] Changes do not occur along price–quantity functions but in the 'constants' of the curves – i.e. in the parametric utilities of income and investment – which express the disposition to supply and to demand labour (pp. 511–16). The determination of wages as equilibrium prices is undermined by the fact that independent supply-and-demand functions cannot be assumed.

The question whether the level of wages is 'natural' or 'institutional' is quite distinct from the question whether a 'normal' level, in the sense of a stable equilibrium, can be found . . . The former is the question whether the 'constants' which provide a solution to the equations are values which depend on nature or can be altered at will by the hand of man. The latter is the distinct question whether the equations can be solved at all . . . But it is at any rate possible that our failure to frame satisfactory equations indicate that the deductive method is not so appropriate, at least to the problem of distribution, as we have habitually supposed. (p. 517, italics added)

Dobb argued that in the case of labour the fact that the constants of the function are the significant objects of analysis, and the fact that the price–quantity functions have no systematic behaviour because 'one curve cannot move without producing a related movement in the other' (p. 518), make the supply-and-demand determination of wages implausible and inconsistent.

The point is made even more clear in *Political Economy and Capitalism* where in the chapter on frictions and expectations Dobb says:

Here the new factor in the situation is treated as though it were an additional constant, altering by a given amount the value of one or more of the variables in

the governing equations . . . then it can properly be regarded as a mere disturbing factor, weakening the precision but not damaging the essential correctness of the previous generalization.
 . . . the introduction of the new element may transform the situation in a much more radical manner, in the sense of altering the character of the actual relations which hold between various quantities. *Its influence can then no longer be properly regarded merely as that of a retarding or displacing friction: it is rather that of a new chemical element, the presence of which alters the character and action of other elements and so transforms the whole composition.* (Dobb, 1937, pp. 188–9, italics added)

Unfortunately, in this context Dobb continues by saying:

But the new situation is capable of being rendered determinate, like the old, provided that the number of equations . . . can be made equal to the number of dependent variables. (p. 189)

As Bharadwaj (1978c) noted, in his early writings Dobb could not completely abandon a supply-and-demand framework. The critique of the neoclassical theory of distribution could not be achieved through discussion of the mathematics of the functions; it had to wait for Sraffa's *Production of Commodities*, which questioned the logic of the neoclassical relationship on the basis of the measurement of heterogeneous commodities given exogenous changes in distribution. Dobb's attempt is interesting anyway, because he refers to the qualitative changes of the economic system in the case of changes in wages.
 Keynes acknowledged the significance of Dobb's attempt and in his article 'On the Question of High Wages' (1930). Referring directly to Dobb's article in the *Economic Journal*, he says:

There is a growing scepticism abroad as to the psychological and theoretical validity of the orthodox theory of value which led others to dispute that there is any natural level of wages at all, or, at any rate, one that is rigidly fixed; and this attitude of mind accords much better with popular aspirations. Limits there are, no doubt, this school would admit; but there is a fairly wide margin, they would maintain, within which the determining factor is, not so much what used to be called economic law, as social and political habits and practices, and the trend of public opinion.
 Advocates of such views are employing two distinct types of arguments. The first of them involves no radical departure from orthodox analysis . . . In raising wages you bring into activity latent energies in the entrepreneur out of which the additional wages can be paid . . .
 The second type of critic makes a much more fundamental attack on the old theory. He questions altogether the rigidity of what economists call the Theory of

127

Social reproduction of labour

Distribution: These relative rates of remuneration are, they contend, the product of historical and social forces. There are no actual physical or psychological laws which compel them to be what they are now . . . there is a large arbitrary element in the relative rates of remuneration, and the factors of production get what they do, not because in any strict sense they precisely earn it, but because past events have led to these rates being customary and usual. So there is nothing sacrosanct about them. If the working classes have the political and bargaining power to get a larger share of the product of industry than formerly, well, this is a new historical fact; historical evolution is this time on their side. The business men will have to get less, and that is all there is to it. (Keynes, 1930, pp. 111–14)[10]

Unfortunately, Keynes in the 1930 article abandons the ground of distribution, shifting the argument from the implications of an exogenously given wage, to the demand for labour and to international competition of capital. As a matter of fact, it often happens in economic theory that the problems which manifest themselves in the labour market are transposed to other levels of analysis, or that the problems which pertain to the supply of labour as a manifestation of its peculiarity are dealt with in terms of the demand for labour. Thus they are shifted from the sector of the reproduction of labour, where the labouring classes have some degree of control, to the sector of production and finance, where – by definition of the capitalist system – they are excluded from decision making. If we start breaking down automatic relationships and the systematic functions relating prices to quantities, this transposition from one aspect to the other and from one level of analysis to another – for instance from the normality of production and distribution to the accidental allocation of scarcity – is no longer legitimate.

The surplus approach questions price–quantity relationships at different levels. It reverses – as a normal case, and not as mere downward rigidity of minimum wages – the relationship between standards of living and wages. It challenges the very notion of a supply function of labour, taking the relationships between wages and standards of living, between quantity of the labour force and standards of living, and between wages and attitudes to work, as historically and institutionally given. The adjustment mechanisms operate not through automatic changes in quantities and relative prices, but through qualitative changes in productive structures and social behaviour which cannot be framed in systematic quantitative functional relationships.[11] The real problems of the labour market no longer need to be treated as exceptions to the general theory of the determination of wages based on scarcity and on the productivity of labour. They can be analysed through generalizations and abstractions based on the historical functioning of the social system.[12] Economic theory provides the analytical location of the problems, and historical enquiry may provide the information for plausible generalizations.

6.5 A different approach

Classical political economists tried to locate in their abstract scheme the problems which emerged as structurally important and persistent in the capitalist system. The nature of the problems of the waged labour market, its conflicts and its adjustment mechanisms, required an analytical treatment of the price of labour which could take some account of the specificity of the labour commodity and the peculiarity of its process of reproduction. Although we do not have a theory of social reproduction, we do have some information on the structure of the process, its agents and inherent conflicts. What is more important, we have an analytical framework in which we can locate the question of the social reproduction of labour in a more adequate way. Nonetheless, many problems arise in using the classical framework as a positive approach to the analysis of modern labour markets.

The classical theory of wages was basically a theory of low wages. This can be explained historically by the heavy dependence of living standards on natural resources, the expropriation of traditional forms of access to the means of subsistence, the relative political weakness of the working classes, and the new forms of organization of the process of social reproduction based on the capitalist restructuring of the family. Today the theory of wages as costs of social reproduction no longer needs to imply low wages, but controlling the process of social reproduction of labour remains a crucial problem for the capitalist system. Thus the notion of wages as costs of social reproduction, within a surplus definition of profit, is still valid precisely because it brings out a real conflict between profit and the social reproduction of labour.

Nonetheless, if we take the classical analytical framework as a starting point for a critical approach to the main-stream analysis of the labour market, we must note some major differences that distinguish the present historical context from the classical one. The first problem that the classical theory of wages encounters in its adaptation to modern labour markets is the enormous increase in the role of the state in the labour market, compared with what it was – and was meant to be – in the first half of the nineteenth century. Nevertheless, despite its naivety with regard to the theory of the state, classical political economy, in accord with its basic methodology, provides some fruitful insights on the role of the state in the economic system. These insights relate both to the complexities of the process of social reproduction and to the assumption of a non-clearing labour market. For Ricardo the assumption of a non-clearing labour market was rooted precisely in the historical and social separation between

Social reproduction of labour

production and reproduction.[13]

The second historical difference encountered in the reappraisal of a surplus approach is the role of unions, now part of an institutionalized apparatus for wage bargaining and the political representation of the working classes. Last but not least is the changing structure of the family, which can no longer be expected to paper over the gap between production and reproduction. But historical changes can be dealt with more readily within a classical framework which from the start takes historical processes as the basis for determination of relative prices, than in the ahistorical neoclassical framework.

In addition to the difficulties arising from the changed historical context, there are some difficulties at an analytical level. For instance the distinction between the part of wages regarded as productive consumption and the part which can be reckoned as surplus, is not worked out.[14] The distinction cannot be traced in the composition of commodities or services; it must be defined in terms of sedimented living standards and their persistence, and in terms of social norms and power relationships. It should be noted, though, that all consumption by the labouring population, however defined, is subtracted from profits which are treated as a residuum. The definition of the labouring population, moreover, is not a clear-cut one, though it is crucial for the analysis of the labour market because it defines its scope and depth. More troublesome is the fact that the modern reappraisal of the surplus approach is based on an input–output commodity model where the relationship between labour processes is not immediately evident and only the wage commodities component of the standard of living is taken into account. That problem can be set aside for the moment, as in this context I am only speculating on the inverse wage–profit relationship, which is fully endorsed by the modern surplus approach.

In spite of the difficulties with some definitions, I think that an approach to the labour market focussed on the perspective of the social reproduction of labour, and based on the definition of wages as costs of social reproduction exogenous to other relative prices, can be very fruitful. This definite analytical stand is what makes my approach different from those of other streams of economic thought which openly criticize neoclassical economics – for example the institutionalists – or which attempt to deal with the reproduction of labour – such as home economics and the human capital approaches.

The institutionalist approach was partly based on the historical works of the Webbs on unions, unemployment, casual labour and state institutions.[15] The institutionalists of the forties questioned the contradictions between theory and facts that were particularly evident in the analysis of the labour market (Dunlop, 1944; Lester, 1946; Ross, 1948). Economists found it increasingly difficult to overcome the disparity between the real complexities of capitalist labour markets and the mechanical adjustments assumed by the theory (McNulty, 1980, p. 159). The core of the problem, as in the wages fund debate, was the analytical determinacy of wages (pp. 110–17) and the role of trade unions in the economic system. Although the old institutionalist economists stressed the special and central role of the labour market, the historical determination of wages and the impact of unions and collective wage bargaining, they did not challenge the general theory of wages and prices. On the whole, they finally accepted Hicks's 'Theory of wages' which, after the institutionalist attack, reassessed the assumption that the price of labour was only a special case of the supply-and-demand determination of relative prices (p. 178). Persistent and general contradictions of the labour market continued to be seen as exceptions and as rigidities of the competitive adjustment mechanisms of the labour market.

Today the new stream of institutionalist economics offers interesting hints for a critical approach to main-stream neoclassical economics. But one does not explicitly challenge the theory of supply-and-demand prices and the basic neoclassical theory of distribution merely by giving attention to institutions, social norms and habits. Moreover, some of the attention formerly focussed on the labour market has been diverted towards other institutions such as firms and commodity and money markets.[16] In my view the classical approach, based on a normal exogenous determination of wages as costs of social reproduction, enables us to benefit from the richness of the institutionalists' research without having to confine historical evidence within a generally ahistorical analytical framework. What I am saying in fact is that wages are exogenous as a general rule, not merely rigid within a context of theoretical flexibility. This difference concerns not only the fluidity of the adjustment mechanisms but the specification of the normal structure: i.e. what the analysis has to say about the very nature of the social system and of value.

The evolutionary form of the institutionalist analysis, which takes into account changes in the parameters induced by the system's dynamics, must also come to terms with the specificity of labour.[17] It would be wasteful merely to change the models without acknowledging once again the difficulty of specifying any endogenous systematic relationship with regard to population and standards of living.

One analytical perspective that focusses directly on the problems of the reproduction of labour is the human capital approach. This approach admits that the reproduction of labour includes exchanges of intellectual energy (Becker, 1965, 1981), but it does not derive any major analytical consequence from this peculiarity. In the human capital approach, the use of time and income for investing in education is seen purely as an allocative problem of maximizing at the margin, analogous to that confronted by the firm. As in the case of home economics, education is considered a commodity just like all the others, and the theory remains unchallenged. The same holds for the considerable literature on fertility (Schultz, 1974, 1981).[18] The extension of the supply-and-demand framework to non-market services is thus only a sign of monotony rather than of scientific rigour. A rigorous enquiry must take full account of the specific nature of the problems under scrutiny. What the neoclassical approaches aim to do is to assume an endogenous process of reproduction which adapts systematically to changes in relative prices.

The problems of social reproduction are also taken directly into consideration in the Basic Needs approach used as a policy base in developing countries (ILO, 1977). Without entering into this area of debate, it is perhaps worth noting that a general analytical framework in which the historical processes of social reproduction of the labouring population are seen as the basis for the structuring of waged labour markets could be very helpful in dealing with the complexities of different social systems. A specific examination of the basic structure of the capitalist labour market and its inherent relationship between production and reproduction might well be crucial for economic systems which are moving rapidly towards an international waged labour market and going through a radical process of increasing insecurity of access to the means of subsistence.

Moreover, a direct focus on the social reproduction of labour could also throw light on some of the problems related to the role of emerging states in the countries of the southern hemisphere. The following passage quoted from a talk given by the Director of ILO, shows that some of the problems facing the countries of the North are familiar to the South as well:

It cannot be denied that as the standards of living improve, and social security expands, people's expectations are becoming increasingly ambitious. The introduction of comprehensive, diversified and relatively generous benefits is paving the way for the emergence of new needs and a generalised desire among the population to obtain even more . . . Moreover all kinds of social–occupational categories are demanding to be placed on equal footing, which in effect means levelling up all benefits to the higher prevailing rates. Thus, like a mirage, the objective recedes as soon as it appears to be within reach. (ILO, 1984, p. vii)

Needless to say, the problem is not the generosity of benefits but the nature of state mediation between the process of reproduction of labour –

The supply of labour

exposed to a revolution of rising expectations – and the still-developing process of commodity production. The concept of the normal price of labour as historically determined could allow us on the one hand to expand the analysis of the process of social reproduction beyond the limited case of subsistence – understood merely as minimum wage rigidity, and on the other hand to remove the analysis of poverty from the supply-and-demand framework, heavily based on the notion of persistent scarcity of resources and surplus population. Thus we can escape the trap of considering as a specific problem of poor countries something which is a general and basic characteristic of the capitalist system.[19]

6.6 A starting point

The social-reproduction perspective opens new avenues for criticism of the capitalist system. To assess its possibilities it is worth recapitulating the main points made by Smith, Ricardo and Malthus with regard to the relationship between production and reproduction. The analytical differences between these authors reflect corresponding differences in their views of the economic system. Surplus, from the Physiocrats on, has been defined as the difference between production and the costs necessary for production: mainly labourers' subsistence. The *Tableau Economique* shows how the surplus is determined in the (agricultural) production process, and brings out the institutionally exogenous nature of the distribution of income and the circular relation between production, distribution and exchange. But the *Tableau* does not distinguish between profits and wages, and in an industrial capitalist system the relation between profits and the subsistence of waged workers and their families is the central and crucial issue for the development of the system.

For Smith (at least in his price theory) that relation was not necessarily conflictual, because his idea of growth was such that increased labour productivity made it possible to keep the relation between production of commodities and reproduction of labour within the limits compatible with capital accumulation. Thus the system can expand indefinitely because it contains a possible solution of the problem of subsistence of the labouring population which satisfies both capitalists and labourers through the expansion of internal and external markets. This is why Smith considered that wages as subsistence did not conflict radically with wages as costs.

Ricardo's view differs because a central element in it is the scarcity of land, a non-producible natural factor; this introduces a basically pessimistic view of the system's possibilities for continuous growth. In that context Ricardo's main concern is on the one hand to transform all consumption into productive consumption, and on the other to bring out clearly the potential conflict between profits and wages, and between

133

profits and rent, so that economic policy could delay the advent of a stationary state.

Ricardo's proposed economic policy pursues the first objective through reduction of rent (and hence non-productive consumption on the part of landowners), and cutting Poor Law public assistance (and hence non-productive consumption by the labouring population). Ricardo sought to provide the analytical clarity necessary to support these measures, by means of a price theory demonstrating that distribution is a zero-sum game within a given product, and that profits and wages are thus mutually complementary for a given unit of product.

Once the historically given possibilities of formation of surplus are maximized, according to Ricardo's scheme there should be no general problems in its realization. Ricardo's attention thus concentrates on wages as costs of production, while still keeping subsistence as a central datum in his theory of relative prices. Pressure on profits, in his view, comes from the awareness that the process of reproduction of labour, unlike that of other means of production, is not directly controllable by the capitalists. Labour is a producible commodity, and thus not a persistently scarce one like land; but it is not producible by the capitalists. This does not mean that the process of reproduction of labour is external to the economic system, but only that the exogeneity of wages is assumed in the determination of relative prices.

Malthus substantially modified the picture of the relation between production and reproduction. While on the one hand he gave plenty of attention to the process of reproduction – in fact, he devoted much of his analysis to the formulation of a specific theory of reproduction – on the other hand he considered subsistence, and hence the process of reproduction, as endogenous to the process of allocation. The problematic nature of the relation between production and reproduction – which in Ricardo's view would lead to a stationary state – was resolved by Malthus, at least analytically, through his supply-and-demand theory of wages. Supply and demand are seen in terms of allocation of persistently scarce resources. Thus the waged labour market, as an analytical concept and as a view of the world, is no longer considered capable of guaranteeing access to the means of subsistence for the population at a level which is appropriate to historical living standards, and the process of social reproduction of labour has to adapt to the needs of capital accumulation.

From this point on, the problem becomes one of demarcating the surplus population and/or of providing for a continuous downward flexibility of wages. Compatibility between profit and reproduction is guaranteed by the allocation of given quantities of population and capital.

All the workers can do is adjust the number of their children, and/or their living standards, to the apparently objective and impersonal forces of supply and demand. From this point of view Malthus and the wages fund theorists were the forerunners of modern economists.

As the wages fund was taken as given and standards of living of the labouring population were said to be contained through the scarcity of natural resources, Malthus saw the unproductive consumption of landowners as a solution to the structural problem of insufficient effective demand. Thus he considers wages both as costs and as subsistence (flexible in response to supply-and-demand variations) and dismisses their effects on the dynamics of aggregate demand.[20]

While in reality it is certainly true that in a capitalist system workers' living conditions depend on the conditions of accumulation, it is not true that this happens impersonally through the interaction of price–quantity relationships. In fact the adjustment is determined through power balances, social norms, habits and institutions. The labour market provides the information necessary for the allocation of labour, but its structure and adjustment mechanisms are necessarily institutional. The following example of a clearing market may help to clarify what I mean. Here we see one way in which the market is cleared when an oversupply of slaves is signalled:

It not infrequently happens that the market is either overstocked with human beings, or no buyers are to be found; in which case the maintenance of the unhappy slave devolves solely on the government. The expense incurred by this means is oftentimes murmured against by the king, who shortly afterwards causes an examination to be made, when the sickly, as well as the old and infirm, are carefully selected, and chained by themselves in one of the factories (five of which, containing upwards of one thousand slaves of both sexes, were at Badagry during my residence there); and next day the majority of these poor wretches are pinioned and conveyed to the banks of the river, where having arrived, a weight of some sort is appended to their necks, and being rowed in canoes to the middle of the stream, they are flung into the water and left to perish, by the pitiless Badagrians. Slaves, who for other reasons are rejected by the merchants, undergo the same punishment, or are forced to endure more lively torture at the sacrifices, by which means hundreds of human beings are annually destroyed. (Lander, 1835, p. 251)

An analysis that looks below the surface of the labour market reveals the profound institutional relations between the price of labour and social reproduction, and between the price of labour and profit. In this connection the concept of wages as a normal price reflecting the social cost of reproduction is of the greatest analytical value for grasping the labour market as an historical institution.

After Ricardo's death the wage fund theorists contributed to the triumph of the Malthusian theories. They not only adopted the theory of population and rent, as Ricardo did, but also confused the market price of labour with its natural price. For economic policy, and in particular for the Poor Law of 1834, there remained the problem of managing the difficult relation between production and reproduction by limiting the access of the poor to the means of subsistence and insisting on the objective necessity of downward flexibility of wages.

While the analysis removed the question of the problematic relation between accumulation and reproduction, policies had to deal with growing and persistent problems which led the state to make radical changes at the beginning of the twentieth century. The problems appeared at various levels. First of all, it became increasingly difficult to explain the exclusion from access to waged labour of the so-called 'involuntary unemployed', who were often skilled adult males. In the second place, the persistent poverty of women, due to their unwaged work of reproduction, became a source of increasing embarrassment. Lastly, market wages were so low as to induce cumulative processes of destitution and could no longer guarantee adequate conditions of reproduction to provide the workers and soldiers required by the Nation.

These facts were not only difficult to justify at the social level (partly because of the growing political representation of workers); they were also a source of increasing costs for the state because the residual population did not quietly disappear but put pressure at various levels on the public administration. In 1905 the appointment of the Royal Committee for the reform of the Poor Laws was prompted by just these economic and political difficulties.

The problem of the market's incapacity to absorb the 'involuntary' unemployed has been and still is the theme of continual debates among economists; but on the subject of women's reproductive work (the real adjustment mechanism between reproduction and accumulation) and their consequent massive exclusion from independent access to the means of subsistence, economists have always maintained a discreet silence. This is why I find it necessary to call attention to this opaque area, disdained by the economic profession.[21]

6.7 A critical perspective

In this book I have used the analytical perspective of the surplus approach to bring out certain contradictions in the production–reproduction relationship, and to analyse two basic adjustment mechanisms of the economic system: (a) the state, and (b) housework.

The supply of labour

In both cases we have seen that it is not enough to add the process of social reproduction of labour to the economic analysis: it is necessary to define the particular relationship that links production and reproduction. The two cases studied illustrate those links as they operate in the waged labour market.

I have used the theory of profit as surplus to provide an analytical framework in which the question of the relation between production and reproduction can be restored to its place among the foundations of political economy. Now the moment has come to assess the limits of the classical theory – a critique which is possible because the concept of the natural price of labour enables us to begin from a broader perspective than that offered by a merely allocative analysis of the labour market.

First of all we should note that classical political economy is vitiated from the start by reductivism. The social thought of the seventeenth and eighteenth centuries focussed on a wide range of basic human needs that motivate individual and collective activity: survival, security, reproduction of the species, growth, beauty ('delicacy of mind'), communication, self-affirmation and sympathy for others. Within this context the problem of social theorists was to explain – or to hide – the fact that they were thinking only in terms of the propertied classes. For instance, the idea of 'delicacy of mind' did not apply to the labouring population: as Mandeville says, 'To make the Society happy . . . it is requisite that great numbers of them should be ignorant as well as Poor' (Mandeville, 1970, p. 294).

In an economic system where access to the means of reproduction was guaranteed by access to land and the aim was to provide luxurious levels of consumption for the propertied classes, the social problem was to limit consumption by the labouring poor and to keep them subservient. In the capitalist system, where subsistence is guaranteed by access to money and the aim is accumulation, the problem is to contain the costs of reproduction of the labouring population for the sake of profit. In this context the focus of social enquiry shifts from human needs and moral sentiments to costs, surplus and markets. The classical economists, except for Marx, restricted human needs to those compatible with accumulation and the functioning of the waged labour market.

Adam Smith transformed exchange from a means for satisfying needs to an instinctive need in itself. In his *Lectures on Jurisprudence* the division of labour was said to be motivated by the natural insatiability of men's needs and by their delicacy of mind. In the draft of the *Wealth of Nations* it appears as the expression of an instinct to exchange:

This division of labour from which so many advantages result, is originally the effect of no human wisdom which foresees and intends that general opulence to which it gives occasion. It is the necessary, tho' very slow and gradual consequence, of a certain principle or propensity in human nature, which has in view no such extensive utility. This is a propensity, common to all men and to be found in no other race of animals, a propensity to truck, barter and exchange one thing for another. That this propensity is common to all men is sufficiently obvious. And it is equally so that it is to be found in no other race of animals, which seems to be acquainted neither with this nor with any other Species of Contract. (A. Smith, 1978b (*c*. 1763), pp. 570-1)

This is a mystification, as is very clear in the case of the labour market. The obvious fact is that workers need wages for subsistence, growth and communication – not because they feel an instinctive need for this form of exchange. The mystification of the labour market as part of the sphere of instinct and natural liberties is reflected in other aspects of the picture of the social system.

Smith's idea that mercantile exchange is one of the inborn elements of human nature and that all men have equal access to exchange, hides the historical determination of the labour market. Exchanging goods is not the same as exchanging commodities, and exchanging commodities is not the same as exchanging labour. In the case of labour, the market implies an exchange of bodies, emotions and intelligence.

The social relations determined by the functioning of the waged labour market are regulated, in their general form, by competition among workers. Social relations between different people tend to be structured on the basis of the market exchange of labour, which has the form of an interchangeable commodity and is treated and used as such. This inevitably leads to a levelling of differences; it works against the affirmation of personal individuality and against solidarity based on the common humanity of different people. Everyone would sympathize with the hunger of an immigrant worker if he/she did not constitute a threat to the prevailing structure of access to the means of subsistence. Given the fear induced by the basic insecurity of the labour market, workers tend to erect barriers against 'outsiders' in order to protect their 'privileged' position in relation to wages and the state.

This is particularly important in a world where an international labour market is being built up, rapidly bringing different races, societies and cultures into contact all over the globe, with physical and cultural differences often being used as lines of demarcation between sections of the population. While with respect to the right of subsistence demarcations are ostensibly based on physical differences, in fact they reflect less visible differences in power relationships with the labour market and the state. Hostility to those who are different is based on insecurity and the fear of being cut off from access to the means of subsistence – which are made scarce not by nature but by the structure of social power.

The issues become clearer when they are defined in terms of the relation between production and the reproduction of labour. This relation must be kept compatible with the formation and accumulation of profit. When the costs of reproduction of labour cannot be contained through reduced consumption, increased housework or lower value of wage goods, the system may use immigrant workers, whose living standards are historically lower and who have less power, to keep down the average costs of reproduction. This segmentation depresses everybody's wages, not only because of competition but because the living standards of the weakest groups dramatically emphasize the insecurity endemic in the system.

Competition on the labour market now operates on a global scale, as marked differences in standards of living and security of access to the means of reproduction create strong incentives towards mobility in the international labour market. 'Economic refugees' are an important structural feature of modern labour markets.

The rise of the market for commodities and labour has also led to a narrowing in the concept of liberty, which more and more tends to be seen in terms of freedom to buy and sell. Of course, the freedom to sell oneself on the labour market does constitute a form of liberty greater than that offered by feudal or familial modes of personal command over labour; but it is hardly the broadest imaginable perspective of liberty. Formal equality of access to the labour market is not sufficient to guarantee a substantial liberty based on secure access to the means of subsistence. Hidden behind the apparent liberty of exchange on the labour market is a profound insecurity in relation to the means of subsistence, which reflects a domination of accumulation over reproduction.

When the object of economic science is defined as the allocation of scarce resources, rational economic behaviour is defined solely in terms of the objectives of market allocation of goods and services. In this context the important information concerns quantities and prices, and other experienced forms of social rationality become invisible. They can be recognized only by specifying the more general objectives which underlie individual choices – for example the choices involved in reproduction and in relations between individuals and groups of different sex, culture, race, etc. In the allocative perspective the choices involved in the process of social reproduction of labour, though they are fundamental for the structure of the labour market, are either placed outside the purview of political economy or treated as market exchanges. The first solution leads to a distorted division of labour between social scientists, based not on a specialization of techniques but on a rigidly compartmentalized view of society. The second induces a particular form of reductivism, in which all social subjects and all institutions are treated as if they were simple buyers and sellers, or enterprises motivated solely by the objective of minimizing costs and maximizing profit.

The questions usually listed in Economics textbooks for first-year students are: what to produce, how much and at what price? Further questions should be added: who produces, for what purpose, for whose benefit, and in what institutional context? If the nature of the waged labour market is revealed by focussing first on the specific production–reproduction relation that characterizes it, these questions must and can be put directly and explicitly.

These are difficult questions which the classical economists tried to answer in different ways. For all of them, including Malthus, the producers were the workers, the aim of production was profit, and the surplus was distributed to the owners of the means of production (producible and non-producible). The institutional context was that of a free market based on private property, through which access to the means of subsistence was filtered. The structure of society involves forms of social cohesion which are not harmonious – because they are based on competition between capitalists and on class conflict. But society was seen as being held together by social consensus and social control, by institutions, and by individual behaviour expressing internalized social norms. This is the basis of the 'invisible hand', and it is a much broader and firmer basis than the idea of equilibrium prices.

Smith, Ricardo and Marx recognized that the wage was a central factor in production, circulation, distribution and – last but not least – the reproduction of the 'race' of labourers. Therefore all these aspects were kept together (though the arguments and relative weights differed) in the concept of the natural price of labour used by all three authors. It is a complex and problematic concept precisely because it reflects the basic contradictions of the system. Removing the concept does not remove the problems and contradictions, but merely eliminates the analytical tool that can deal with them directly. The difficulties re-emerge at other analytical levels as partial rather than general, as accidental rather than systematic phenomena.

To abolish the general concept of wages as costs of social reproduction means to deprive economic analysis of one of its foundations. First of all, because political economy is cut off from its original sources, which were rooted in studies of population, labour, poverty, needs, etc. Secondly, because it wrecks the analytical scheme which the classical economists used to analyse the market as a structure reflecting different levels with a certain scale of relative importance. And, lastly, because it obscures and mystifies a crucial aspect of reality: the contradiction between production and reproduction.

With the achievement of greater lucidity about the nature of the production–reproduction relation, it becomes harder to accept a definition of the economic system in terms of systematic relationships with quantities interacting on the basis of defined causal relations. A view of the system that takes in social reproduction and exogenous distribution between classes must necessarily be based on a system of rules as well as a system of causes.[22] The rules in fact serve to mediate the conflicts between objectives and between social subjects of unequal power.

To identify the specific relation between production and reproduction as one of the contradictory aspects of the capitalist system does not mean to claim that socialism offers a model of social organization capable of reversing that relation. No one, in these times, can be as naive as that.

While this is not the place to discuss the 'socialist' economies or the definition of socialism, a few observations should be made. The cold-war climate favoured polarization between free market and 'socialist' economies. Roughly this means: (a) private versus state ownership of the means of production, and (b) free market versus planning. The direction of the relationship between production and reproduction has been ignored on both sides. If attention were given to that question perhaps the differences between the two economic systems would appear less striking. Both are based on a waged labour market, where wages are the main costs of production and therefore need to be kept within limits compatible with the formation and accumulation of surplus. The great difference is that in the western countries insecurity of access to the means of reproduction is the ultimate tool of control over labour, while in the eastern countries the disciplinary tools have been low standards of living and severe political repression.

We have seen a general rejection, on the part of the populations of East European countries, of an economic development which aimed at state accumulation and support of the bureaucratic and military apparatus rather than at workers' consumption. In those countries, the lack of channels for expression of social conflicts contributed to the extreme rigidity of central planning. The lack of grass-roots democracy blocked any communication between the citizens and the state apparatus with regard to people's real needs. Given this lack of communication between the workers and those responsible for production, the western experience of the free market based on private property probably represents a more efficient and democratic system for the allocation of goods. Indeed, it is so precisely because it implies the possibility of building protest movements and channels for direct bargaining over wages and services.

An analysis that takes account specifically of the relation between production and reproduction may help to clarify the processes now unfolding in Eastern Europe. In the current process of restructuring in the 'socialist' countries not only is the market for goods and capital being liberalized, but the labour market is being reorganized into a form which is based not only on exploitation (an element common to private capitalism and state capitalism), but also on insecurity of wages and access to basic subsistence goods. This aspect is seen as an effect of scarcity of resources, but it is actually essential for the construction of a free market. The flexibility of production required by an open market requires a strong command over labour. This command has to be guaranteed either by forms of direct repression, which today are difficult to impose, or by an internalization of command which is attainable only through a general, though not homogeneous, social insecurity.

The overall costs of this process are difficult to foresee. What is not difficult to foresee, however, is that women will be presented with the task of absorbing, with their housework, the costs and conflicts inherent in the restructuring process. From this point of view, despite the great differences in the structure of their markets for labour, goods and services, private capitalism and state capitalism have always behaved in a similar way. In the 'socialist' countries women's load of housework has been generally maintained, despite higher levels of female employment and high levels of education (McCauley, 1981). The overall load of daily work (paid and unpaid) has been further increased by the scarcity of consumer goods and housing.

In the East European countries the people have massively demonstrated their rejection of the experiences of 'socialism', as a reaction to the prolonged repression and the mortification of their living conditions. After years of containment the contradiction between state accumulation and social reproduction has found public expression. The widespread aspiration for a greater quantity and variety of consumer goods has been translated, understandably, into unconditional support for the free market.

The freedom to buy is a reductive form of liberty, but it can certainly transmit more detailed information about the needs of those who have money to buy things, than 'socialist' planning was able to do. The problems of the free labour market will have to be faced when the social costs become more evident and those excluded from the feast begin to be counted.

These very problems, however, are today the object of direct attention in the western countries, where the issues of security, poverty, work times, standards of living and social norms are politically 'hot' ones and the structure of possible social alliances is open and dynamic. Women in particular are moving on a wide range of issues with many different initiatives. They are contesting the historical relation between men and women; far from accepting the status quo, they daily question the relation between waged work and housework; they campaign internationally for 'wages for housework'; they have more ways of controlling their bodies; from within and without they are challenging the almost exclusively male control of institutions; they have a powerful voice in the cultural and theoretical debate. In short, women are no longer invisible and can no longer be silenced. Their political visibility helps to make visible the political nature of the sector of reproduction.

The introduction of policies deregulating the labour market is today forcing the trade unions to face the problems of social security, distribution of social labour, guaranteed income for those excluded from the labour market, and standards of living (Deakin and Wilkinson, 1990). For example, these issues are involved in the negotiations on the Social Charter passed by the Member States of the European Community for 'integration of social policies'. But the trade-union platform on the social wage is not yet defined. The debate is still open, especially with regard to the question of guaranteed income and the order of importance of the different problems (Standing, 1986). Moreover, housework is not yet clearly included as social labour, and access to an independent income for housewives is not yet recognized as a right (Gorz, 1989). But one thing that emerges clearly from the trade-union debate is that the issue of security is being brought up in new ways, though these are not radically critical of the basic structure of the labour market and of the relation between waged and wageless sections of the labouring population.

The ecological movement, for its part, has posed at an international level the question of the relation between economic development and the natural environment. In the interest of defending the natural environment people have begun to criticize the nature of the capitalist economic system (Ekins, 1986). The conflict is seen mainly as one between economic growth and the environment as a natural system. In this context the living standards of the labouring population are classified as depending on production, and thus to be contained within the natural limits of growth. This approach forfeits the possibility of analysing some basic aspects of the capitalist mode of production, which precisely by ruling out a 'humanistic' relation between production and reproduction leads to accelerated exploitation of natural resources, of the human species as a whole and of its individual members – all used as instruments of production and reproduction. While some ecologists are aware of labour exploitation in production, they are generally uncritical with regard to the exploitation of women as means of reproduction (Illich, 1981, 1982).

Moreover, the typically capitalist conflict between the need to contain the market for wage goods within the limits of accumulation and the need to continually expand the size of the markets for produced goods, leads to massive waste. The responsibility for this waste belongs to those who own the means of production, organize its processes and appropriate the surplus – not to those who work for wages or those who work for the reproduction of the wage earner. If the aim of the system were the reproduction of persons rather than the accumulation of profit and the global extension of the market, the rush towards a devastating exploitation of the natural environment might be restrained by the pleasure of living in harmony with nature.

Lastly, in these times when we are faced with new forms of the arms race introduced by the Gulf war, we should remember that the right to 'subsistence', for all persons, populations and minorities, requires the abolition of war. The possibility of killing millions in order to defend the conditions of accumulation at international level is one more sign of the profound cynicism generated by the production–reproduction relation under capitalism.

Notes

Introduction

1   On the central role of the labour market in the development of the capitalist system and of classical political economy, see: Dobb, 1937, 1946; Marx, 1961 (1867).

2   The general scientific context is also changing: the methodological schemes of the natural sciences have been opened to the problem of time and the qualitative modifications of complex dynamic systems (Jacob, 1982; Prigogine and Stengers, 1984).

1. Wages as exogenous costs of social reproduction

1   On the relationship between the individual and collective subjects, Arendt (1958) introduces seminal ideas. For a recent contribution to the debate on the concept of class, Miliband, 1989.

2   This dualism between tradition and innovation was noted by McPherson (1980, p. 71) with regard to Burke's observations on Political Economy.

3   Recently there have been several attempts to link Smith's works on jurisprudence, ethics, rhetory and methodology, to the *Wealth of Nations* – see, among many: Christie, 1987; Hont and Ignatieff, 1983; Meek, 1976; A. Skinner, 1979; Wiles, 1968; Winch, 1978.

4   Basic sources on the establishment of the waged labour market are: Steuart, 1966 (1767); Eden, 1797; Marx, 1961 (1867).

   Eden's *State of the Poor* is a precious source on the structuring of the labouring population and of the labour market from the fifteenth century till the late eighteenth. The long study of this work has been particularly important in shaping my ideas on the nature of the capitalist labour market. For a recent reappraisal of the issue of primitive accumulation, Hobsbawm, 1980; Perelman, 1984.

5   In precapitalist forms of exploitation of labour the objective of production was the consumption of surplus, i.e. the luxurious reproduction of the ruling classes.

6   The labour market is a democratic institution if compared with forms of direct command over persons, as markets in general imply relatively democratic relationships (Hirschman, 1977, 1982; McPherson, 1973). Nonetheless, deep insecurity over the means of

reproduction and the general dependence on employers for subsistence are the basis for new forms of control over people which limit individual freedom.

7   In the eighteenth-century debate, Millar and Ferguson had already called attention to the risks involved in the loss of autonomy of the labouring population and to the combinations of the rich against the poor. On standards of living in the industrial revolution see Taylor, 1975 and Linder and Williamson, 1983.

8   In this paragraph I rely on Federici and Fortunati (1985) who draw a powerful connection between witch hunts and the rise of capitalism. Important references on witch hunts are: Mandrou, 1979; Trevor-Roper, 1984. On the role of men in witch hunts, Hester, 1990.

9   A basic source for the understanding of the profound changes that occurred with the establishment of the waged labour system, focussing on the changes that occurred in women's lives and in their degree of economic dependence, is the classic Pinchbeck (1930) from which the following quotation is taken:

> The industrial revolution, which was to establish a new order of things, introduced changes of vital importance to women. One industry after another was taken from the home by invention and the development of large scale industry; in the process the family wage disappeared, and agrarian and industrial changes combined to deprive women of their earning capacity in the home. (Pinchbeck, 1930, p. 4)

10 It is interesting to note that the differentiation used by Smith as the basis of his theory of prices is also used by him in his vision of the juridical system. Here too he is more interested in the foundations of the legal system, i.e. on the constitutional level, than in current lobbying (West, 1976).

11 On the relationship between the problem of justice and the analytical perspectives which framed the market economy Hirschman (1977, 1982) is illuminating. The debate on the different rankings of the right of property as civil right, and the right to subsistence as natural right, has a long tradition in Locke, Grotius and Pufendorf. With regard to these issues, within a political economy context, Burke is of some interest (McPherson, 1980); moreover, the work of Paley, *The Principles of Moral and Political Philosophy* (1785), focussing on the question of the right to subsistence, sets the scene of the early nineteenth-century debate on welfare (Horne, 1985).

12 On the issue of the role of the modes of subsistence in Smith and in the Scottish Enlightenment the works of Meek are seminal (Meek, 1967b, 1976). For a critical review of Meek see Q. Skinner, 1976.

13 The literature on the Ricardian model of the determination of wages

is vast. Relevant references can be found in Caravale, 1985. The controversy on the legacy of Ricardo is far from settled; see for instance Garegnani, 1982; S. Hollander, 1990; Peach, 1990.

14　A. Smith, 1976 (1776), p. 82; on the fundamental role of such a separation in the classical picture of the capitalist system see Dumont, 1977.

15　The strength and the persistency of the urge towards a continuous refinement of standards were recognized also by Hume and Millar (Gobetti, 1983), while the necessity of restraining the pressure towards higher standards of living of the labouring population was fully acknowledged by Mandeville.

16　On the relationship between the Scottish Enlightenment and natural history, Bryson, 1945, P.B. Wood, 1989.

17　Smith's idea of delicacy of mind as the basis for arts and growth in productive processes is well expressed by Frye in the following passage:

> Civilization is not merely an imitation of nature, but the process of making a total human form out of nature, and it is impelled by the force that we have just called desire. The desire for food and shelter is not content with roots and caves: it produces the human forms of nature that we call farming and architecture. Desire is not a simple response to needs, for an animal may need food without planting a garden to get it, nor is it a simple response to want, or desire for something in particular. It is neither limited to nor satisfied by objects, but it is the energy that leads human society to develop its own form. Desire in this sense is the social aspect of what we met on the literal level as emotion, an impulse towards expression which would have remained amorphous if the poem had not liberated it by providing the form of its expression. The form of desire, similarly is liberated and made apparent by civilization. The efficient cause of civilization is work, and poetry in its social aspect has the function of expressing, as a verbal hypothesis, a vision of the goal of work and the forms of desire. (Frye, 1957, pp. 105–6)

18　For a critique of Lewis's 'classical' model see Picchio Del Mercato (1975).

19　Smith cites numerous cases in which prices differ from natural prices, even for long periods, because of accidental events which are seen in general as exceptions limiting free competition, 'the action of which may however last for many consecutive years' (A. Smith, 1976 (1776), pp. 73–5). The same holds for Ricardo (1951a (1817), pp. 94–5).

20　Rowthorn seems unaware of this: he accuses Marx of confusion because he does not stick to one indicator and changes his opinion on the tendencies of wages and standards of living (Rowthorn, 1980, pp. 205–21). The essential point, however, is the difference between the exogenous historical processes which set the norm for standards of living, and endogenous changes of the market price for labour.

21 A definition of Ricardo's natural price of labour radically different from the one presented in this work is used by Rowthorn:

> We can summarise Ricardo's general theory of wages as follows. Wages are determined in the first instance by supply and demand in the labour market. (Rowthorn, 1980, p. 187)

22 The crucial problem of the control of population was the object of deep and widespread speculations of social theorists in the seventeenth and eighteenth centuries. Among the numerous eighteenth-century works: Wallace, 1753, 1761; Godwin, 1793; Malthus, 1976 (1798). For an interesting collection of materials on the population debate see: Société de Démographie Historique, 1980.

23 Mandeville, for instance, says:

> The Plenty and Cheapness of Provisions depends in a great measure on the Price and Value that is set upon this Labour, and consequently the Welfare of all Societies, even before they are tainted with Foreign Luxury, requires that it should be perform'd by such of their Members as in the first Place are sturdy and robust and never used to Ease or Idleness, and in the second, soon contented as to the necessaries of Life; . . .
>
> If such People there must be, as no great Nation can be happy without vast Numbers of them, would not a Wise Legislature cultivate the Breed of them with all imaginable Care, and provide against their Scarcity as he would prevent the Scarcity of Provision itself? (Mandeville, 1970, p. 293)

24 Malthus's population law plays a crucial role in the shift towards an analytical framework based on a supply-and-demand determination of wages, introduced into the Ricardian framework with the theory of the wages fund. We shall come back to this in the next chapter.

25 Ideas of nature have their own history which reflect the ideas of man in society (R. Williams, 1980, pp. 70–1). Hence even the concept of nature is inherently political.

26 These problems of aggregation have not been recognized in recent debates on the labour-supply function. On the one hand, S. Hollander (1979) has assumed a positively sloped supply schedule as part of his effort to introduce an endogenous theory of wages and of profit in Ricardo. Stigler (1981) criticizes Hollander, defining what he assumes to be the real Ricardian supply function, i.e. an infinitely elastic one. The writers who characterize the supply of labour as a function have to take into account not only the problem of finding the right parameters to shift the supply schedule or change its elasticity, but

also the fact that at any given wage there can be different quantities of labour supplied and different characteristics depending on changes in power relationships between sexes, classes and sections of the same class. The concept of parameters is linked to the concept of function which is alien to the Ricardian analytical framework.

27 The concept of a given supply is often interpreted in different ways. As we have seen, Ricardo defines the natural price of labour, in relation to the size of population, as the price which 'is necessary to enable the labourers, one with another, to persist and to perpetuate their race, without either increase or diminution' (Ricardo, 1951a (1817), p. 93).

In the 'Notes on Malthus', he says: 'By natural price I do not mean the usual price but such a price that is necessary to supply constantly a given demand' (Ricardo, 1966 (1820), p. 227).

Thus the natural price is defined by an exogenously given quantity of labouring population, and it is not persistently and systematically perturbed by supply and demand. The quantitative adjustment mechanism in the case of scarcity is around the given quantity historically defined by, and reflected in, the natural price of labour. This is in turn consistent with what happens in the case of standards of living and of natural prices in general which are not systematically affected by variations in quantities.

28 On the role of the state in Smith's analysis see Wilson and Skinner, 1976. On the role of the state in the history of political economy, see Deane, 1989.

29 Important references on the historical development of machinery are: Landes, 1969; Berg, 1980. Berg argues that the technological development of new machinery was the origin of classical political economy. The control of the labour process introduced with mechanical fixed capital and the greater insecurity inherent in the displacement of labour are indeed important factors in the structure of the labour market. Nonetheless, they developed after the establishment of agricultural capitalism, hence when the main characteristics of the capitalist labour market were already consolidated (Tribe, 1978, 1981). An interesting review of Berg is Claeys and Kerr, 1981.

30 O'Brien puts it very clearly, although in a different context:

The first thing to recognise is that while the Classical writers were the earliest to appreciate the allocative mechanism of the market and the power, subtlety, and efficiency of this mechanism, they were perfectly clear that it could only operate within a framework of restrictions. Such restrictions were partly legal and partly religious, moral, and conventional, and they were designed to ensure the coincidence of self and community interest. (O'Brien, 1975, p. 272)

31 Classical political economists at different times and with different roles were directly involved in preparing the ground of the 1834 Poor Law Act (Collini, Winch and Burrow, 1983; Blaug, 1963, 1964; Coats, 1971, 1972; Fetter, 1980; Himmelfarb, 1984; Mallet, 1921; Winch, 1978).

32 Some of the difficulties encountered in the definition of the natural price of labour are due to its complexity. This makes attention to the context in which it is used more important. The problem, in fact, is not to determine a quantity which solves a mathematical model, let alone to give a precise definition of the concept 'natural wage', but to use the history of the term to trace the historical complexities of the labour market.

With regard to the danger of vagueness Raymond Williams is reassuring:

> Some people when they see a word think that the best thing to do is to define it . . . But while it may be possible to do this, more or less satisfactorily, with certain simple names of things and effects, it is not only impossible but irrelevant in the case of more complicated ideas. What matters in them is not the proper meaning but the history of complexity of meanings: the conscious changes, or consciously different uses: and just as often those changes and differences which, masked by a nominal continuity, come to express radically different and often unnoticed changes in experience and history. (R. Williams, 1980, pp. 67–8)

2. The displacement effect of the wages fund theory

1 Smith's precise formulation reads: 'every species of animal multiplies in proportion to the means of their subsistence, and no species can ever multiply beyond it' (A. Smith, 1976 (1776), p. 97).

2 For a very stimulating approach relating Malthus's population theory to the debate on the public assistance of his times, see Halevy, 1972, pp. 204–48.

3 Marx and the Marxist tradition seem to have followed Ricardo on this path by considering the labour of reproduction of labour as productive only insofar as it has the result of producing wage goods rather than of transforming them into reproductive services in the family.

4 Marx's attribution to Bentham of the responsibility for the wages fund has left his modern translators unconvinced (Marx, 1969–72 (1861–63), translator's note, p. 674). In support of Marx, see Halevy,

1972, p. 222.

5 Once the exogeneity of wages was removed from the Ricardian framework, the theory of profit also became more confused (Bharadwaj, 1983a; De Vivo, 1984).

6 James Mill was well acquainted with Smith's social anthropological tradition, having attended John Millar's lectures on Smith in Edinburgh.

7 The significance of the wages fund theory did not last very long but this attitude, together with some other Malthusian scarcity-based views, proved very resistant. As Dobb remarks,

> It is at least significant of the bias of economists that when the wage level is in question it is the customary standards of the propertied class which are treated as the constant factor and working class standards of life as adaptable at the behests of a purely text-book 'equilibrium'. (Dobb, 1929, p. 516)

8 Taussig also commented on J. Mill's attempt to separate wages and capital: 'If this first step had been followed up, we might have had with James Mill, a new and important stage in the development of the theory of capital and wages' (Taussig, 1896, pp. 184–5).

9 This indirect link between wages and productivity was to have great impact on future developments.

10 On the history of the Irish Famine see Edwards and Williams, 1957.

11 Nor was Ricardo politically innocent: in parliamentary debates he was inclined to forget his analytical precision and follow his Political Economy Club colleagues, as can be seen from the following quotation:

> Gentlemen ought, however, to inculcate this truth on the minds of the working classes that the value of labour, like the value of the other things, depends on the relative proportion of supply and demand.
>
> If the supply of labour were greater than could be employed, then the people must be miserable. But the people had the remedy in their own hands. A little forethought, a little prudence (which probably they would exert, if they were not made such machines of by the Poor Laws), a little of that caution which the better educated felt necessary, would enable them to cure their situation. (Ricardo, 1952 (1816–18), p. 32)

12 Longe's critique was based on his acquaintance with employers' and workers' views, which he gained as a barrister in labour law cases and as a member of the Children's Employment Commission (J.H. Hollander, 1903). The question as to who contributed to Mill's refutation of the wages fund is not easily answered. Thornton published his articles in the *Fortnightly Review* after Longe's pamphlet, with a change in his own previous ideas about wages, but

never acknowledged that he had read it. Mill for his part never mentioned having received Longe's pamphlet, which had been sent to him (J.H. Hollander, 1903, pp. 3–5). On Longe and Thornton see Picchio, 1986b, 1986c.

13   Neither economist finds any improvement over the arithmetical ratio between capital and population (used by James Mill and McCulloch) in the more sophisticated concept of equilibrium wage expressed by J. S. Mill:

> Thus we see that the idea of a ratio between demand and supply is out of place, and has no concern in the matter: the proper mathematical analysis is that of an equation. Demand and supply, the quantity demanded and the quantity supplied, will be made equal. If unequal in any moment, competition equalises them, and the manner in which this is done is by an adjustment of the value. (J.S. Mill, 1965 (1848), p. 466)

14   Fawcett's argument shows that the adoption of the wages fund theory did not necessarily mean repressive and conservative labour policies. On his position see Becattini, 1984; Deane, 1984. On Mill's recantation and his political considerations, see Forget, 1990.

15   In the case of a social system the risks of reductionism do not lie only in the kind of biological model used, i.e. genetic or group evolution (Hodgson, 1991) – but in the use of the biological metaphor itself.

In this regard, what Jacob has to say is of great interest:

> Natural selection has no analogy with any aspect of human behavior. If one wanted to use a comparison, however, one would have to say that this process resembles not engineering but tinkering, *bricolage* we say in French. While the engineer's work relies on his having the raw materials and the tools that exactly fit his project, the tinkerer manages with odds and ends . . . In contrast with the engineer's tools, those of the tinkerer cannot be defined by a project . . .
> In some respects, the evolutionary derivation of living organisms resembles this mode of operation. In many instances, and without any well-defined long-term project, the tinkerer picks up an object which happens to be in his stock and gives it an unexpected function. (Jacob, 1982, p. 34)

16   I have deliberately not gone into Malthus's theory of population and his view of poverty. On this subject there is an ample literature (Dupaquier, 1983; James, 1979; Pullen, 1982). The object of my analysis is not the dynamics of quantities within a particular theory of reproduction but the structural relation between production and reproduction.

17   This continuity between Malthus and modern economics with regard to population is clearly pointed out by Perlman, 1981. A recent

version of a Malthusian endogenous theory of reproduction can be found in Becker, Murphy and Tamura, 1990.

3. The role of the state in the labour market, i.e. social insecurity

1   The following sections on the Poor Law are based on some general references on the history of the Poor Law and particularly on: Bruce, 1961, 1973; Fraser, 1973, 1976; Gilbert, 1976; Nicholls, 1898; M.E. Rose, 1972; Thane, 1978a, 1978b; Webb and Webb, 1963 (1927–9).

2   The conflict between the COS and the Webbs is clearly manifested in the following passage:

> The majority proposal of a Public Assistance Authority actually hid under a new label the old practices of the Poor Law, heavily dependent on private charities: 'The non-elected Public Assistance Committees are themselves to be virtually controlled by statutory "Voluntary Aid Committees," to be constituted on the lines of the Charity Organization Society, and to be eligible for grants from the Public Assistance Authority out of the rates. To these committees, we are told, applicants are to go in the first instance . . . the new Charity Organization Committee is to have the power of setting the standards of what the Poor Relief is to be.' (Webb and Webb, 1909, Part I, p. xvi)

On the political and personal aspects of the relationship between the Bosanquets and the Webbs, McBriar (1987) is illuminating.

3   It is interesting to read her words:

> At first sight it appears as if the long series of reports and proceedings of royal commissions and parliamentary or departmental committees, extending over a whole century, would afford to the social student a perfect mine of facts, about every conceivable subject of social investigation, almost dispensing with any other sources of information. Unfortunately this is not the case. (Webb and Webb, 1975 (1932), p. 142)

> It must also be remembered that these bodies are seldom designed for scientific research; they are primarily political organs with political objects . . . they are frequently set up as a safety valve, or as a channel for current agitations and counter agitations, so as to enable the Government, Parliament and public opinion to test the value of, and estimate the force behind, each of these agitations. (pp. 156–7)

4   In the 1909 Report the difficulty of a clear definition of able-bodied is recognized: 'The indoor paupers classed as able-bodied are practically those to whom the Medical Officer assigns a certain diet', and further on: 'What is an able-bodied pauper is still in doubt. We first of all exclude those who are sick but of the remnant, how many

are men who actually are able to do a day's work and earn their own living we do not know' (House of Commons, 1909, p. 211).

5   An interesting contribution on the ideology of work in the nineteenth century is McClelland, 1987.

6   It is interesting to note the acknowledgement of a difference in the behaviour of men and women.

> This difference between the methods adopted for the relief of men and women is found at all ages. Widows with children are mostly given outdoor relief, and in the case of older persons left alone, a woman can more often manage for herself, and is given outdoor relief, where a man could not, and is consequently drawn into the Poor Law institution. Moreover, in the case of younger persons there is often greater danger of encouraging idleness in giving outdoor relief to men than to women. And in the case of incapacitating sickness a man is more likely to seek infirmary treatment than his wife would be. (House of Commons, 1909, p. 19)

7   On the Chartist Movement see Edsall, 1971; Hunt, 1981, pp. 215–18, Ward, 1973.

8   The development of separate Poor Law infirmaries, has, probably, rendered the receipt of indoor medical treatment less distasteful, and many who would not previously have accepted such treatment now take advantage of new institutions. (House of Commons, 1909, p. 44)

> For some references on the history of health see: Abel Smith, 1964; Gilbert, 1965; Navarro and Berman, 1983.

9   It is interesting to note that concern for health standards was particularly alert in times of war, showing that the State sometimes worries more about the physical and psychological capability to kill – and to be killed – than to live.

10   The price index (base 1885) was respectively: 112 in 1834 and 91 in 1909 (Mitchell and Deane, 1962, pp. 471, 473).

> Sidney Webb in his 'Address to the Royal Economic Society' in 1909, gives the figure of 70 million for public expenditure in goods and services. For more information on the growth of goods and services over Public Expenditure and of Public Expenditure over the National Product, see Peacock and Wiseman (1961), chapters 5–6.

11   What the Poor Law Authorities are doing for the infants, the children, the sick, the mentally defective, the aged and the infirm, and the unemployed able-bodied man or woman respectively, already forms (or is on the point of forming) only a fractional part of the public provision made from the rates and taxes for each of those very classes; and a part that cannot be marked off from the rest by any significant characteristic – not even by the 1834 attribute of 'being in a state of destitution'. (Webb and Webb, 1909, Part I, p. xv)

12   In this context, it is interesting to cite an episode referred to in the introduction to the Webbs' *History of the Poor Laws*:

> When Keynes came up to greet Mrs. Webb . . . she said: 'Ah, Mr. Keynes, we are awaiting with great interest your economic theory to cure unemployment.' To which Keynes replied, 'Oh, it is all in the Minority Report, Mrs. Webb.' (Webb and Webb, 1963 (1927–9), p. xii)

4. Women and the Poor Law

1   On the radical changes which occurred in the second half of the nineteenth century in the structure of the capitalist system, in Britain and elsewhere, see Hobsbawm, 1975. This book is also important for the attention given to the social processes which contributed to the establishment of bourgeois ideas and norms of behaviour.
   An interesting review of Hobsbawm can be found in Stedman Jones, 1977.
2   To the occupied women we must add women occupied for money in other activities such as renting rooms, family shops, washing, prostitution, etc. The addition of these other traditional female sources of income would increase activity rates but also stress the point that the work of reproduction is a major element in women's paid work.
3   On women's subordinate position in production due to their role in reproduction before the separation between household and work place, Berg, 1987.
4   On the specific problem of birth control, Maclaren, 1978; on women's sexuality, Fee, 1973; on legislation, Kenrick, 1981, pp. 178–81; O'Donovan, 1979, and on body politics in general, Jacobus, Keller and Shuttleworth, 1990.
5   The institutionalization did not lead to a substitution between women's housework and state services as Zaretsky (1982) seems to suggest.
6   The woman question was generally unmentioned by the 1834 policy-makers.

> Clearly women provided some of the more intractable problems in the poor law administration. However, the male authors of both the Royal Commission's Report of 1834 and the ensuing Poor Law Amendment Act had remarkably little to say about the female half of the population. The rules and regulations of the central poor law authority had therefore to fill the gaps left by legal enactment, because, in practice, male guardians found that considerable numbers of paupers were women. (Digby, 1978, p. 150)

7 The Bill was amended in 1910 in the Battered Wives Bill.
8 On the question of how and when the wage bargaining shifted from customary norms to the market 'rules of the game', based on productivity, Hobsbawm, 1964, pp. 345–63.
9 On Beatrice Webb and her relationship with the women's movement, Caine, 1982

5. Women's work at the core of the labour market

1 The activity rates are defined as the percentage of women in the labour market (employed and unemployed) compared to the total population of working age.
2 The similarity is noticed by Hakim, 1981.
3 In the seventies there was an intense debate on housework which originated in the militant feminist context (Dalla Costa and James, 1972; Federici, 1976), and then moved to a more orthodox Marxist and academic one (Molineaux, 1979; Himmelweit and Mohun, 1977; Folbre, 1982). A collection of readings on the housework debate can be found in Malos (1982), with special attention to Federici.

While the political discussion was conducted within – and against – the Wages for Housework Campaign, the academic debate was mainly focussed on the application to housework of a Marxian theory of exploitation and of labour-value. It soon became a formal debate interested more in the quantitative than in the innovative aspects of a political feminist perspective.

4 On the issue of well-posed questions within scientific communities, see Jardine, 1986, pp. 120–33.
5 The data were collected on the basis of a research financed in 1925 by the Federal Government. Women were asked to work out time budgets on the basis of guidelines provided by the US Bureau of Home Economics. The same methodology was followed in the studies of the thirties, forties, fifties and sixties (Vaneck, 1980, pp. 82–3).
6 Child care is not included among the duties and hence the figures represent only a part of the total housework.
7 In the study by Gershuny and Jones the comparisons between men and women are made on the basis of: (a) formal work, i.e. paid work including work at home, second job training and travel to and from work; (b) domestic work, which includes cooking and washing up, housework, odd jobs, gardening, shopping, child care and domestic travel; (c) personal care, including dressing, personal services, meals and snacks, sleep and rest (Gershuny and Jones, 1986, pp. 17–18).

8   Sen distinguishes between negative liberties – in relation to the
     impediments to freedom of action – and positive liberties reflecting
     the basic conditions of security. He defines the standard of living not
     only in terms of goods and services but also in terms of entitlements,
     that is to say the possibility of making full use of one's own life
     (Sen, 1987). From this point of view his framework might be useful
     for partially interpreting women's relation with housework and waged
     work.

6. The supply of labour as a process of social reproduction

1   Atkinson continues by quoting Smith:

     By necessities I understand not only the commodities which are
     indispensably necessary for the support of life, but whatever the custom of
     the country renders it indecent for creditable people, even of the lowest
     order, to be without. (A. Smith, 1976 (1776), pp. 869–70)

2   In the seventies there was an intense debate on the question of social
     needs: see, among others, Fitzgerald (1977). For a recent reappraisal,
     see Doyal and Gough (1986).
3   The conflict between houseworkers and employers became apparent,
     for instance, during the 1984–5 Miners' Strike when the organization
     of the Miners' Wives held pickets and campaigned all over Europe
     not only in solidarity with their husbands' struggle but also directly
     on women's issues.
4   The distribution of income inherent in the process of reproduction is
     not a clear-cut one, since social services can be paid out of taxes
     both on property and on wages. If taxes on wages were then
     compensated by higher wages, in a pure Ricardian fiscal model, it
     would not make much difference to profits since in both cases they
     would decrease.
5   The history of the Poor Laws and the Welfare State hides a long
     story of struggles of the wageless. Some records can be found in:
     Fox Piven and Cloward, 1971, 1977; H. Rose, 1978; M. E. Rose,
     1970.
6   The women's movement has questioned union practices in relation to
     women; some valuable sources for grasping the real issues are:
     Campbell, 1984; James, 1975a; Land, 1978.
7   It must be remembered that in modern states the unions also play the
     role of legitimizing social policies by taking part in their formulation,
     and by disciplining their membership (Panitch, 1976).
8   Dobb's art as an historian is evident in his later works, *Political*

Economy and Capitalism (1937) and *Studies in the Development of Capitalism* (1946). On Dobb's historical works see Brenner, 1978 and Kowalik, 1978.

9   Dobb cites Sraffa with regard to the effects on demand of a change in the utilization of a factor employed in great quantities, in particular:

> since commodities into the production of which a common special factor enters are frequently, to a certain extent, substitutes for one another . . . the modification in their price will not be without appreciable effects upon demand in the industry concerned. (Sraffa, 1926, p. 539)

10   Keynes's diplomatic assessment of the relevance of the critique is also quite interesting:

> Now I am not here concerned to defend the orthodox hypothesis against these attacks. To a large extent I sympathise with the attacks. I think there is a great deal in what the critics say. I believe that the best working theories of the future will own these assailants as their parents. All those, who want to improve economic theory and to make a contribution to it, ought to pay a great deal of attention to what Mr Dobb and Mr Rowe and others are saying.
> My present purpose is, to propose certain qualifications . . .
> For the High-Wage Party forget that we belong not to a closed system, moreover for which we have deliberately contrived a very high degree of mobility of international lending. (Keynes, 1930, pp. 114–15)

11   For some analogies between economic logic and physics, see Mirowsky, 1984, 1989.

12   It must be noted that there is a vast amount of literature on the possibility that wages differ from marginal productivity. However, the interpretation of this fact is put forward in terms of 'sticky wages', and its effects are analysed in terms of disequilibria. Thus although the fact is controversial the analytical implications are not.

    For some interesting examples of this literature, Akerlof and Yellen, 1986.

13   In any case, the issue of clearing labour markets entered the political economy debate later with the formalization of supply and demand (Mirowsky, 1990, p. 69).

14   Sraffa adopted the line of considering the whole of the wage as surplus and hence wage goods were no longer basic commodities (Sraffa, 1960, pp. 9–10).

15   With regard to the first institutionalists I largely rely on McNulty, 1980.

16   A very interesting institutionalist approach can be found in Hodgson, 1988.

17 For instance, Allen explicitly recognizes that changes in people's expectations and life-styles cannot be included in his model of economic evolution, as it is not easy 'to say when and in what way people may modify their values and adopt new goals' (Allen, 1988, p. 116).

18 Marxist economists, too, have paid attention to the question of human capital and its implications for the analysis of heterogeneous labour (Bowles and Gintis, 1975). Their approach is based on the problem of training skilled labour rather than on the household process of reproduction of the labouring population, which they usually help to conceal.

19 For a critical approach to the analysis of economic development based on the radical needs of survival and autonomy, see Doyal and Gough (1986, pp. 69–80).

20 Keynes followed Malthus against Ricardo in acknowledging the possibility of a general excess of production; but he used wages as the pivot of aggregate demand.

21 For the benefit of those who think economics is just a logical game or an aesthetic pursuit, and who declare their satisfaction with elegant formalisms, I maintain that this return to the origins of the subject can be very deeply satisfying to the aesthetic sense. Economists may discover that taste can be satisfied by many aesthetic schemes: for example, alongside the rationalism of a Mondrian we have the classic primitivism of a Henry Moore.

22 On this point see Q. Skinner, 1972.

References

Abel Smith, B., 1964. *The Hospitals, 1880–1948*, London, Heinemann

Abel Smith, B., and Townsend, P., 1965. *The Poor and the Poorest*, London, Bell and Sons

Akerlof, R. C., and Yellen, A. R., 1986. eds., *Efficiency Models of the Labour Market*, Cambridge, Cambridge University Press

Alexander, S., 1983. *Women's Work in Nineteenth Century London. A Study of the Years 1820–50*, London, The Journeyman Press

Alexander, S., and Davin, A., 1976. 'Feminist History', in *History Workshop*, No. 1, pp. 4–6

Allen, P., 1988. 'Evolution, Innovation and Economics', in G. Dosi *et al*, eds., *Technical Change and Economic Theory*, London, Pinter Publ.

Anderson, M., 1971. *Family Structure in Nineteenth Century Lancashire*, Cambridge University Press

1980. *Approaches to the History of the Western Family*, London, Macmillan

Arendt, H., 1958. *The Human Condition*, Chicago, Chicago University Press

Aries, P., 1962. *Centuries of Childhood. A Social History of Family Life*, New York, Vintage Books

Ashley, W. J., 1926. 'Wages Fund', in H. Higgs, ed., *Palgrave's Dictionary of Political Economy*, vol. III, London, Macmillan

Atkinson, A. B., 1969. *Poverty in Britain and the Reform of Social Security*, Cambridge, Cambridge University Press

1989. *Poverty and Social Security*, New York, Harvester Wheatsheaf

Bailward, W. A., 1912. 'Recent Developments of Poor Relief', in *Economic Journal*, vol. 22, pp. 542–53

Bain, A., 1882. *James Mill: a Biography*, London, Longman

Balbo, L., 1987. 'Crazy Quilts: Rethinking the Welfare State Debate from a Woman's Point of View', in Showstack Sassoon, ed., *Women and the State*, London, Hutchinson

Barton, J., 1817. *Condition of the Labouring Classes of Society*, reprint, Baltimore, Johns Hopkins University Press, 1934

Becattini, F., 1984. 'Henry Fawcett and the Labour Question', in L. Goldman, ed., *The Blind Victorian: Henry Fawcett and British Liberalism*, Cambridge, Cambridge University Press

References

Becker, G., 1960. 'An Economic Analysis of Fertility', in *Demographic and Economic Change in Developed Countries*, NBER, Princeton, Princeton University Press

    1965. 'A Theory of the Allocation of Time', in *Economic Journal*, vol. 70, pp. 493–517

    1981, *A Treatise on the Family*, Cambridge, Harvard University Press

    1987. 'Family', in J. Eatwell, M. Milgate and P. Newman, eds., *The New Palgrave Dictionary of Political Economy*, London, Macmillan

Becker, G., Murphy, K., and Tamura., R., 1990. 'Economic Growth', in *Journal of Political Economy*, vol. 98, pp. 513–37

Beechey, V., and Perkins, T., 1987. *Women, Part-Time Work and the Labour Market*, Cambridge, Polity Press

Benston, M., 1969. 'The Political Economy of Women's Liberation', in *Monthly Review*, vol. 21, pp. 13–27

Berg, M., 1980. *The Machinery Question and the Making of Political Economy 1815–1848*, Cambridge, Cambridge University Press

    1987. 'Women's Work, Mechanisation and the Early Phases of Industrialization in England', in P. Joyce, ed., *The Historical Meanings of Work*, Cambridge, Cambridge University Press

Bettio, F., 1988. *The Sexual Division of Labour: the Italian Case*, Oxford, Clarendon Press

Beveridge, W. H., 1909. *Unemployment: a Problem of Industry*, London, Longmans, Green and Co.

    1942. *Report on Social Insurance and Allied Services*, London, HMSO

    1943. 'Children's Allowances and the Race', in W.H. Beveridge, *The Pillars of Security*, London, Allen and Unwin

    1953. *Power and Influence*, London, Hodder and Stoughton

Bharadwaj, K., 1978a. *Classical Political Economy and the Rise to Dominance of Supply and Demand Theories*, Calcutta, Orient Longman

    1978b. 'The Subversion of Classical Analysis: Alfred Marshall's Early Writing on Value', in *Cambridge Journal of Economics*, vol. 2, pp. 253–72

    1978c. 'Maurice Dobb's Critique of Theories of Value and Distribution', in *Cambridge Journal of Economics*, vol. 2, pp. 153–74

    1983a. 'On a Controversy over Ricardo's Theory of Distribution', in *Cambridge Journal of Economics*, vol. 7, pp. 11–36

    1983b. 'Ricardian Theory and Ricardianism', in *Contributions to Political Economy*, vol. 2, pp. 49–77

References

1985. 'Sraffa's Return to Classical Theory: Change and Equilibrium', in *The Surplus Approach*, vol. 1, pp. 3–31

1986. 'Subsistence', in J. Eatwell, M. Milgate and P. Newman, eds., *The New Palgrave Dictionary of Political Economy*, London, Macmillan

1989. *Themes in Value and Distribution: Classical Theory Reappraised*, London, Unwin Hyman

Blaug, M., 1958. *Ricardian Economics*, Yale, Yale University Press

1963. 'The Myth of the Old Poor Law and the Making of the New', in *Journal of Economic History*, vol. 23, pp. 151–84

1964. 'The Poor Law Report Reexamined', in *Journal of Economic History*, vol. 24, pp. 229–45

Borchorst, A., and Siim, B., 1987. 'Women in the Advanced Welfare State – a New Kind of Patriarchal Power?', in Showstack Sassoon, ed., *Women and the State*, London, Hutchinson

Bowles, S., and Gintis, H., 1975. 'The Problem with Human Capital Theory, a Marxian Critique', in *American Economic Review*, vol. 65, pp. 74–82

Bowley, A., 1921. 'Earners and Dependants in English Towns', in *Economica*, vol. 1, pp. 101–12

Braidotti, R., 1991. *Patterns of Dissonance*, Cambridge, Polity Press

Braudel, F., 1974. *Capitalism and Material Life*, London, Fontana

Breines, W., Cerullo, M., and Stacey J., 1978. 'Social Biology, Family Studies, and Antifeminist Backlash', in *Feminist Studies*, vol. 4, pp. 43–67

Brenner, R., 1978. 'Dobb's Transition from Feudalism to Capitalism', in *Cambridge Journal of Economics*, vol. 2, pp. 121–40

Briggs, A., 1967. 'The Language of Class in Early Nineteenth Century England', in A. Briggs and J. Saville, eds., *Essays in Labour History*, London, Macmillan

1968. *Victorian Cities*, Harmondsworth, Penguin

Brocas, A. M., Cailloux, A. M., and Oget, V., 1990. *Women and Social Security*, Geneva, ILO

Brown, C., and Preece, A., 1986. 'Housework', in J. Eatwell, M. Milgate and P. Newman, eds., *The New Palgrave Dictionary of Political Economy*, London, Macmillan

Brown, K. D., 1971. *Labour and Unemployment 1900–1914*, Newton Abbot, David and Charles

Bruce, M., 1961. *The Coming of the Welfare State*, London, B. T. Batsford

1973. *The Rise of the Welfare State; English Social Policy 1601–1971*, London, Weidenfeld and Nicolson

References

Brydon, L., and Chant, S., 1989. *Women in the Third World: Gender Issues in Rural and Urban Areas*, Aldershot, Edward Elgar

Bryson, G., 1945. *Man and Society: the Scottish Inquiry of the Eighteenth Century*, Princeton, Princeton University Press

Burn, R., 1764. *The History of the Poor Laws, with Observations*, London, A. Millar

Burrow, J. W., 1970. *Evolution and Society: a Study in Victorian Social Theory*, Cambridge, Cambridge University Press

Butler, J. E., ed., 1869. *Woman's Work and Woman's Culture*, London, Macmillan

Cain, G., 1976. 'The Challenge of Segmented Labor Market Theories to Orthodox Theory: A Survey', in *Journal of Economic Literature*, vol. 14, pp. 1215–57

Caine, B., 1982. 'Beatrice Webb and the "Woman Question"', in *History Workshop*, vol. 14, pp. 23–43

Campbell, B., 1980. 'Feminist Sexual Politics', in *Feminist Review*, vol. 5, pp. 1–18

1984. *Wigan Pier Revisited. Poverty and Politics in the 80s*, London, Virago

Caravale, G. A., ed., 1985. *The Legacy of Ricardo*, Oxford, Oxford University Press

Carr, E. H., 1951. *The New Society*, London, Macmillan

Cartelier, L., 1982. 'The State and Wage Labour', in *Capital and Class*, vol. 18, pp. 39–54

Casarosa, C., 1978. 'A New Formulation of the Ricardian System', in *Oxford Economic Papers*, vol. 30, pp. 38–63

Chadwick, E., 1836. 'The New Poor Law', in *Edinburgh Review*, vol. 63, pp. 487–537

Checkland, S. G., 1949. 'The Propagation of Ricardian Economics', in *Economica*, vol. 16, pp. 40–52

Checkland, S. G., and Checkland, E. O. A., 1974. 'Introduction', in S.G. Checkland and E.O.A. Checkland, eds., *The Poor Law Report of 1834*, Harmondsworth, Penguin

Chodorow, N., 1978. *The Reproduction of Mothering*, Berkeley, University of California Press

Christie, J. R. R., 1987. 'Adam Smith's Methaphysics of Language', in A.E. Benjamin, G.N. Cantor and J.R.R. Christie, eds., *The Figural and the Literal*, Manchester, Manchester University Press

Claeys, G., and Kerr, P., 1981. 'Mechanical Political Economy (review of Maxime Berg, *The Machinery Question and the Making of Political Economy 1815–1848*)', in *Cambridge Journal of Economics*, vol. 5, pp. 251–72

References

Clapham, J. H., 1938. *An Economic History of Modern Britain: Machines and National Rivalries (1887–1914), with an Epilogue (1914–1929)*, Cambridge, Cambridge University Press

Coats, A. W., 1971. *The Classical Economists and Economic Policy*, London, Methuen and Co.

1972. 'The Classical Economists, Industrialization and Poverty', in *The Long Debate on Poverty*, IEA, Readings, No. 9, London, IEA

1976. 'The Relief of Poverty, Attitudes to Labour, and Economic Change in England, 1660–1782', in *International Review of Social History*, vol. 21, pp. 98–115

Cohen, S., and Schnelle, T., 1986. *Cognition and Fact, Materials on Ludwik Fleck*, Boston, D. Reidel Publ.

Coleman, D., and Schofield, R., 1986. *The State of Population Theory; Forward from Malthus*, Oxford, Basil Blackwell

Collini, S., Winch, D., and Burrow, J., 1983. *That Noble Science of Politics: A Study in Nineteenth Century Intellectual History*, Cambridge, Cambridge University Press

Connell, R. W., 1987. *Gender and Power: Society, the Person and Sexual Politics*, Cambridge, Polity Press

Coward, R., 1983. *Patriarchal Precedents*, London, Routledge and Kegan Paul

Cowherd, R. G., 1977. *Political Economists and the English Poor Laws, an Historical Study of the Influence of Classical Economics on the Formation of Social Welfare Policy*, Athens Ohio, Ohio University Press

Crouch, C., 1979. *State and Economy in Contemporary Capitalism*, London, Croom Helm

Crowther, M. A., 1982. 'Family Responsibility and State Responsibility in Britain before the Welfare State', in *Historical Journal*, vol. 25, pp. 131–45

Dalla Costa, M., 1983. *Famiglia, Welfare e Stato tra progressismo e New Deal*, Milan, Franco Angeli

Dalla Costa, M., and James, S., 1972. *The Power of Women and the Subversion of the Community*, Bristol, Falling Wall Press

Dardi, M., 1984. *Il giovane Marshall, accumulazione e mercato*, Bologna, Il Mulino

Davidoff, L., 1983. 'Class and Gender in Victorian England', in J. Newton, M. Ryan and J. Walkowitz, eds., *Sex and Class in Women's History*, London, Routledge and Kegan Paul

Davin, A., 1978. 'Imperialism and Motherhood', in *History Workshop 5*, pp. 9–65

164

References

1983. 'Feminism and Labour History', in Samuel, ed., *People's History and Socialist Theory*, History Workshop Series, London, Routledge and Kegan Paul

Deakin, S., and Wilkinson, F., 1990. *After Deregulation: Social and Economic Rights in the Labour Market*, Institute of Employment Rights, Mimeo

Deane, P., 1984. 'Henry Fawcett: the Plain Man's Political Economist', in L. Goldman, ed., *The Blind Victorian: Henry Fawcett and British Liberalism*, Cambridge, Cambridge University Press

1989. *The State and the Economic System. An Introduction to the History of Political Economy*, Oxford, Oxford University Press

Deane, P., and Cole, W. A., 1962. *British Economic Growth, 1688–1959: Trends and Structure*, Cambridge, Cambridge University Press

Deere, C. D., 1976. 'Rural Women's Subsistence Production in the Capitalist Periphery', in *Review of Radical Political Economy*, vol. 8, pp. 9–17

Defoe, D., 1704. *Giving Alm No Charity and Employing the Poor, a Grievance of the Nation*, London, Booksellers of London and Westminster

Del Re, A., ed., 1989. *Stato e rapporti sociali di sesso*, Milan, Franco Angeli

De Marchi, N., 1970. 'The Empirical Content and Longevity of Ricardian Economics', in *Economica*, vol. 37, pp. 257–76

1988. 'Introduction', in N. De Marchi, ed., *The Popperian Legacy in Economics*, Cambridge, Cambridge University Press

Department of Employment and Productivity, 1971. *British Labour Statistics. Historical Abstract, 1886–1968*, London, HMSO

De Vivo, G., 1984. 'Ricardo and His Critics. A Study of Classical Theories of Value and Distribution', in *Studi e Ricerche dell' Istituto Economico*, vol. 23, Modena

Dickinson, J., and Russell, B., eds., 1986. *Family, Economy and State*, London, Croom Helm

Digby, A., 1978. *Pauper Palaces*, London, Routledge and Kegan Paul

Dobb, M., 1928. *Wages*, London, Cambridge Economic Handbooks

1929. 'A Sceptical View on Wages', in *Economic Journal*, vol. 39, pp. 506–19

1937. *Political Economy and Capitalism. Some Essays in Economic Tradition*, London, Routledge and Kegan Paul

1944. 'Review of J. T. Dunlop's *Wage Determination under Trade Unions*', in *Economic Journal*, vol. 54, pp. 411–14

1946. *Studies in the Development of Capitalism*, London, Routledge and Sons

References

1973. *Theories of Value and Distribution since Adam Smith*, Cambridge, Cambridge University Press

Donini, E., 1990. *La nube e il limite, donne, scienza, percorsi nel tempo*, Turin, Rosenberg and Sellier

Donzelot, J., 1980. *The Policing of Families*, London, Hutchinson

Douglas, M., and Isherwood, B., 1979. *The World of Goods. Towards an Anthropology of Consumption*, London, Allen Lane

Doyal, L., and Gough, I., 1986. 'Human Need and Strategies for Social Change', in Ekins, ed., *The Living Economy*, London, Routledge and Kegan Paul

Dresher, S., 1986. *Capitalism and Antislavery*, London, Macmillan

Dubois, E., 1975. 'The Radicalism of the Women's Suffrage Movement: Toward the Reconstruction of the Nineteenth Century Feminism', *Feminist Studies*, vol. 3, pp. 63–71

Dudden, F. E., 1983. *Serving Women: Household Service in Nineteenth Century America*, Middletown, Connecticut, Wesleyan University Press

Dumont, L., 1977. *From Mandeville to Marx. The Genesis and Triumph of Economic Ideology*, Chicago, Chicago University Press

Dunlop, J., 1944. *Wage Determination under Trade Unions*, New York, Kelley, 1950

Dupaquier, J., 1983. *Malthus Past and Present*, London, Academic Press

Dyos, H., and Wolff, M., 1973. *The Victorian City*, London, Routledge and Kegan Paul

Eatwell, J., 1977. 'The Irrelevance of Returns to Scale in Sraffa's Analysis', in *Journal of Economic Literature*, vol. 15, pp. 61–8

1982. 'Competition', in I. Bradley and M. Howard, eds., *Classical and Marxian Political Economy*, London, Macmillan

1987. 'Natural and Normal Conditions', in J. Eatwell, M. Milgate and P. Newman, eds., *The New Palgrave Dictionary of Political Economy*, London, Macmillan

Eden, T. M., 1797. *The State of the Poor, or an History of the Labouring Classes in England from the Conquest to the Present Period in which are particularly considered their Domestic Economy with Respect to Diet, Dress, Fuel, and Habitation*, London, Davies; reprinted in London, Frank Cass, 1966

Edsall, N. C., 1971. *The Anti Poor Law Movement 1834–44*, Manchester, Manchester University Press

Edwards, R. D., and Williams, T. D., eds., 1957. *The Great Famine; Studies in Irish History*, Dublin, Brown and Holm

Ehrenreich, B., and English, D., 1979. *For Her Own Good: 150 Years of Experts' Advice to Women*, New York, Doubleday Anchor

166

References

Ekins, P., ed., 1986. *The Living Economy: a New Economics in the Making*, London, Routledge and Kegan Paul

Engels, F., 1958 (1892). *The Condition of the Working Class in England in 1844*, W.O. Henderson and W.H. Chaloner, eds., Oxford, Basil Blackwell

1972 (1884). *The Origin of the Family, Private Property and the State*, London, Lawrence and Wishart

Equal Opportunities Commission, 1987. *New Earnings Surveys; Women and Men in Britain, a Statistical Profile*, London, HMSO

EUROSTAT, 1989. *Employment and Unemployment*, Brussels, EEC

Fadiga Zanatta, A. L., 1988. 'Donne e lavoro', in ISTAT, Associazione Italiana di Sociologia, *Immagini della Societa' Italiana*, Rome, ISTAT

Federici, S., 1976. *Counterplanning from the Kitchen*, Bristol, Falling Wall Press

1982. 'Wages against Housework', in Malos, ed., *The Politics of Housework*, London, Allison and Busby

1984. 'La caccia alle streghe', in Federici and Fortunati, *Il grande Calibano*, Milan, Franco Angeli

Federici, S., and Fortunati, L., 1985. *Il grande Calibano*, Milan, Franco Angeli

Fee, E., 1973. 'The Sexual Politics of Victorian Social Anthropology', in *Feminist Studies*, vol. 1, pp. 23–39

Fenstermaker, S., ed., 1980. *Women and Household Labor*, Beverly Hills, Sage Publications

Fetter, F. W., 1980. *The Economists in Parliament*, Durham, Duke University Press

Finch, J., 1983. *Married to the Job: Wives' Incorporation in Men's Work*, London, Allen and Unwin

Finch, J., and Groves, D., eds., 1983. *A Labour of Love: Women Work and Caring*, London, Routledge

Fitzgerald, R., ed., 1977. *Human Needs and Politics*, Oxford, Pergamon

Fleck, L., 1979. *Genesis and Development of a Scientific Fact*, Chicago, University of Chicago Press

1986. 'On the Crisis of Reality', in Cohen and Schnelle, eds., *Cognition and Fact*, Boston, D. Reidel Publ.

Fleming, S., 1986. 'Spokeswoman for a Movement', in E. Rathbone, *The Disinherited Family*, Bristol, Falling Wall Press

Flew, A. G. N., 1957. 'The Structure of Malthus' Population Theory', in *Australasian Journal of Philosophy*, vol. 35, pp. 1–20

Folbre, N., 1982. 'Exploitation Comes Home: a Critique of the Marxian Theory of Family Labour', in *Cambridge Journal of Economics*, vol. 6, pp. 317–29

Forget, E., 1990. 'J. S. Mill and the Tory School', Paper presented at the History of Economic Thought Conference, Norwich

Foster, J., 1974. *Class Struggle and the Industrial Revolution*, London, Weidenfeld and Nicolson

Foucault, M., 1979. *The History of Sexuality*, vol. 1, London, Allen Lane

Fox Keller, E., 1985. *Reflections on Gender and Science*, New Haven, Yale University Press

Fox Piven, F., and Cloward, R. A., 1971. *Regulating the Poor*, New York, Pantheon

1977. *Poor People's Movements*, New York, Pantheon

Fraser, W. M., 1950. *The History of English Public Health, 1834–1909*, London, Macmillan

1973. *The Evolution of the British Welfare State*, London, Macmillan

1976. ed., *The New Poor Law in the Nineteenth Century*, London, William Claves

Freeden, M., 1986. *Liberalism Divided*, Oxford, Clarendon Press

Frye, N., 1957. *Anatomy of Criticism*, Princeton, Princeton University Press

Furniss, E. S., 1920. *The Position of the Laborer in a System of Nationalism. A Study in the Labor Theories of Late English Mercantilists*, Boston, Cambridge University Press

Fuz, J. K., 1952. *Welfare Economics in English Utopias*, The Hague, Martinus Nijhoff

Garegnani, P., 1976. 'On a Change in the Notion of Equilibrium in Recent Work on Value and Distribution', in M. Brown, K. Sato, and P. Zarembka, eds., *Essays in Modern Capital Theory*, Amsterdam, North Holland

1978–9. 'Notes on Consumption, Investment and Effective Demand, 1–2', in *Cambridge Journal of Economics*, vol. 2, pp. 335–53

1982. 'On Hollander's Interpretation of Ricardo's Early Theory of Profits', in *Cambridge Journal of Economics*, vol. 6, pp. 65–77

1983. 'The Classical Theory of Wages and the Role of Demand Schedules in the Determination of Relative Prices', in *American Economic Review*, vol. 73(2), pp. 309–13

1984. 'Value and Distribution in the Classical Economists and Marx', in *Oxford Economic Papers*, vol. 36, pp. 291–325

1987. 'The Quantity of Capital', in J. Eatwell, M. Milgate and P. Newman, eds., *The New Palgrave Dictionary of Political Economy*, London, Macmillan

References

Garside, W. R., 1980. *The Measurement of Unemployment in Great Britain, 1850–1979. Methods and Sources*, Oxford, Basil Blackwell

Gershuny, J., and Jones, S., 1986. *Time Use in Seven Countries*, Dublin, European Foundation for the Improvement of Living and Working Conditions

Giddens, A., 1980. *The Class Structure of Advanced Societies*, London, Hutchinson

  1985. *Nation-State and Violence*. Volume Two of *A Contemporary Critique of Historical Materialism*, Cambridge, Polity Press

Gilbert, B., 1965. 'Health and Politics: the British Physical Deterioration Report of 1904', in *Bulletin of the History of Medicine*, vol. 39, pp. 143–53

  1976. *The Evolution of National Insurance in Great Britain: the Origins of the Welfare State*, London, Michael Joseph

Gobetti, D., 1983. 'Sfera domestica e sfera politica nella riflessione del pensiero politico britannico del '700', in *Annali della Fondazione Einaudi*, vol. 18, pp. 291–331

Godelier, M., 1981. 'The Origin of Male Domination', in *New Left Review*, vol. 127, pp. 3–17

Godwin, W., 1793. *Enquiry Concerning Political Justice*, London

  1964 (1820). *Of Population. An Inquiry Concerning the Power of Increase in the Numbers of Mankind, Being an Answer to Mr Malthus's Essay on that Subject*, New York, Kelley

Goldschmidt-Clermont, L., 1982. 'Unpaid Work in the Household: a Review of Economic Evaluation Methods', in *Women, Work and Development Series*, Geneva, ILO

Goode, W., 1971. 'Force and Violence in the Family', in *Journal of Marriage and the Family*, vol. 33, pp. 624–36

Goody, J., 1976. *Production and Reproduction. A Comparative Study of the Domestic Domain*, Cambridge, Cambridge University Press

  1983. *The Development of Family and Marriage in Europe*, Cambridge, Cambridge University Press

Gorz, A., 1989. *Critique of Economic Reason*, London, Verso

Gosden, P. H., 1961. *The Friendly Societies in England, 1815–1875*, Manchester, Manchester University Press

Gough, I., 1979. *The Political Economy of the Welfare State*, London, Macmillan

Gronau, R., 1977. 'Leisure, Home Production and Work: the Theory of the Allocation of Time Revisited', in *Journal of Political Economy*, vol. 85, pp. 1099–123

References

Habakkuk, H. J., 1971. *Population Growth and Economic Development since 1750*, Leicester, Leicester University Press

Hakim, C., 1981. 'Job Segregation Trends in the 1970s', in *Department of Employment Gazette*, vol. 89, pp. 521–9

Halevy, E., 1972. *The Growth of Philosophic Radicalism*, London, Faber and Faber

Hall, P., Land, H., Parker, R., and Webb, A., 1975. *Change, Choice and Conflict in Social Policy*, London, Heinemann

Hall, R., 1985. *Ask Any Woman. A London Enquiry into Rape and Sexual Assault*, Bristol, Falling Wall Press

Hall, R., James, S., and Kertesz, J., 1981. *The Rapist Who Pays the Rent. Evidence Submitted by Women Against Rape, Britain, to the Criminal Law Revision Committee*, Bristol, Falling Wall Press

Hamburger, J. D., 1963. *James Mill and the Art of Revolution*, New Haven, Yale University Press

Hamilton, C., 1909. *Marriage as a Trade*, London, The Women's Press, 1981

Hamilton, C. J., 1910. 'The Poor Law Controversy', in *Economic Journal*, vol. 20, pp. 472–9

Hamilton, M. A., 1932. *Sidney and Beatrice Webb: a Study in Contemporary Biography*, London, Sampson Low, Martson and Co.

Hammond, J. L., and Hammond, B., 1966. *The Town Labourer 1760–1832*, London, Longman

Harcourt, G. C., 1972. *Some Cambridge Controversies in the Theory of Capital*, Cambridge, Cambridge University Press

Harding, S., 1986. *The Science Question in Feminism*, Ithaca, Cornell University Press

Hareven, T. K., 1976. 'Modernization and Family History: Perspectives of Social Changes', in *Sign*, vol. 2, pp. 190–206

Harris, J., 1972. *Unemployment and Politics, 1886–1914*, Oxford, Oxford University Press

Hartmann, B., 1987. *Reproductive Rights and Wrongs. The Global Politics of Population Control and Contraceptive Choice*, New York, Harper and Row

Hartmann, H., 1979. 'Capitalism, Patriarchy, and Job Segregation by Sex', in Z. Eisentein, ed., *Capitalist Patriarchy and the Case for Socialist Feminism*, New York, Monthly Review Press

Hartman, H., and Reskin, B., 1986. *Women's Work, Men's Work. Sex Segregation on the Job*, Washington, National Academy Press

Hartsock, N., 1983. *Money, Sex and Power. Toward a Feminist Historical Materialism*, New York, Longman

Hay, J. R., 1975. *The Origins of the Liberal Welfare Reforms, 1906–1914*, London, Macmillan

Hernes, H. M., 1987. 'Women and the Welfare State: the Transition from Private to Public Dependence', in Showstack Sassoon, ed., *Women and the State*, London, Hutchinson

Hester, M., 1990. 'The Dynamics of Male Domination, using the Witch Craze in Sixteenth and Seventeenth Century England as a Case Study', in *Women's Studies International Forum*, vol. 13, pp. 9–19

Hewitt, M., 1930. *Wives and Mothers in Victorian Industry*, London, Barrie and Rockliff

Hicks, J. R., 1932. *The Theory of Wages*, London, Macmillan

Hicks, J. R., and Hollander, S., 1977. 'Mr. Ricardo and the Moderns', in *Quarterly Journal of Economics*, vol. 91, pp. 351–69

Himmelfarb, G., 1984. *The Idea of Poverty*, London, Faber and Faber

Himmelweit, S., and Mohun, S., 1977. 'Domestic Labour and Capital', in *Cambridge Journal of Economics*, vol. 1, pp. 15–31

Hirschman, A. O., 1977. *The Passions and the Interests*, Princeton, Princeton University Press

1982. 'Rival Interpretations of Market Society: Civilizing, Destructive or Feeble', in *Journal of Economic Literature*, vol. 20, pp. 1463–84

Hobsbawm, E. J., 1964. *Labouring Men*, London, Weidenfeld and Nicolson

1974. *Labour's Turning Point, 1880–1900*, Brighton, Harvester Press

1975. *The Age of Capital 1848–1875*, London, Weidenfeld and Nicolson

1980. 'Scottish Reformers of the Eighteenth Century and Capitalist Agriculture', in E.J. Hobsbawm, ed., *Peasants in History: Essays in Honour of Daniel Thorner*, Calcutta, Orient Longman

1981. 'Looking Forward: History and the Future', in *New Left Review*, vol. 125, pp. 3–19

Hodgson, G., 1988. *Economics and Institutions*, Oxford, Polity Press

1991. 'Hayek's Theory of Cultural Evolution', in *Economics and Philosophy*, vol. 7, pp. 67–82

Hogben, L., 1938. *Political Arithmetic. A Symposium of Population Studies*, London, G. Allen and Unwin

Holcombe, L., 1983. *Wives and Property: Reform of Married Women's Property Law in Nineteenth-Century England*, Toronto, University of Toronto Press

Hollander, J. H., 1903. 'Introduction', in Longe, *A Refutation of The Wage Fund Theory*, Baltimore, Johns Hopkins Press

Hollander, S., 1979. *The Economics of David Ricardo*, Toronto and Buffalo, University of Toronto Press

1984. 'Marx and Malthusianism: Marx's Secular Path of Wages', in *American Economic Review*, vol. 74, pp. 139–51

1990. 'Ricardian Growth Theory: a Resolution of Some Problems in Textual Interpretation', in *Oxford Economic Papers*, vol. 42, pp. 730–50

Hollis, P., 1979. *Women in Public 1850–1900: Documents of the Victorian Women's Movement*, London, Allen and Unwin

Hont, I., and Ignatieff, M., 1983. 'Introduction', in I. Hont and M. Ignatieff, eds., *Wealth and Virtue*, Cambridge, Cambridge University Press

Horne, T. A., 1985. 'The Poor Have a Claim Founded in the Law of Nature: William Paley and the Rights of the Poor', in *Journal of the History of Philosophy*, vol. 33, pp. 51–70

Horrel, S., Rubery, J., and Burchell, B., 1989. *Working-Time Patterns, Constraints and Preferences*, Department of Applied Economics, University of Cambridge, mimeo

House of Commons, 1817. *Report from the Select Committee on the Poor Laws*, London, HMSO

1824. *Report from the Select Committee on Labourers' Wages*, London, HMSO

1909. *Report of the Royal Commission on the Poor Laws and Relief of Distress. Majority*, London, HMSO

Hubback, E. M., 1949. 'The Family Allowances Movement, 1924–1947', in E. Rathbone, ed., *Family Allowances*, London, Allen and Unwin

Humphries, J., 1977. 'Class Struggle and the Persistence of the Working Class Family', in *Cambridge Journal of Economics*, vol. 1, pp. 241–58

1981. 'Protective Legislation, the Capitalist State and Working Class Men: the Case of the 1842 Mines Regulation Act', in *Feminist Review*, vol. 7, pp. 1–33

Humphries, J., and Rubery, J., 1984. 'The Reconstitution of the Supply Side of the Labour Market: the Relative Autonomy of Social Reproduction', in *Cambridge Journal of Economics*, vol. 8, pp. 331–46

Hunt, E. H., 1981. *British Labour History 1815–1914*, London, Weidenfeld and Nicolson

Hutchins, B. L., 1909. *The Public Health Agitation*, London, A. C. Fifield

1915. *Women in Modern Industry*, London, Bell and Sons

Illich, I., 1981. *Shadow Work*, London, Marion Boyars Publications

References

1982. *Gender*, London, Marion Boyars Publications

ILO, 1977. *Meeting Basic Needs. Strategies for Eradicating Mass Poverty and Unemployment*, Geneva, ILO

1984. *Report of the Director General*, Geneva, ILO

ISTAT, 1985. *Indagine sulle strutture e i comportamenti familiari*, Rome, ISTAT

Jacob, F., 1982. *The Possible and the Actual*, Seattle, University of Washington Press

Jacobus, M., Keller, E., and Shuttleworth, S., 1990. *Body Politics. Women and the Discourses of Science*, New York, Routledge

Jaget, C., 1980. *Prostitutes: our life,*, Bristol, Falling Wall Press

James, P., 1979. *'Population' Malthus: His Life and Times*, London Routledge and Kegan Paul

James, S. 1975a. *Women, the Unions and Work*, London, Crest Press

1975b. *Sex, Race and Class*, Bristol, Falling Wall Press and Race To-Day

1975c. 'Wageless of the World', in W. Edmonds and S. Fleming, eds., *All Work and No Pay*, Bristol, Falling Wall Press

Jardine, N., 1986. *The Fortunes of Enquiry*, Oxford, Clarendon Press

Jessop, B., 1977. 'Recent Theories of the Capitalist State', in *Cambridge Journal of Economics*, vol. 1, pp. 353–73

Jones, G., 1980. *Social Darwinism and English Thought: the Interaction between Biological and Social Theory*, Brighton, Harvester Press

Jordanova, L. J., 1981. 'The History of the Family', in Cambridge Women's Study Group, *Women in Society, Interdisciplinary Essays*, London, Virago

Kames, H. Home, Lord, 1774. *Sketches of the History of Man*, Edinburgh

Kenrick, J., 1981. 'Politics and the Construction of Women as Second-Class Workers', in F. Wilkinson, ed., *The Dynamics of Labour Market Segmentation*, London, Academic Press

Keynes, J. M., 1930. 'On the Question of High Wages', in *Political Quarterly*, vol. 1, pp. 110–24

Kindleberger, C. P., 1976. 'The Historical Background: Adam Smith and the Industrial Revolution', in Wilson and Skinner, eds., *The Market and the State*, Oxford, Clarendon Press

Kowalik, T., 1978. 'The institutional framework of Dobb's Economics', in *Cambridge Journal of Economics*, vol. 2, pp. 141–52

Kropotkin, P., 1906. *The Conquest of Bread*, London, Chapman and Hall

Lachlan, G. M., and McKeown, T., 1971. *Medical History and Medical Care*, Oxford, Oxford University Press

Land, H., 1978. 'Who Cares for the Family?' in *Journal of Social Policy*, vol. 7, pp. 257–84

References

1980. 'The Family Wage', in *Feminist Review*, vol. 6

Lander, R., 1835. Quoted in 'Correspondence Relating to the Slave Trade', in *Quarterly Review*, vol. 55, pp. 25–285

Landes, D., 1969. *The Unbound Prometheus, Technological Change and Industrial Development in Western Europe from 1750 to the Present*, Cambridge, Cambridge University Press

Laslett, P., ed., 1972. *Household and Family in Past Time*, Cambridge, Cambridge University Press

Leacock, E., 1972. 'Introduction', in Engels, *The Origin of the Family, Private Property and the State*, London, Lawrence and Wishart

Lecourt, D., 1981. 'Biology and the Crisis of the Human Sciences', in *New Left Review*, vol. 125, pp. 90–6

Lester, R., 1946. 'Shortcomings of Marginal Analysis for Wage-Employment Problems', in *American Economic Review*, vol. 36, pp. 63–82

Levine, D., 1985. 'Industrialization and the Proletarian Family in England', in *Past and Present*, vol. 2

1987. *Reproducing Families*, Cambridge, Cambridge University Press

Lewis, W. A., 1954. 'Economic Development with Unlimited Supplies of Labour', in *Manchester School*, vol. 26, pp. 1–23

Linder, P. H., and Williamson, J. G., 1983. 'English Workers' Living Standards during the Industrial Revolution: a New Look', in *Economic History Review*, vol. 36, pp. 1–25

Longe, F. D., 1903 (1866). *A Refutation of the Wage Fund Theory*, Baltimore, Johns Hopkins Press

McAuley, A., 1981. *Women's Work and Wages in the Soviet Union*, London, Allen and Unwin

McBriar, A. N., 1987. *An Edwardian Mixed Doubles: the Bosanquets versus the Webbs: a Study in British Social Policy 1890–1929*, Oxford, Clarendon Press

McClelland, K., 1987. 'Time to Work and Time to Live: Some Aspects of Work and Re-formation of Class in Britain 1850–1880', in P. Joyce, ed., *The Historical Meanings of Work*, Cambridge, Cambridge University Press

McCloskey, D., 1983. 'The Rhetoric of Economics', in *Journal of Economic Literature*, vol. 31, pp. 434–61

McCulloch, J. R., 1854. *A Treatise on the Circumstances which Determine the Rate of Wages and the Condition of the Labouring Classes*, reprint, New York, Kelley, 1954

MacDonald, J., 1910. 'Oral Evidence', in House of Commons, Royal Commission on the Poor Laws, *Appendix*, vol. VIII, pp. 227–41, London, HMSO

References

Mackintosh, M., 1977. 'Reproduction and Patriarchy. A Critique of Meillassaux, *Femmes, greniers et capitaux*', in *Capital and Class*, vol. 2, pp. 119–27

1978. 'The State and the Oppression of Women', in A. Kuhn and A. Wolpe, eds., *Feminism and Materialism*, London, Routledge and Kegan Paul

Maclaren, A., 1978. *Birth Control in the Nineteenth Century*, London, Croom Helm

McNicol, J., 1980. *The Movement of Family Allowances*, London, Heinemann

McNulty, P. J., 1980. *The Origins and Development of Labor Economics. A Chapter in the History of Social Thought*, Cambridge Mass., MIT Press

MacPherson, C. B., 1973. 'Market Concept in Political Theory', in C.B. MacPherson, *Democratic Theory: Essays in Retrieval*, Oxford, Clarendon Press

1977. 'Needs and Wants: an Ontological or Historical Problem', in Fitzgerald, ed., *Human Needs and Politics*, Oxford, Pergamon

1980. *Burke*, Oxford, Oxford University Press

1985. *The Rise and Fall of Economic Justice and Other Papers*, Oxford, Oxford University Press

Mallet, J. L., ed., 1921. *Centenary Volume, Political Economy Club*, London

Malos, E., 1982. *The Politics of Housework*, London, Allison and Busby

Malthus, T. R., 1820. *Principles of Political Economy, considered with a View to their Practical Application*, London, Murray; reprint, *Principles of Political Economy*, J. Pullen, ed., Variorum Edition, vol. 1, Cambridge, Cambridge University Press, 1989

1963 (1808–25). *Occasional Papers on Ireland, Population, and Political Economy*, B. Semmel, ed., New York, Burt Franklin

1976 (1798). *An Essay on the Principle of Population*, Harmondsworth, Penguin

Mandeville, B., 1970. *Fable of the Bees*, Harmondsworth, Penguin

Mandrou, R., 1979. *Possession et sorcellerie ou XVIIè siècle: textes inédits*, Paris, Fayard

Marshall, A., 1887. 'A Fair Rate of Wages', in M. Pigou, ed., *Memorials of Alfred Marshall*, New York, Kelley, 1956

Martin, A., 1911. 'The Married Working Women – A Study', in *The Nineteenth Century and after*, vol. LXIX, pp. 108–22

Martineau, H., 1834. 'Trades Unions and Strikes', in *The Edinburgh Review*, vol. 59, pp. 341–59

References

Marx, K., 1961 (1867). *Capital. Critical Analysis of Capitalist Production*, Moscow, Foreign Languages Publishing House
1969–72 (1861–63). *Theories of Surplus Value*, vols. 1–3, London, Lawrence and Wishart
1975 (1865). *Wages, Price and Profit*, Peking, Foreign Languages Press
Maurin, E., 1989. 'Types de pratique quotidiennes, types de journées et determinants sociaux de la vie quotidienne', in *Economie et statistique*, No. 223, pp. 41–61
Meek, R. L., 1953. *Marx and Engels on Malthus*, London, Lawrence and Wishart
1962. *The Economics of Physiocracy. Essays and Translations*, London, Allen and Unwin
1967a. 'The Scottish Contribution to Marxist Sociology', in R.L. Meek, ed., *Economics, Ideology and Other Essays*, London, Chapman and Hall
1967b. 'The Decline of Ricardian Economics in England', in R.L. Meek, ed., *Economics, Ideology and Other Essays*, London, Chapman and Hall
1971. 'Smith, Turgot, and the Four Stages Theory', in *History of Political Economy*, vol. 3, pp. 9–27
1976. *Social Science and the Ignoble Savage*, Cambridge, Cambridge University Press
1977. 'The Rise and Fall of the Concept of the Economic Machine', in R.L. Meek, ed., *Smith, Marx, and after*, London, Chapman and Hall
Meek, R. L., and Skinner, A. S., 1973. 'The Development of Adam Smith's Ideas on the Division of Labour', in *Economic Journal*, vol. 83, pp. 1094–1116
Meillassoux, C., 1972. 'From Reproduction to Production: a Marxist Approach to Economic Anthropology', in *Economy and Society*, vol. 1, pp. 93–105
1977. *Femmes, greniers et capitaux*, Paris, Maspero
Merchant, C., 1980. *The Death of Nature, Women, Ecology, and the Scientific Revolution*, London, Harper and Row
Miliband, R., 1989. *Divided Societies. Class Struggle in Contemporary Capitalism*, Oxford, Oxford University Press
Mill, James, 1817a. 'Colonies', in the Supplement to the *Encyclopaedia Britannica*
1817b. *History of British India*, London
1937 (1820). *An Essay on Government*, Cambridge, Cambridge University Press
1965 (1821). *Elements of Political Economy*, New York, Kelley

References

Mill, J. S., 1869. 'Thornton on Labour and Its Claims', in *Fortnightly Review*, vol. 5 (New Series), pp. 505–18 and 680–700

1964 (1873). *Autobiography*, London, Oxford University Press

1965 (1848). *Principles of Political Economy, with Some of Their Applications to Social Philosophy*, J.M. Robson, ed., Toronto, University of Toronto Press

Millar, J., and Glendinning, J., 1987. 'Invisible Women, Invisible Poverty', in *Women and Poverty in Britain*, Brighton, Wheatsheaf

Mirowsky, P., 1984. 'Physics and the Marginalist Revolution', in *Cambridge Journal of Economics*, vol. 3, pp. 361–79

1989. *More Heat than Light: Economics as Social Physics*, New York, Cambridge University Press

1990. 'Smooth Operator', in R. McWilliams Tullberg, ed., *Alfred Marshall in Retrospect*, Aldershot, Elgar

Mitchell, B. R., and Deane, P., 1962. *Abstract of British Historical Statistics*, Cambridge, Cambridge University Press

Mohun, S., and Himmelweit, S., 1977. 'Domestic Labour and Capital', in *Cambridge Journal of Economics*, vol. 1, pp. 15–31

Molineaux, M., 1979. 'Beyond the Housework Debate', in *New Left Review*, vol. 116, pp. 3–27

Mowat, C. L., 1961. *The Charity Organization Society*, London, Methuen

Mullion, M., 1826. *Some Illustrations of Mr. McCulloch's Principles of Political Economy*, Edinburgh

Navarro, V., 1978. *Class Struggle between State and Medicine*, Martin Robertson

Navarro, V., and Berman, D. N., eds., 1983. *Health and Work under Capitalism: an International Perspective*, New York, Baywood

Nicholls, G., 1898. *A History of the Poor Law in Connection with the Legislation and Other Circumstances Affecting the Condition of the People*, New York, Kelley, 1967

Oakley, A., 1974. *Woman's Work: the Housewife, Past and Present*, New York, Vintage

1982. *Subject Women*, London, Fontana Paperbacks

O'Brien, D. P., 1975. *The Classical Economists*, Oxford, Clarendon Press

O'Donovan, K., 1979. 'The Male Appendage: Legal Definitions of Women', in S. Burman, ed., *Fit Work for Women*, London, Croom Helm

Oren, L., 1973. 'The Welfare of Women in Laboring Families, England, 1860–1950', in *Feminist Studies*, vol. 1, pp. 107–25

Osborn, F., 1940. *Preface to Eugenics*, London, Harper

Pahl, J., 1978. *Battered Women*, DHSS, London, HMSO

1980. 'Patterns of Money Management within Marriage', in *Journal of Social Policy*, vol. 9, pp. 313–35

1989. *Money and Marriage*, London, Macmillan

Pahl, R. L., 1984. *Divisions of Labour*, Oxford, Basil Blackwell

Paley, W., 1785. *The Principles of Moral and Political Philosophy*, Dublin, Exshaw, White, etc.

Panitch, L., 1976. *Social Democracy and Industrial Militancy*, Cambridge, Cambridge University Press

Parker, W. N., ed., 1986. *Economic History and the Modern Economist*, Oxford, Basil Blackwell

Pateman, C., 1988. *The Sexual Contract*, Cambridge, Polity Press

Peach, T., 1984. 'David Ricardo's Early Treatment of Profitability. A New Interpretation', in *Economic Journal*, vol. 94, pp. 733–51

1990. 'Samuel Hollander's "Ricardian Growth Theory": a Critique', in *Oxford Economic Papers*, vol. 42, pp. 751–64

Peacock, A., and Wiseman, J., 1961. *The Growth of Public Expenditure in the United Kingdom*, NBER, Princeton, Princeton University Press

Peattie, L., and Rein, M., 1983. *Women's Claims: a Study in Political Economy*, Oxford, Oxford University Press

Perelman, M., 1984. *Classical Political Economy: Primitive Accumulation and the Social Division of Labour*, London, Rowman and Allan Held

Perlman, M., 1981. 'Population and Economic Change in Developing Countries: a Review Article', in *Journal of Economic Literature*, vol. 19, pp. 74–82

Petersen, W., 1979. *Malthus*, London, Heinemann

Phelps Brown, H., 1977. *The Inequality of Pay*, Oxford, Oxford University Press

Picchio, A., 1984. 'The Political Economy of the Social Reproduction of Labour', in *Studi e Ricerche del Dipartimento di Economia Politica*, vol. 29, Modena

1986a. 'Poor Laws', in J. Eatwell, M. Milgate and P. Newman, eds., *The New Palgrave Dictionary of Political Economy*, London, Macmillan

1986b. 'Longe', in J. Eatwell, M. Milgate and P. Newman, eds., *The New Palgrave Dictionary of Political Economy*, London, Macmillan

1986c. 'W. T. Thornton', in J. Eatwell, M. Milgate and P. Newman, eds., *The New Palgrave Dictionary of Political Economy*, London, Macmillan

References

Picchio Del Mercato, A., 1975. 'Il modello di Lewis e la teoria classica della distribuzione', in *Rivista Internazionale di Scienze Economiche e Commerciali*, vol. 22, pp. 1048–74
1981a. 'Il prezzo naturale del lavoro nell'Economia Politica Classica', in *Ricerche Economiche*, gennaio
1981b. 'Wages as Costs of Social Reproduction', in University of Cambridge, Faculty of Economics and Politics, *Research Papers*, vol. 17
1981c. 'Social Reproduction and Labour Market Segmentation', in F. Wilkinson, ed., *The Dynamics of Labour Market Segmentation*, London, Academic Press
Pigou, M., 1910. 'Memorandum on Some Economic Aspects and Effects of Poor Law Relief', in House of Commons, Royal Commission on the Poor Laws and Relief of Distress, *Appendix*, vol. IX, pp. 981–1000, London, HMSO
Pinchbeck, I., 1930. *Women Workers and the Industrial Revolution, 1750–1850*, London, Virago, 1981
Polanyi, K., 1944. *The Great Transformation*, New York, Rinehart
1977. *The Livelihood of Man*, New York, Academic Press
Porter, R., 1987. *Disease, Medicine and Society in England 1550–1860*, London, Macmillan
Poynter, H., 1969. *Society and Pauperism: English Ideas on Poor Relief 1795–1834*, London, Routledge and Kegan Paul
Prigogine, I., and Stengers, I., 1984. *Man's New Dialogue with Nature*, London, Heinemann
Prochaska, F. K., 1980. *Women and Philanthropy in Nineteenth Century England*, Oxford, Clarendon Press
Pullen, J. R., 1982. 'Malthus and the Doctrine of Proportions and the Concept of Optimum', in *Australian Economic Papers*, vol. 21, pp. 270–86
Ramelson, M., 1967. *Petticoat Rebellion. A Century of Struggle for Women's Rights*, London, Lawrence and Wishart
Rapp, R., Ross, E., and Bridenthal, R., 1983. 'Examining Family History', in J. Newton, M. Ryan and J. Walkowitz, eds., *Sex and Class in Women's History*, London, Routledge and Kegan Paul
Rathbone, E., 1917. 'The Remuneration of Women's Services', in *Economic Journal*, vol. 27, pp. 55–68
1947 (1924). *The Disinherited Family*, London, Allen and Unwin
Reskin, B., and Hartmann, H., eds., 1986. *Women's Work, Men's Work. Sex Segregation on the Job*, Washington, National Academy Press

References

Ricardo, D., 1951a (1817). 'On the Principles of Political Economy and Taxation', in P. Sraffa, ed., *Works and Correspondence*, vol. I, Cambridge, Cambridge University Press

1951b (1823). 'Absolute Value and Exchangeable Value', in P. Sraffa, ed., *Works and Correspondence*, vol. IV, Cambridge, Cambridge University Press

1952 (1816–18). 'Speeches and Evidence', in P. Sraffa, ed., *Works and Correspondence*, vol. VII, Cambridge, Cambridge University Press

1966 (1820). 'Notes on Malthus', in P. Sraffa, ed., *Works and Correspondence*, vol. II, Cambridge, Cambridge University Press

Riley, D., 1981. 'Feminist Thought and Reproductive Control: the State and the Right to Choose', in Cambridge Women's Study Group, *Women and Society*, London, Virago

Robbins, L., 1933. *Wages*, London, Jarrold

1958. *Robert Torrens and the Evolution of Classical Economics*, London, Macmillan

Roberts, D., 1960. *Victorian Origins of the British Welfare State*, Yale University Press

Robinson, J. P., and Converse, P. C., 1972. 'Social Change Reflected in the Use of Time', in A. Campbell and P.C. Converse, eds., *The Human Meaning of Social Change*, New York, Sage

Roncaglia, Alessandro, 1972. 'Introduzione', in R. Torrens, *Saggio sulla produzione della ricchezza*, Milan, Isedi

Rose, H., 1978. 'In Practice Supported, in Theory Denied: an Account on an Invisible Urban Movement', in *International Journal of Urban and Regional Research*, vol. 2, pp. 521–37

1981. 'Re-reading Titmuss: the Sexual Division of Labour', in *Journal of Social Policy*, vol. 10, pp. 477–502

1983. 'Hand, Brain, and Heart: a Feminist Epistemology for the Natural Sciences', in *Signs*, vol. 9, pp. 73–90

Rose, M. E., 1970. 'The Anti-Poor Law Agitation', in Ward, ed., *Popular Movements, 1830–50*, London, Macmillan

1972. *The Relief of Poverty, 1834–1914*, London, Macmillan

Rosenberg, C., 1975. *The Family in History*, University of Pennsylvania Press

Ross, A. M., 1948. *Trade Union Wage Policy*, Berkeley, University of California Press

Rossi Doria, A., 1985. 'Uguali o diverse? La legislazione vittoriana sul lavoro delle donne', in *Rivista di Storia Contemporanea*, vol. 1

Rousse, H. and Roy, C., 1981. 'Activités ménagères et cycle de vie', in *Economie et statistique*, vol. 131, pp. 59–67

180

References

Rowbotham, S., 1990. *The Past Is before Us*, Harmondsworth, Penguin
Rowntree, B. S., 1918. *The Human Needs of Labour*, London, Nelson and Sons
Rowthorn, B., 1980. 'Marx's Theory of Wages', in *Capitalism, Conflict and Inflation*, London, Lawrence and Wishart
Roy, C., 1982. 'L'emploi du temps des mères et pères de famille nombreuse', in *Economie et statistique*, vol. 142, pp. 59–78
    1989. 'La Gestion du temps des hommes et des femmes, des actifs et des inactifs', in *Economie et statistique*, vol. 223, pp. 5–40
Rubery, J., 1978. 'Structured Labour Markets, Market Organization and Low Pay', in *Cambridge Journal of Economics*, vol. 2, pp. 17–36
Rude, G., 1981. *The Crowd in History. A Study of Popular Disturbances, 1730–1848*, London, Lawrence and Wishart
Ryan, M., 1983. 'The Power of Women's Networks', in J. Newton, M. Ryan and J. Walkowitz, eds., *Sex and Class in Women's History*, London, Routledge and Kegan Paul
Ryan, M., and Walkowitz, J., 1979. 'Crossing Borders: Transnational Advances in the History of Women', in *Feminist Studies*, vol. 5, pp. 1–6
Samuel, R., ed., 1981. *People's History and Socialist Theory*, History Workshop Series, London, Routledge and Kegan Paul
Samuels, W. J., 1988. 'Introduction', in W.J. Samuels, ed., *Institutional Economics*, London, Edward Elgar
Saraceno, C., 1987. 'Division of Family Labour and Gender Identity', in Showstack Sassoon, ed., *Women and the State*, London, Hutchinson
Schultz, T. W., ed., 1974. *Economics of the Family: Marriage, Children and Human Capital*, NBER, Chicago, University of Chicago Press
    1981. ed., *Investing in People: the Economics of Population Quality*, Berkeley, University of California Press
Schumpeter, J. A., 1954. *History of Economic Analysis*, New York, Oxford University Press
Schwartz Cowan, R., 1983. *More Work for Mother. The Ironies of Household Technology from Open Hearth to the Microwave*, New York, Basic Books
Seccombe, W., 1983. 'Marxism and Demography', *New Left Review*, vol. 137, pp. 22–47
Sen, A., 1983. 'Poor Relatively Speaking', in *Oxford Economic Papers*, vol. 35, pp. 153–69
    1985a. *Commodities and Capabilities*, Amsterdam, North Holland
    1985b. *Resources, Values and Development*, Oxford, Basil Blackwell

References

1987. 'The Standard of Living', in G. Hawthorn, ed., *The Tanner Lectures, Clare Hall College*, Cambridge, Cambridge University Press

Sen, A. K., and Williams, B., eds., 1982. *Utilitarianism and Beyond*, Cambridge, Cambridge University Press

Sen, G., and Grown, C., 1988. *Development, Crises and Alternative Visions*, London, Earthscan Publications

Senior, N. W., 1831. *Three Lectures on the Rate of Wages, delivered before the University of Oxford in Easter Term, 1830. with a preface on the causes and remedies of the present disturbances*, London, John Murray

Showstack Sassoon, A., ed., 1987. *Women and the State*, London, Hutchinson

Simon, H. A., 1983. *Reason and Human Affairs*, Oxford, Basil Blackwell

Skinner, A., 1979. *A System of Social Science: Papers Related to Adam Smith*, Oxford, Clarendon Press

Skinner, Q., 1972. 'Social Meaning and the Explanation of Social Action', in T.P.R. Laslett, W.G. Runciman and Q. Skinner, eds., *Philosophy, Politics and Society*, Oxford, Basil Blackwell

1976. 'Standards of Living', in *Times Literary Supplement*, 13 Feb.

Smith, A., 1976 (1776). *An Inquiry into the Nature and Causes of the Wealth of Nations*, A.S. Skinner and R.H. Campbell, eds., Oxford, Clarendon Press

1978a (1767). *Lectures on Jurisprudence*, R.L. Meek, D.D. Raphael and P.G. Stein, eds., Oxford, Clarendon Press

1978b (c. 1763). 'Early Draft of Part of the *Wealth of Nations*', in R.L. Meek, D.D. Raphael and P.G. Stein, eds., *Lectures on Jurisprudence*, Oxford, Clarendon Press

Smith, K., 1978. *The Malthusian Controversy*, New York, Octagon Books

Snowden, P., 1912. *The Living Wage*, London, Hodder and Stoughton

Société de Demographie Historique, 1980. *Catalogue of the Exhibition 'De Malthus au Malthusianism'*, Paris

Soffer, R. N., 1978. *Ethics and Society in England. The Revolution in the Social Sciences, 1870–1914*, Berkeley, University of California Press

Solow, R. M., 1985. 'Economic History and Economics', in *American Economic Review*, vol. 75, pp. 328–31

1990. *The Labour Market as a Social Institution*, Oxford, Basil Blackwell

Soloway, R. A., 1982. *Birth Control and the Population Question in England, 1877–1930*, Chapel Hill, University of North Carolina Press

References

Sraffa, P., 1926. 'The Laws of Returns under Competitive Conditions', in *Economic Journal*, vol. 36, pp. 535–50

1951. 'Introduction' to Ricardo, *On the Principles of Political Economy and Taxation*, London, Cambridge University Press

1960. *Production of Commodities by Means of Commodities*, Cambridge, Cambridge University Press

Standing, G., 1986. 'Meshing Labour Flexibility with Security: an Answer to British Unemployment?', in *International Labour Review*, vol. 125, pp. 87–105

Stedman Jones, G., 1971. *Outcast London*, Oxford, Clarendon Press

1977. 'Society and Politics at the Beginning of the World Economy, Review of E. Hobsbawm, *The Age of Capital*', in *Cambridge Economic Journal*, vol. 1, pp. 77–92

Stephen, Leslie, 1900. *The English Utilitarians, vol. 2: 'James Mill'*, reprinted London, London School of Economics, 1950

Steuart, J., 1966 (1767). *An Inquiry into the Principles of Political Economy*, A.S. Skinner, ed., Chicago, University of Chicago Press

Stevenson, J., 1974. 'Food Riots in England, 1792–1818', in R. Quinault and J. Stevenson (eds.), *Popular Protest and Public Order*, London, George Allen and Unwin

Stigler, G., 1981. 'Hollander: the Economics of David Ricardo', review in *Journal of Economic Literature*, vol. 19, pp. 100–102

Stikney Ellis, S., 1850. *The Wives of England, Their Relative Duties, Domestic Influence and Social Obligations*, New York, Edward Walker

Strachey, L., 1921. *Queen Victoria*, London, Chatto and Windus

Strasser, S. M., 1982. *Never Done: a History of American Housework*, New York, Pantheon

Szalai, A., 1975. 'Women's Time. Women in the Light of Contemporary Time-Budget Research', in *Futures*, October, vol. 7, pp. 385–99

Szalai, S., 1972. *The Use of Time*, The Hague, Mouton

Tarling, R., and Wilkinson, F., 1982. 'The Movement of Real Wages and the Development of Collective Bargaining in the UK 1855–1920', in *Contributions to Political Economy*, vol. 1, pp. 1–23

Taussig, F. W., 1896. *Wages and Capital*, New York, Appleton

Taylor, A. J., ed., 1975. *The Standard of Living in Britain in the Industrial Revolution*, London, Methuen

Thane, P., 1978a. 'Women and the Poor Law in Victorian and Edwardian England', in *History Workshop*, vol. 6, pp. 29–51

1978b. ed., *Origins of British Social Policy*, London, Croom Helm

Thomis, M., and Grimmer, J., 1982. *Women in Protest, 1800–1850*, London, Croom Helm

References

Thompson, E. P., 1969. *The Making of the English Working Class*, Harmondsworth, Pelican
1971. 'The Moral Economy of the English Crowd', in *Past and Present*, vol. 50, pp. 76–136
Thompson, W., 1825. *Appeal of one Half of the Human Race, Women, against the Pretensions of the other Half, Men, to retain them in Political and hence in Civil and Domestic Slavery*, reprinted London, Virago, 1983
Thornton, W. T., 1869. *On Labour*, London
Tilly, L., and Scott, J., 1978. *Women, Work and Family*, New York, Holt, Rinehart and Winston
Titmuss, R. M., 1963. *Essays on the Welfare State*, London, Unwin Books
Titmuss, R. M., and Titmuss, K., 1942. *Parents' Revolt*, London, Secker and Warburg
Tool, M. R., ed., 1988. *Evolutionary Economics. Foundations of Institutional Thought*, vols. *I–II*, New York, Sharpe Inc.
Torrens, R., 1829. *An Essay on the External Corn Trade, with an Appendix on the Means of Improving the Condition of the Labouring Classes*, London, Longman
1834. *On Wages and Combination*, reprinted New York, Kelley, 1969
1837. *A Letter to the Right Hon. Lord John Russell on the Ministerial Measure for Establishing Poor Laws in Ireland and on the Auxiliary Means which it will be Necessary to Employ in Carrying that Measure into Effect*, London, Longman
1843a. *A Letter to the Right Honourable Sir Robert Peel on the Condition of England and on the Means of Removing the Causes of Distress*, London, Smith Elster
1843b. *Postcript to a Letter to the Right Honourable Sir Robert Peel on the Condition of England, etc.*, London, Smith and Co.
Townsend, J., 1786. *A Dissertation on the Poor Laws*, London, C. Dilly
Townsend, P., 1985. 'A Sociological Approach to the Measurement of Poverty. A Rejoinder to Amartya Sen', in *Oxford Economic Papers*, vol. 37, pp. 659–68
Trevor-Roper, H., 1984. *The European Witch-Craze of the 16th and 17th Centuries*, Harmondsworth, Penguin
Tribe, K., 1978. *Land, Labour and Economic Discourse*, London, Routledge and Kegan Paul
1981. *Genealogies of Capitalism*, London, Macmillan
Tristan, F., 1980. *London Journal. A Survey of London Life in the 1830s*, London, George Prior
Tucker, G. L. S., 1960. *Progress and Profits in British Economic Thought 1650–1850*, Cambridge, Cambridge University Press

References

Turner, M., 1986. *Malthus and His Time*, London, St. Martin Press
Ullmann-Margalit, E., 1977. *The Emergence of Norms*, Oxford, Clarendon Press
UN, 1985. 'Economic Role of Women in the EEC Region', in *Economic Bulletin for Europe*, vol. 37, no. 1
Vaggi, G., 1986. 'Natural Rate and Market Rate', in J. Eatwell, M. Milgate and P. Newman, eds., *The New Palgrave Dictionary of Political Economy*, London, Macmillan
Vaneck, J., 1980. 'Time Spent in Housework', in A.H. Amsden, ed., *The Economics of Women and Work*, Harmondsworth, Penguin
Vercelli, A., 1988. 'Homo economicus oppure Homo sapiens, comportamentismo e razionalismo in economia politica', in *Economia Politica*, vol. 5, pp. 169–75
Vicinus, M., 1977. *A Widening Sphere: Changing Roles of Victorian Women*, Bloomington, University of Indiana Press
    1985. *Independent Women: work and community for single women, 1850–1920*, London, Virago
Walby, S., 1990. *Theorizing Patriarchy*, Oxford, Basil Blackwell
Walker, F. A., 1876. *The Wages Question*, New York, Henry Holt
Walkowitz, J., 1980. *Prostitution and Victorian Society: Women, Class and the State*, Cambridge, Cambridge University Press
Wallace, R. 1753. *A Dissertation on the Number of Mankind in Ancient and Modern Times*, London
    1761. *Prospects of Mankind, Nature and Providence*, London
Ward, J. Y., ed., 1970. *Popular Movements, 1830–50*, London, Macmillan
    1973. *Chartism*, London, Macmillan
Webb, B., 1907. 'The Decline of the Birth Rate', in *Fabian Tracts*, vol. 131
    1910. *Memoranda*, in House of Commons, Royal Commission on the Poor Laws and Relief of Distress, Appendix, vol. XII, pp. 113–327, London, HMSO
    1926. *My Apprenticeship*, London, Longman and Green
Webb, B., and Webb, S., eds., 1909. *The Minority Report, Poor Law Commission: Part I, The break-up of the Poor Law; Part II, The Public organization of the labour market*, London, Longman and Green; reprint, Clifton, Kelley, 1974
    1963 (1927–9). *English Poor Law History*, vol. 2, London, Frank Cass
    1975 (1932). *Methods of Social Study*, Cambridge, Cambridge University Press
Webb, S., 1909. 'Address to the Royal Economic Society', in *Economic Journal*, vol. 19, pp. 313–15

References

1910. 'Oral Evidence', in House of Commons, Royal Commission on the Poor Laws, *Appendix*, vol. IX, pp. 182–98, London, HMSO

Wermel, M., 1939. *The Evolution of the Classical Wage Theory*, New York, Columbia University Press

West, E. G., 1976. 'Adam Smith's Economics of Politics', in *History of Political Economy*, vol. 8, pp. 515–39

Weyland, J., 1807. *A Short Inquiry into the Policy, Humanity and Past Effects of the Poor Law*, London, Hatchard

1816. *The Principles of Population and Production*, London

Wiles, R. C., 1968. 'The Theory of Wages in Later English Mercantilism', in *Economic History Review*, vol. 21, pp. 113–26

Wilkinson, F., 1981. 'Preface', in F. Wilkinson, ed., *The Dynamics of Labour Market Segmentation*, London, Academic Press

1988. 'Where Do We Go from Here? Real Wages, Effective Demand and Economic Development', in *Cambridge Journal of Economics*, vol. 12, pp. 179–91

Williams, K., 1981. *From Pauperism to Poverty*, London, Routledge and Kegan Paul

Williams, R., 1980. 'Ideas of Nature', in *Problems of Materialism and Culture*, London, Verso

Willis, R., 1987. 'What Have We Learned from the Economics of the Family', in *American Economic Review*, vol. 77, pp. 68–81

Wilson, E., 1979. *Women and the Welfare State*, London, Tavistock

Wilson, T., and Skinner, A., eds., 1976. *The Market and the State*, Oxford, Clarendon Press

Winch, D., 1966. 'Introduction', in D. Winch, ed., *James Mill, Selected Economic Writings*, Scottish Economic Society, Edinburgh, Oliver and Boyd

1978. *Adam Smith's Politics: an Essay in Historiographic Revision*, Cambridge, Cambridge University Press

1987. *Malthus*, Oxford, Oxford University Press

Winter, J. M., 1975. 'The Economic and Social History of War', in J.M. Winter, ed., *War and Economic Development*, Cambridge, Cambridge University Press

Wollstonecraft, M., 1970 (1792). *The Rights of Woman*, London, Everyman's Library

Wood, J. C., ed., 1986. *Thomas Robert Malthus: Critical Assessments*, London, Croom Helm

Wood, P. B., 1989. 'The Natural History of Man in the Scottish Enlightenment', in *History of Science*, vol. 27, pp. 89–123

Young, M., 1952. 'Distribution of Income within the Family', in *British Journal of Sociology*, vol. 3, pp. 305–21

References

Young, K., 1988. *Women and Economic Development: Local, Regional and National Planning Strategies*, Oxford, UNESCO

Zaretsky, E., 1976. *Capitalism, the Family and Personal Life*, New York, Harper and Row

    1982. 'The Place of the Family in the Origins of the Welfare State', in B. Thorne and M. Yalom, eds., *Rethinking the Family*, New York, Longman

Zopf, P. E., 1989. *American Women in Poverty*, New York, Greenwood Press

Zweig, F., 1975. *Labour, Life and Poverty*, East Ardsley, E. P. Publishing Limited

Index

defined in terms of interest 36
moral rate of 40, 42
and reproduction 34–5
surplus theory of 2, 49, 117,
137
versus wages 41, 43
prostitution 77–8
public expenditure increase 66,
72–3
public works projects 70–1

Rathbone, E. 82–3
rent, theory of 31
reproduction, *see* social
reproduction
Ricardo, D. 26, 31–5, 36–7, 43,
54, 129
natural and market prices 12,
13, 20, 48, 136, 140
the politician 151
supply of labour 24–5, 27–9
surplus approach 6, 8, 133–4
theory of distribution 31, 34,
49
theory of value 11
on wages 14–23
Robinson, J. P. 103
Rowntree, S. 118

scarcity 92
Schumpeter, J. A. 20
Senior, N. W. 52, 54, 55, 62
servants 78–9, 81
sexual habits 77
Sidgwick, H. 54
slavery 15–16, 35, 135
Smith, A. 4, 9, 30, 97, 107, 118
class conflicts 11
instinct to exchange 137–8
State intervention 26
supply of labour 25
on wages 12–23, 29, 140

social experimentation 119
social insurance 68
social relations, and the labour
market 9, 138–9
social reproduction
and capital accumulation 9
classical approach 88
costs of 14, 16, 21, 31, 85, 121
and the labour market 20–1
political views of 91
and rate of profit 34–5
redistribution of resources
towards 110
and the state 10, 58, 85–6,
112-13
and supply of labour 117–44
time factor in 50–1
wages as costs of 3, 130
the work of 95–9
see also
production–reproduction
relationship
social services 61, 76
socialist economies 141–2
Solow, R. 2
Sraffa, P. 1, 40, 125, 126, 127
standard of living 16, 18, 117–21
basis of 21
determinants of 135
dual nature 118, 120
flexible 44–5, 62, 89
historical 40
and housework 121
increase in 118–19
indicator of capital–population
ratio 45–7
inflexibility of 31
and power relationships 22–3
subsistence 117–18
and wages 111
see also living conditions
state 5, 137

Printed in the United States
By Bookmasters